SOE IN THE NETHERLANDS

SOE IN THE NETHERLANDS

THE SPECIAL OPERATIONS EXECUTIVE'S DUTCH SECTION IN WW2

AN OFFICIAL HISTORY

FRONTLINE
BOOKS

SOE IN THE NETHERLANDS
The Special Operations Executive's Dutch Section in WW2

This edition published in 2024
by Frontline Books,
An imprint of
Pen & Sword Books Ltd,
47 Church Street, Barnsley, S. Yorkshire, S70 2AS,

This book is based on file references HS 7/159 and HS 7/161 which are held at
The National Archives, Kew, and are licensed under the Open Government
Licence v3.0.

Text alterations and additions © Frontline Books

ISBN: 978-1-03611-085-7

Pen & Sword Books Ltd incorporates the imprints of Air World Books, Pen
& Sword Archaeology, Atlas, Aviation, Battleground, Discovery, Family
History, History, Maritime, Military, Naval, Politics, Social History, Transport,
True Crime, Claymore Press, Frontline Books, Praetorian Press, Seaforth
Publishing and White Owl.

For a complete list of Pen & Sword titles please contact:

PEN & SWORD BOOKS LTD
47 Church Street, Barnsley, South Yorkshire, S70 2AS, UK.
E-mail: enquiries@pen-and-sword.co.uk
Website: www.pen-and-sword.co.uk
or
PEN AND SWORD BOOKS,
1950 Lawrence Road, Havertown, PA 19083, USA
E-mail: Uspen-and-sword@casematepublishers.com
Website: www.penandswordbooks.com

CONTENTS

PUBLISHER'S NOTE

This official history is based on two files, and, as far as possible, they are reproduced in the form and format that they were originally written in the relevant documents. Aside from correcting obvious spelling mistakes or typographical errors, we have strived to keep the edits and alterations to the absolute minimum.

INTRODUCTION

The Section became an independent entity on December 20th, 1940, when Mr. R.V. Laming was placed in charge.

Situation on Establishment vis-à-vis The Netherlands Authorities

Grave difficulties immediately confronted the Section, due mainly to the opposition of the chief of the Dutch Secret Service, Mr. Van't Sant, whose influence was extremely great, and whose obstructive attitude made it impossible to obtain the services of Dutchmen of military age, whilst, at the same time, it closed valuable sources of general information. As a result of this attitude the prevailing outlook of Dutch officials was one of non-co-operation based partly on fear of Van't Sant, and partly on considerations set forth in the following paragraph.

Nature of Dutch Official Circles

All authority naturally derived from Queen Wilhelmina. The appointment of minsters had to be approved by her. The circle from which they could be recruited was of necessity limited to the relatively few possible candidates already in the U.K., most of whom were politicians of the old parties. The influence of Van't Sant on the Queen was quite uncanny and permeated many spheres in which he was not directly interested.

Gerbrandy, the Prime Minister, was sincere but weak. Thus, many ministers and functionaries were imbued with the necessity for confining their activities to the strict limits of their official duties, fearing that any extraneous commitments might involve displeasure and possible dismissal. Obviously, their underlings followed the same line. The result was complete apathy so far as such schemes as ours were concerned.

This state of affairs rendered it necessary for the Section to decide to go forward with the preliminary work without consulting the Dutch. It is, however, highly probable that such activities as were initiated were known to Van't Sant, whose system of espionage was notoriously thorough.

Recruiting

The situation as above outlined made it essential to confine efforts at recruitment to people not connected with the Netherlands Government, thus reducing the available field to an unhealthily small circle.

Preliminary Reconnoitring

Consideration was given to the possibility of landing agents by sea, and the support of the R.A.F. was enlisted for reconnaissance flights over the northern islands of Holland. This plan was fraught with difficulties of all kinds. It was a hazardous undertaking at the best, and preparations for it were complicated by the lack of local knowledge.

In March 1941, the question of dropping agents by parachute was discussed. This proposal had previously been rejected as the opinion was that the topography and population density of Holland were unfavourable. Another reason was that it was extremely difficult to secure the right type of man for this highly specialised type of infiltration.

As landing by sea turned out impracticable when attempted in July 1941, parachuting was decided upon and training arrangements instituted.

Personnel

During the period Dec 1940 – Dec 1941 the staff of the Dutch Section at H.Q. consisted of the following individuals:

Mr. R.V. Laming (Chief)
Lieutenant R. Laming
Major Loewe
Major Pinnock
Lieutenant Dawson   } Conducting
Lieutenant Kay   } Officers
Mr. Bingham
Lieutenant Rupert

Chapter 1

1941

Agents Sent September 1941

On the night of September 7th two agents were dropped, viz. Henning and Steen, constituting Operation *Glasshouse A*.

Mission: Apart from sundry possible contacts for securing general intelligence, they were to contact one Jan Bottema, who was to be advised of this organisation's existence and general intentions. They were also to sound Bottema about sea communications.

Field History: Nothing was heard from either of the agents, or about them, until on January 4th 1942 a W/T operator sent out with a subsequent operation (*Catarrh*) reported that one of them had set out for the U.K. The other was said to have been caught in early October, escaped and gone into hiding. It subsequently transpired that Steen left by boat on Nov 13th. No more was ever heard of him, and he was presumed lost. Henning was successfully exfiltrated on a trawler and landed in the U.K. on February 20th 1942, bringing with him two more Dutchmen who were put into training as agents.

Henning brought back certain general information about internal conditions, but it was impossible to send him back again as he was too well-known to escape detection.

Agents Sent October 1941

No despatches.

Agents Sent November 1941

This is the next month in which agents were sent. The operation was known as *Catarrh* and consisted of: Timmer – Organiser [and] Looman – W/T Operator. They left on 8th November 1941.

Mission: Their mission was divided into two parts. A) To contact the two *Glasshouse* couriers sent in September and to assist them to return. B) Thereafter to proceed with the organisation of sabotage groups in the West of Holland.

Field History: Nothing was heard from these agents until January 4th 1942, when the message about *Glasshouse* arrived. Traffic proceeded in a reasonably satisfactory manner and *Catarrh* reported good progress with the proposed sea-route to be arranged via Bottema (then known as *Brandy*).

By January 1942, the Germans were aware that attempts were being made to build up sabotage organisations under guidance from London. Their prime source of information was a Dutchman named Ridderhof who acted for them in penetrating an existing organisation near Nijmegen. As a result, they found out about a projected dropping of containers from London scheduled for the end of February.

Two containers were dropped on the 27th and were handed over to Ridderhof by Captain van den Berg, chief of the reception committee "for safe keeping". This seems to have been done unwittingly by van den Berg. This incident convinced the German counter-espionage, led by Oberstleutnant Giskes and Sonderfuehrer Huntemann, that somebody was in direct communication by W/T with the U.K. Priority was accordingly given to locating the operator. By the beginning of March, the street in the Hague where Looman was transmitting was discovered. The district was raided and, on the 6th March, Looman was arrested.

According to two reports made since the capitulation by Giskes and Huntemann (as well as one by a certain Kup, who will be referred to in another section of this history), Looman was soon persuaded to turn and operate under German control. On the 18th March, he sent message No. 17 calling for more supplies and stating that a previously agreed dropping point was too dangerous. Thenceforward all his traffic was German controlled. The implications of this are apparent but will be referred to in more detail in the subsequent comments on the general situation in the field during 1942-3.

In fairness to Looman, it must be added that he endeavoured to attract the attention of London H.Q. to the fact that he was controlled, by omitting to give identity checks when sending his telegrams.

Looman was moved from Holland to Germany in the summer of 1944. He was in Rathenow when the Russians arrived and was liberated on April 25th, 1945, arriving in England on May 21st.

Timmer, after working successfully with Looman, had the misfortune to get into touch with an agent provocateur known as Johnny, who caused him to be shadowed. On the 18th March 1942, Timmer made an attempt to rescue one of his group from German captivity; he was arrested during the attempt. The Germans did not, at the time, appreciate the importance of their capture. Timmer refused to talk at first, but later on, being convinced that the whole organisation was blown, he gave details of his mission. His soldierly behaviour was described by Giskes as exemplary.

Details of his subsequent movements are not clearly established, but he was eventually sent to Mauthausen Concentration Camp, where he was shot on September 6th 1944.

Agents Sent December 1941
No despatches.

Chapter 2

1942

Dutch Section, General
The personnel of the H.Q. Section, January – February 1942 were:
  Mr. R.V. Laming (Chief)
  Major Pinnock
  Major Loewe
  Lieutenant Dawson
  Lieutenant Kay
  Captain Bingham
  Lieutenant Knight

The personnel of the H.Q. Section, March – December 1942 were:
  Major Blizard (Chief)
  Captain Bingham
  Lieutenant Knight
  Sub. Bond (A.T.S.)
  Lieutenant Snewing
  Lieutenant Mills
  Lieutenant Kay   } Conducting
  Lieutenant Parr   } Officers

Relations with the Dutch Authorities
The situation at the end of 1941 could not be described as satisfactory. It seemed apparent that until we could get our affairs segregated from the mass of high-level intrigue and allocated to a specific chief with a suitable and adequate department in close contact with our section, little progress could be made. Our efforts were, accordingly, directed to that end. In February 1942, with the advent of the new section chief of S.O.E. H.Q., Major Blizard, efforts were intensified to reach an understanding with the Dutch.

4

Eventually Colonel de Bruyne, the Netherlands Marines, was placed in charge of the M.I.D. (Militaire Inlichtings-Dienst, or Military Intelligence Service), assisted by Captain Lieftinck, also of the Netherlands Marines, and Lieutenant Schilp of the Netherlands Navy.

Co-operation between the M.I.D. and H.Q. Dutch Section was cordial and close, but for some time de Bruyne's position was insecure and unhappy, due to intrigues against him on high levels. In these intrigues the hand of Van't Sant was again evident. He resented the encroachment on his previously unchallenged supremacy in "secret" affairs, and also disliked de Bruyne personally. There was also the fact that military circles viewed with disfavour the assumption by a naval man of power in a sphere which, considered theoretically, could not be called connected with the Navy.

In May the intrigues had reached such a pitch that de Bruyne, in spite of his anxiety to co-operate with us, was fast finding his position untenable. He was an honest, open kind of man who was unable to cope with the "palace intrigue" in which he became entangled. His desire was to get on with the job and he suffered from an undermining of his authority and position by powerful self-seeking people of limited vision and mediocre minds. Negotiations on a high level took place aiming at a clarification of the position, culminating in the intervention of Prince Bernhard. The result was, eventually, that de Bruyne's position was strengthened, with a consequent revival of his enthusiasm. More energetic steps were taken to provide us with suitable recruits, and the standard of the men sent to us for training was, on the average, high.

In April a plan was worked out known as the "Plan for Holland". It was elaborated in collaboration with the Dutch and Col. de Bruyne spent much time in discussing it with us, so that co-operation between S.O.E. Dutch Section and his office was very close. It continued so during the whole year in spite of vicissitudes in de Bruyne's career.

Outline of Planning for the Field in 1942

During the first three months of the year, as is evidenced by the details of the agents' missions, efforts were directed towards establishing in Holland a nucleus of men who could undertake preparatory work for future operations on a large scale, to follow a concerted plan. This preparatory work may be analysed as follows:

The establishment of satisfactory arrangements for the reception of personnel and stores.

The establishment of efficient lines of communication between the U.K. and the Field.

The recruiting of helpers prepared to participate in more extensive action later.

The commission of undetectable acts of sabotage along specific lines.

The instruction and training of men in sabotage and subversive work generally.

All this programme was designed gradually to lead up to the introduction of much more ambitious and far-reaching schemes to be eventually worked out in conjunction with the plans of the Allied High Command.

In April the first draft of the "Plan for Holland" was drawn up and submitted to Col. de Bruyne's office for consideration and discussion. It was eventually completed in its final form and the agent commissioned to initiate it in the filed was Jurgens (Operation *Marrow*). The salient points of the Plan were as follows:

It has as its object the creation of a "Secret Army". The activities of the Secret Army are divided into two phases:

Phase A – The disruption of enemy communications on or soon after D-Day, according to the strategic plan and the tactical situation. The prevention, by this disruption, of the removal to Germany of Dutch locomotives rolling-stock.

Phase B – Ater D-Day, the provision of direct support, behind the enemy's lines, to forces in the field. The prevention of demolitions by the enemy: (i) of objectives (bridges, power-stations, dock facilities etc) which the advancing Allied armies will wish to use. (ii) of other objectives constituting scorched-earth policy.

The plan was supported by a wealth of military and industrial intelligence and, commencing with agent Jurgens, (Operation *Marrow*) organisers and instructors were given all facilities for a detailed study of its objects and implications.

Apart from this Plan, a directive was issued by General Gubbins covering the general policy to be followed during the last quarter of the year. This was:

To extend contact and communication with the Orde Dienst so as to cover as many districts as possible, endeavouring at the same time to deliver arms and stores to them.

To continue to build up the sabotage organisations and to deliver arms and stores to them as far as possible without endangering their security.

To undertake undetectable sabotage of all forms of transport and of establishments working for the enemy, although railway lines should not be attacked until further orders.

Special Note re Operation *Parsley*

This agent was given a special mission at the request of the Dutch authorities. Under the details of his mission are given the main headings of his tasks, which were designed to provide the Dutch and us with up-to-date and complete details of all aspects of German measures in Occupied Holland – defences, communications, troop concentrations, movements, petrol stores, living conditions, Luftwaffe dispositions, Naval situations, war industries etc. The value of such information for general purposes, as well as in relation to the development of the "Plan for Holland", is apparent.

Actual Position in the Field during 1942

The lines along which it was supposed and intended that activity in the field should develop are seen from the agents' missions, which were based on the plans formulated, details of which are found in the "Outline of Planning" attached to this history.

In reality, as is evident from the fate of the agents despatched during 1942, the position was that the German so-called "Ast-Niederlande", under the direction of one Oberstleutnant Giskes, had control over the whole of our organisation. Through that control, they were aware of our plans, and were able to carry out large numbers of arrests throughout the country, thereby stifling the development of resistance in general.

They concentrated on forcing or persuading W/T operators to work for them and appear to have been largely successful. At the same time, by threats and cajolery they extracted as much information as possible about our organisation in England, and our plans for subversive action in Holland.

The original penetration was on the occasion of the capture of Looman (Operation *Catarrh* q.v.). From the "turning" of that agent dates the gradual assumption by the Germans of control over our activities, and this control continued undetected the whole of the year. Having all the cards in their hands, the Germans played them cleverly. They maintained heavy traffic on all circuits and described the "successful" completion of sabotage projects which, of course, had never been carried out. In the case of Operation *Parsley* they realised that the fictitious collection of intelligence and its transmission to London would involve an enormous amount of laborious work and a waste of W/T traffic to little or no purpose. They accordingly decided to eliminate him and his mission in a convenient way by advising us of his death as a consequence of an accident on landing. Actually, of course, he was in prison.

This is typical of the many ruses to which they resorted and with which they managed to support the façade which they had built. It follows that our plans were rendered nugatory and that during the year under review, we were under a completely false impression.

Agents Sent January 1942
No despatches.

Agents Sent February 1942

Operation *Carrot*

Agent: Dessing.

Date of departure: 27.2.42.

Mission: Reconnoitring of southern sea-route possibilities; Arranging for the escape of some important Dutchmen such as Dr. Colijn or Minister van Dijk; Contacting Mr. L.J. van Looy, a prominent social-democrat and Trade Unionist; Organising sabotage cells in the Rotterdam Dordrecht area, especially in shipbuilding and shipping circles.

Field History: Dessing contacted van Looy, who was running an underground paper called *Verzet*. He assisted van Looy in the preparation and distribution of this paper. He also looked for suitable landing grounds and did a certain amount of intelligence work.

In general, he did what he could to further the cause, but he never found a suitable W/T operator, so that he did not get into touch with London. (He was to have communicated through the W/T operator of Operation *Turnip*, despatched shortly after him. but who was killed on landing). He felt isolated and lost heart, eventually arranging his own escape via Switzerland whence he was exfiltrated via Gibraltar to the U.K. His interrogation revealed that he did contact the *Turnip* organiser, Andringa, but as the latter was accompanied by a Gestapo agent and indicated so to Dessing, *Carrot* dropped the attempt and never saw Andringa again. He was thus without W/T communication and without contact with those agents from London with whom he expected to work.

He found himself continually short of money, this in itself cramping his activities. As he was in no position to supply any sabotage organisation with material, he thought it futile to undertake the building-up of groups.

His investigation of possible sea-routes in the South convinced him that movement restrictions and defence measures precluded such a scheme being successful. To attempt the exfiltration of important people was also a task beyond his capacity.

The mission must be considered a failure due partly to bad luck and partly to Dessing's losing heart and consequently adopting a passive rather than an active attitude. He arrived back in the U.K. on 2nd September 43 and has since been employed in the Netherlands Ministry of Finance.

Agents Sent March 1942

Operation *Turnip*

Agents: Andringa (Organiser), Molenaar (W/T).

Date of departure: 28.3.42.

Mission: To investigate the possible opening of a new sea-route for in- and ex-filtration; To reconnoitre specified targets in Brabant and to recruit men willing to sabotage them.

Field History: Molenaar was killed on landing. Andringa was arrested by the Sipo in early April 1942, on information supplied by a woman in Utrecht. Details are not known. Andringa had recruited a local W/T operator known as *Swede*, and it is thought that the Germans, by discovering the *Turnip* signal plan on Molenaar's body, were able to track down *Swede* whom they operated.

Andringa was first sent to Haren Concentration Camp, then to Rawicz, Silesia and finally to Mauthausen, where he was executed in September 1944.

Operation *Watercress*

Agent: Baatsen.

Date of departure: 27.3.42.

Mission: To reconnoitre the telephone exchange near Voorburg (suburb of the Hague); To deal with the Hotel Aurora, H.Q. of the German Nachrichtdienst, containing an important telephone exchange; To destroy or damage a large store of provisions and clothing for German Naval personnel at Rijnsburg, near Leiden; To damage as much as possible the petrol dock serving the aerodrome at Ypenburg, near the Hague; After completion of these tasks to return to the U.K. by a route to be arranged by us.

Field History: The impending departure of *Watercress* was signalled to *Catarrh* on March 19th in telegram No. 21. He dropped on March 27th to a Dutch reception committee under S.D. control. *Catarrh* advised London of his "safe" arrival in his telegram of 28th March 42.

He is alleged by the Germans to have offered voluntarily to work for them, and to have been used by the Sipo for spying on his fellow prisoners at Haren Concentration Camp. This may be true but nevertheless, we have been advised that he was shot at Mauthausen in September 1944.

Operation *Lettuce*

Agents: Ras (Organiser), Jordaan (W/T).

Date of departure: 28.3.42.

Mission: Organisation of sabotage groups and selection of dropping grounds.

Field History: Ras. Arrested early May 1942 due to information given to the Sipo by a Dutch traitor, Dr. Stemkel, of Utrecht. He was not heard of again until reported shot at Mauthausen in September 1944.

Jordaan. Arrested at the same time as Ras, and also as a result of denunciation by Dr. Stemkel. First sent to Haren and subsequently traced in May 45 to one of the Mauthausen camps, and was still alive then. He was alleged to have been transferred to an American hospital, but it has so far proved impossible to locate him and he must be regarded as "missing".

Agents Sent April 1942

Operation *Leek*

Agents: Kloos (Organiser), Salberg (Assistant organiser and instructor).

Date of departure: 5.4.42.

Mission: Both men were to work in Overijssel and to carry out immediate acts of sabotage to hinder the enemy war effort and acts which would hamper and hinder the Germans in the event of their invading England from Holland or of our invading the Continent via Holland.

Field History: Kloos and Salberg were arrested soon after arrival. Both were first sent to Haaren Concentration Camp and executed at Mauthausen in September 1944.

Operation *Potato*

Agent: De Haas.

Date of departure: 19.4.42.

Mission: Organisation of ferry service between England and Holland; Arranging of suitable accommodation addresses where agents could leave messages asking to be brought back to U.K.

Field History: Due to the arrest of Jordaan in April, the Germans were able to decipher messages sent on the *Trumpet* circuit. It is known that *Potato* contacted *Trumpet* and it is thought that it was through this contact that *Potato* was arrested on April 28th.

He was held at Den Haag for some time before being sent to Haaren Concentration Camp. From there, he probably went to Rawicz, but this is not certain. He was eventually transferred to Mauthausen Camp, where he was executed in September 1944.

Agents Sent May 1942

Operation *Beetroot*

Agents: Parlevliet and Van Steen (Sub-organisers).

Date of departure: 29.5.42.

Mission: To investigate the possibilities of opening a new sea-route for in- and ex-filtration, and to assist *Turnip*; To prepare plans and collect stores for the interruption of railway traffic when instructed by London; To carry out sabotage acts in general.

Field History: The two agents dropped to a German reception committee, so were arrested on arrival. Parlevliet was imprisoned at Haaren, but we do not know his ultimate fate, and he is still considered "missing".

Van Steen was seen at Rawicz Concentration Camp, in Silesia, in July 1944, but we have no subsequent news, so that he also is posted as "missing".

Agents Sent June 1942

Operation *Spinach*

Agent: Buizer (W/T).

Date of departure: 22.6.42.

Mission: To act as W/T operator to *Parsnip*, as well as to assist him generally; To act, if necessary, as W/T operator to *Potato*.

Field History: Dropped at the same time as *Parsnip* and arrested with him. Subsequently reported executed at Mauthausen Concentration Camp in September 1944.

Operation *Parsnip*

Agent: Van Rietschoten.

Date of departure: 22.6.42.

Mission: Organising and instructing groups of men for sabotage in the province of Zuid Holland; Arranging reception transport and storage of arms and material; Acts of opportunistic sabotage; Maintaining touch with *Potato* and *Spinach* (see under *Spinach*).

Field History: From London's telegram of 15th June 1942 No. 28 to *Trumpet*, the Germans learned of the impending arrival of *Parsnip*. He was arrested on arrival as the reception committee was German. He was imprisoned in Haren Concentration Camp, whence he escaped on Nov 22nd 1943. He apparently left there with Van der Giessen of Operation *Cabbage*. A German source states that he was arrested with *Cabbage* whilst travelling in the train from Rotterdam to Zeeland, and that he was subsequently executed. No confirmation of this exists and he is listed as "missing".

Operation *Marrow*

Agents: Jambroes (Organiser), Bukkens (W/T).

Date of departure: 26.6.42.

Mission: To contact leaders of the "Orde Dienst" and to explain to them the "Plan for Holland" which had been complied in London and agreed between the British and Dutch authorities. Thereafter, to organise the recruiting of suitable bodies of men to implement the plan. Details of this Plan are given under the heading "Outline of Planning". Thirdly, to organise reception committees.

Field History: London advised *Catarrh* on June 15th, in telegram No. 61, of the proposed despatch of these two agents as from June 24th. They were both arrested on arrival, their "safe" landing being advised to us by *Catarrh* on June 27th.

Jambroes was transferred from Haren Concentration Camp to Rawicz, in Silesia, where he was seen in June-July 1944. He was subsequently reported to have been executed at Mauthausen in September 1944.

Bukkens was also transferred to Rawicz and shot at Mauthausen in September 1944.

Agents Sent July 1942

Operation *Leek A*

Agent: Van Hemert.

Date of departure: 23.7.42.

Mission: To amplify the instructions given to Kloos (Operation *Leek*) before departure, and to have a report made out as to his progress, such report to be enciphered and collected by us.

Field History: Arrested on landing, July 24th, 1942. No further news of him until May 1945, when he was reported executed at Mauthausen in September 1944.

Agents Sent August 1942
No despatches.

Agents Sent September 1942

Operation *Kale*

Agents: Beukema, Thoe, Water.

Date of departure: 24.9.42.

Mission: Having studied exhaustively the "Plan for Holland" given to *Marrow*, *Kale* was to be prepared to relieve *Marrow* of his duties and to take over from him as soon as possible, continuing his work. *Marrow* was to be exfiltrated, but this was not *Kale's* task but that of *Mangold* (see Operation *Mangold*).

Field History: Dropped to a German controlled reception committee and arrested on the 25th September 1942. He was seen at Rawicz Concentration camp in July 1944, but in May 1945 he was reported executed at Mauthausen in September 1944.

Operation *Mangold*

Agents: Drooglever, Fortuyn.

Date of departure: 24.9.42.

Mission: Based on the "Plan for Holland". To work in with *Kale* and *Cauliflower* (see notes re *Cauliflower* Operation). Specific tasks were: a) To organise without delay two reception committees for stores and men; b) To arrange for transport of such stores to suitable places in the region; c) To tell *Marrow* by what means he can arrange to be exfiltrated; d) To tell *Marrow* of the impending arrival of his successor and of organiser-instructors for the operation of the "Plan for Holland"; e) To assist *Marrow* in all possible ways.

Field History: Dropped to German controlled reception committee and arrested at once (25.9.42). After being held for a time in Holland, he was transferred to Rawicz, Silesia, and is known to have been there in June 1944. He was ultimately sent to Mauthausen where he was executed in September 1944.

Operation *Parsley*

Agent: Jongelie.

Date of departure: 24.9.42.

Mission: This man, an older type unusual and extremely reliable was sent at the request of the Dutch authorities. His tasks were to contact the leaders of the Inlichtingsdienst ("I.D"), the Secret Intelligence Organisation in Holland. To explain to them that he was to act as liaison officer of the Dutch Military Intelligence Service, and as such to be the channel for instructions from London to the "I.D". This organisation to be told at once to give all possible assistance to Jongelie by providing reports, information, agents and any other help necessary for him in the execution of his duties as the Dutch Government's official envoy.

Field History: Dropped to German controlled reception committee and arrested 25th September 1942. The Germans, finding Jongelie's mission too involved for them to pretend in their traffic back to England that it was being carried out, decided to report that he was killed on landing.

Our latest information is to the effect that he was eventually shot at Mauthausen Concentration Camp on the 6th September 1944.

Operation *Cauliflower*

Agent: Mooy.

Date of departure: 24.9.42.

Mission: To assume the duties of Regional Commander for Overijssel or Gelderland in connection with the "Plan for Holland". The decision as to the region allotted to be made by *Marrow*. In this capacity to give guidance and instruction to the personnel already recruited; To organise the reception of personnel and stores; To do the groundwork necessary for the eventual exfiltration of *Marrow* by Lysander.

Field History: Dropped to German controlled Reception Committee. Arrested at once and imprisoned at Haaren Camp. Nothing further is known of him and he is considered "missing".

Agents Sent October 1942

Operation *Cabbage*

Agent: Van der Giessen.

Date of departure: 1.10.42.

Mission: To join *Parsnip* and to assist him in organising sabotage in the province of Zuid Holland, concentrating on transport in all forms; Reconnoitring possible reception grounds in the area.

Field History: Van der Giessen was arrested on arrival, the Reception Committee being German controlled. He was imprisoned in Haren Concentration Camp but escaped on the night of Nov 22/23, 1943. Since that time reports of his whereabouts have been circumstantial and varied. It is confirmed that he did escape and that he made his way to the Rotterdam area.

He endeavoured there to help underground activities. According to one German interrogation, he became involved with an organisation dealing in the manufacturer of false documents.

He was proceeding by train from Rotterdam towards South Beveland, accompanied by one Wegener (Operation *Lacrosse*, to be referred to under that operation), when he was arrested. The same source stated that he was shot later on, but we have no proof and still regard him as "missing".

Operation *Celery*

Agents: Steeksma (Instructor), Koolstra (Instructor), Macare (W/T).

Date of departure: 21 and 24.10.42.

Mission: The two instructors' duties were: a) Reconnoitring of targets; b) Instruction of sabotage groups in handling of weapons, explosives, and incendiaries; c) General steps to raise efficiency.

Field History: Dropped to German controlled committees and arrested at once. All three agents were reported by a returned French agent to have been sent to Rawicz Concentration Camp in Silesia, in July 1944. Steeksma and Koolstra were subsequently shot at Mauthausen Concentration Camp in September 1944. Nothing is known of Macare who is still "missing".

Operation *Pumpkin*

Agent: Pals.

Date of departure: 21.10.42.

Mission: Regional organiser for any area in the South of Holland to be decided by the leader of the "Secret Army", in connection with the "Plan for Holland" already mentioned.

Field History: Arrested on arrival by German controlled committee. Sent to Haaren Concentration Camp. Seen in July 1944 at Rawicz Concentration Camp. Reported shot at Mauthausen Camp in September 1944.

Operation *Tomato*

Agents: Hofstede (Instructor), Kamphorst (Instructor), Pouwels (W/T).

Date of departure: Hofstede and Pouwels 24.10.42; Kamphorst 21.10.42.

Mission: To assist leaders in reconnoitring targets and considering best methods of attacking them; To instruct sabotage groups in the handling of weapons, explosives and incendiaries; Generally, to help to bring all aspects into an efficient state. All these points in the light of the "Plan for Holland".

Field History: Arrested on arrival. Hofstede was sent to Haaren, whence he was moved to Rawicz, Silesia, where he was seen by an escaped French agent. He was executed at Mauthausen Camp in September 1944. Kamphorst was also at Haren and Rawicz, and eventually suffered the same fate as Hofstede, being executed at Mauthausen in September 1944.

Pouwels was imprisoned at Haren and then supposedly moved to Rawicz, but this is not certain. His fate is unknown.

Operation *Cucumber*

Agents: Bakker (W/T), Dane (Organiser).

Date of departure: 27.10.42.

Mission: In connection with the "Plan for Holland", to take charge, as Regional Organiser, of the Provinces of Friesland, Groningen and Drenthe. In this capacity, to organise, train and instruct bodies of suitable men and to perfect the organisation according to instructions from the leader as well as in the light of his own discretion. To organise the reception of the necessary stores.

Field History: Both dropped to a German controlled reception committee and were arrested on 28.10.42.

Bakker disappeared thereafter so far as any news was concerned, but we have recently heard from Dutch sources that he died in Vienna from tuberculosis, shortly after the liberation of that city.

Dane – Advice has been received that he was executed at Mauthausen Concentration Camp in September 1944.

Operation *Broccoli*

Agent: Ruseler.

Date of departure: 28.10.42.

Mission: In connection with the "Plan for Holland", to act as W/T operator for the leader under whom he was placed, and to obey his orders.

Field History: Dropped to a German controlled reception Committee and arrested on 29th November 1942. Sent to Haaren and thence to Rawicz, Silesia. Subsequently executed at Mauthausen in September 1944.

Agents Sent November 1942

Operation *Mustard*

Agent: De Kruyff.

Date of departure: 28.11.42.

Mission: On the basis of the "Plan for Holland", to reconnoitre targets and consider how best to attack them; To instruct groups of saboteurs and trainees in the use of weapons and explosives; To act with initiative under the orders of a designated leader.

Field History: Arrested immediately on arrival, 29th Nov 1942, by German controlled reception committee. No news since until June 1945 when we ascertained that he was executed at Mauthausen in September 44.

Operation *Chive*

Agent: Ubbink (W/T Operator).

Date of departure: 29.11.42.

Mission: To work as W/T operator for the secret military organisation envisaged under the "Plan for Holland".

Field History: Arrested at once by a German reception committee. He was taken to Haaren and subjected to intensive interrogation, thereafter, being placed in a cell and kept there until August 29th 1943, when he escaped with Dourlein, of Operation *Sprout*, (referred to under that operation). He made his way to Switzerland, where he arrived on the 19th November, reaching England, on 1st February 1944.

His interrogation, with Dourlein, was very thorough and prolonged and revealed a mass of information which made it clear that the Germans were in control of our organisation. The implications are obvious and will be referred to in detail under the "General" paragraph relative to the time of the interrogation.

The agent was under a cloud for a long time, and eventually transferred to the Dutch West Indies in some position connected with the Netherlands Merchant Marine.

Agents Sent December 1942
No Despatches.

Operations 1942 Totals

Total "successful" sorties	57
Aircraft lost	3
Total containers	282
Stores delivered:	
H.E.	6,968 lbs.
Stens	460
T.SMG	19
Grenades	3,170
Pistols	1,305
Incendiaries	45 cells.
Clams	495
Limpets	68

Chapter 3

1943

Dutch Section, General

The personnel of the H.Q. Section, January – February 1943 were:
   Major Blizard (Chief)
   Major Bingham
   Captain Knight
   Captain Mills
   Mr. Olink
   Lieut. Snewing
   Lieut. Parr
   Jnr. Cdr. Bond A.T.S.

The personnel of the H.Q. Section, March – December 1943 were:
   Major Bingham (Chief)
   Captain Knight
   Captain Mills
   Mr. Olink
   Lieut. Snewing
   Lieut. Parr
   Jnr. Cdr. Bond A.T.S.
   Lieut. Mortlock (U.S.A.)

Relations with the Dutch Authorities

These continued good throughout the year. Col. de Bruyne and Captain Lieftinck co-operated closely with us, but the former was never free from the cramping influence of "back-stage" intrigues against him. Eventually he relinquished his duties as chief of the M.I.D. (towards the end of 1943) and Captain Lieftinck, assisted by Lieutenant Schilp, carried on. As will be seen from the attached summary of the real position in the field, towards the end of the year certain facts came to light which eventually showed that our organisation was hopelessly penetrated. In addition, losses in aircraft were heavy, and for a period of about three months, air operations were suspended on this account.

Thus, whilst our relations with the Dutch personnel continued good, the amount of operational contact with them, was not great due to the paucity of dispatches, this in turn being a result of the causes above mentioned.

Outline of Planning for the Field in 1943

In general, the "Plan for Holland", details of which are given under the "Outline of Planning for 1942", was the basis of our activities. This is also evident from the agents' missions, as described under the relevant headings.

In May, Major-General Gubbins issued a further directive. The decision had been reached to adopt a more aggressive policy so far as sabotage was concerned.

The Section was, therefore, instructed to extend sabotage activities to include active sabotage as opposed to the previous undetectable kind. The Field was to be instructed to undertake no operations which might prejudice the plans for D-Day and to attack no target if the result of the attack was likely to do more damage to the Dutch population than to German war effort. Furthermore, no attacks were to be made involving the use of arms to overcome resistance by armed guards, unless the target could be shown to be a vital importance.

Selection of targets was to be made in the following order of priority:

Targets directly or indirectly connected with the construction, maintenance, and supply of U-boats.

Fuel oil in storage or in transit by water or rail.

Interference with inland waterways and railways subject to the afore-mentioned conditions.

Mines producing bituminous coal, but not those producing domestic coal.

Shipbuilding yards, working for the Germans.

Other establishments known to be doing work of importance to the German war effort.

Agents Sent January 1943

No despatches.

Agents Sent February 1943

Operation *Endive*

Agent: Van de Bor.

Date of departure: 16.2.43.

Mission: To act as organiser/instructor for groups of sabotage men; To assist in arranging for the reception of arms, their transport and storage; To advise group leaders and their men on the latest technique for handling arms, explosives etc.; To introduce an improved type of Eureka.

Field History: Arrested on arrival to German controlled reception committee. Transferred to Haaren Concentration Camp and ultimately shot at Mauthausen Camp in September 1944.

Operation *Radish*

Agent: Van Hulsteyn.

Date of departure: 16.2.43.

Mission: To act as instructor for Secret Army men and to train them in the latest methods of using explosives.

Field History: Dropped to German reception committee and not heard of since, until May 1945 when information was received of his execution at Mauthausen in September 1944.

Operation *Parsley A*

Agent: Braggar (W/T).

Date of departure: 16.2.43.

Mission: To carry on the work of contacting the I.D. (Dutch Intelligence Service) interrupted by the supposed death of Jongelie (*Parsley*), and to act as W/T channel.

Field History: Immediately arrested by the reception committee and imprisoned at Haren. No news of him after that until we heard in May 1945 that he had been shot at Mauthausen in September 1944.

Operation *Hockey*

Agent: Kist.

Date of departure: 18.2.43.

Mission: To contact, through *Kale*, the leaders of the I.D. and to carry on with Jongelie's (*Parsley's*) work, on similar lines to *Parsley (A)*, except that Kist was not a W/T operator.

Field History: Received by a German controlled committee. Subsequently seen at Rawicz Concentration Camp. No news since. Still regarded as "missing".

Operation *Tennis*

Agent: Van der Wilden, P.

Date of departure: 18.2.43.

Mission: To act as W/T operator for Kist, of Operation *Hockey*.

Field History: Landed to German reception committee and imprisoned at Haaren. Sent to Rawicz where he was seen in June 1944. Shot at Mauthausen in September 1944.

Operation *Golf*

Agent: Van der Wilden, W.

Date of departure: 18.2.43.

Mission: To act as W/T operator for Van Os (Operation *Broadbean*).

Field History: After being received by a German controlled committee, he was not heard of until July 1944 when he was reported as having been seen at Rawicz Concentration Camp. Thereafter, no news until in May this year we heard of his execution at Mauthausen in September 1944.

Operation *Broadbean*

Agent: Van Os.

Date of departure: 18.2.43.

Mission: In connection with the "Plan for Holland", to reconnoitre targets and consider the best means of attacking them. To give instruction in the handling of weapons and explosives. To organise lines of communication, pigeon service and safe houses.

Field History: Arrested at once by the reception committee. Taken from Haren Camp to Rawicz. Eventually executed at Mauthausen in September 1944.

Operation *Lacrosse*

Agent: Wegner.

Date of departure: 18.2.43.

Mission: Organiser/instructor for the Secret Army, in connection with the "Plan for Holland".

Field History: Captured on arrival. Imprisoned at Haaren. He escaped on the night of 22/23 Nov 1943. His intention was to get back to the U.K. and warn us of the penetration which had taken place. The next occasion when he was heard of was when he called on the father of Drooglever-Fortuyn, in Maastricht and told him that his son was in Haaren. Circumstantial evidence at that time attributed anti-patriotic activities to Wegner, but there is far too little evidence to support this.

Thereafter he disappeared and the next we heard was from an interrogation of a German S.D. man from Haaren who said that Wegner had been re-captured on the train between Rotterdam and Zeeland, with Van der Giessen (Operation *Cabbage*) and shot. There is no other support for this statement than the German's assertion. This agent is still considered "missing".

Agents Sent March 1943

Operation *Kohlrabi*

Agent: Boogart.

Date of departure: 9.3.43.

Mission: Organiser/instructor for the Secret Army.

Field History: Arrested on landing. Kept at Haaren for a time and thence transferred to Rawicz. Shot at Mauthausen in September 1944.

Operation *Seakale*

Agent: Arendse.

Date of departure: 9.3.43.

Mission: Organiser/instructor for the Secret Army.

Field History: Suffered the same misfortune as many others by landing to a German controlled committee. He was first shut up in Haaren and then sent to Rawicz. He was executed at Mauthausen in September 1944.

Operation *Sprout*

Agent: Dourlein.

Date of departure: 9.3.43.

Mission: Instructor for the Secret Army organisation.

Field History: Dourlein was captured on landing. He was taken to Driebergen where he was interrogated and then imprisoned at Haaren. On 29th Aug 1943 he escaped with Ubbink (*Chive*) and made his way to Switzerland where he arrived on Nov 11th 1943. He was brought over to the U.K. and landed with *Chive* on 1st Feb 1944. He was thoroughly interrogated, and his story revealed the state of affairs which had been prevalent for the past fifteen months at least. He was subsequently sent to the Dutch West Indies to a job connected with the Netherlands Merchant Marine.

Agents Sent April 1943

Operation *Gherkin*

Agent: Van Uytvanck.

Date of departure: 21.4.43.

Mission: To act as organiser to the Secret Army.

Field History: Arrested at once and sent to Haaren. Nothing further heard of him until May 1945 when we received notice that he had been shot at Mauthausen in September 1944.

Operation *Netball*

Agent: Rouwers.

Date of departure: 21.4.43.

Mission: To act as W/T operator for the Secret Army.

Field History: Dropped to the Germans. After being kept at Haaren, was transferred to Rawicz, where he was seen in June 1944. Since then, we have no news, and he is considered "missing".

Agents Sent May 1943

Operation *Croquet*

Agent: De Brey.

Date of departure: 21.5.43.

Mission: Organiser/instructor for the Secret Army.

Field History: Received by the Germans. No news of his subsequent movements until June 1945 when it was learnt that he had been sent to Mauthausen and shot in September 1944.

Operation *Squash*

Agent: Punt.

Date of departure: 21.5.43.

Mission: Organiser/instructor for the Secret Army.

Field History: The same as that of De Brey, with whom he was dropped, viz: captured at once by the Germans and eventually executed at Mauthausen in September 1944.

Operation *Polo*

Agent: Mink.

Date of departure: 21.5.43.

Mission: Organiser/instructor for the Secret Army.

Field History: Parachuted to German reception committee and imprisoned. Seen at Rawicz in June 1944. Shot at Mauthausen in September 1944.

Agents Sent June 1943
No despatches.

Agents Sent July 1943
No despatches.

Agents Sent August 1943
No despatches.

Agents Sent September 1943

Operation *Soccer*

Agent: Cnoops.

Date of departure: 18.9.43.

Mission: To check the address of a contact given to us by *Catarrh* on 27th Aug 1943, to which funds could be delivered for the Secret Army. The address was: Reeser-Cuperus, Olympia Plein, Amsterdam. If satisfied, to establish contact and circumspectly to observe whether the circle in which Cuperus moved and the organisation of which he formed a part, could be considered reliable. Also, to hand over Hfl.30,000 to that address for the use of the organisation. If not satisfied to return to U.K., bring back the money and report fully.

Field History: Dropped to Reception Committee near Paris and apparently genuinely received. Cnoops decided that Cuperus was not reliable and eventually handed over the money to another contact given by London, whom he trusted. He returned to the U.K. on Nov 12th, 1943.

Agents Sent October 1943

Operation *Badminton*

Agent: Van Schelle.
Date of departure: 18.10.43.

Mission: To deliver money to *passeurs* in Brussels and Holland, who were running an escape line from Holland. To follow and report on an escape line in Belgium which had recently failed to pass out some airmen delivered to it.

Field History: The 'plane was shot down by a German night-fighter. Van Schelle made his way to Brussels and was picked up by Van Vliet a Dutchman acting for the Germans and, throughout his time in Holland was shadowed by him. He eventually returned to the U.K. via Paris, bringing back a report, which was useful, as intelligence, but did not appear trustworthy owing to the fact that all Van Schelle's activities were shepherded by Van Vliet. The reason that he was allowed to return and was not arrested, was that the Germans wished to restore London's confidence by allowing a genuine agent, who had been in touch with the resistance groups, to travel in and out unscathed.

He reached the U.K. on the 20th of December 1943.

Operation *Rugger*

Agent: Gruen.

Date of departure: 18.10.43.

Mission: To contact the Underground Press to give it funds and to find out the best way in which we could co-operate and supply advice, funds, paper, cliches, etc.

Field History: Gruen who travelled with Van Schelle (*Badminton*) was in the 'plane which was shot down in Belgium. He made his way to Brussels and there was found by Van Vliet who persuaded him that he was a genuine contact and who knew all the passwords and answers. He was introduced to several people through Van Vliet and put into touch with the Underground Press, but the whole affair turned out to be a cat-and-mouse game and he was eventually arrested by the German security police and taken to a Concentration Camp.

He was taken to the Gestapo H.Q. at the Hague, ill-treated and interrogated under conditions of duress, at the end of December 1943. Then he was sent to Haaren, and thence to Vught. Afterwards he was transferred to Hamelin and finally later Hanover where he was released by the Germans on the 5th of April 1945. He contacted the British and was eventually flown to the UK arriving on May the 7th.

Agents Sent November 1943
No despatches.

Agents Sent December 1943
No despatches.

Actual Position in the Field During 1943
From the fate of the majority of agents sent during 1943, it will be apparent that the Germans continued to capture and imprison our men as they arrived, and that we were in fact accomplishing nothing at all on the lines of the plans formulated at London H.Q.

The first suspicion that all was not well was when, on June 23rd, a message reached the "C" organisation via an O.D. W/T channel to the effect that eight parachutists had been arrested "some time ago". A meeting was at once called between S.O.E. security and "C", Section V, in order to compare notes and to decide which channels have communication were to be trusted.

On the 30th June, another message over the O.D. line stated that the information given in the message of June 23rd had originated from Haren. The next day, Berne again telegraphed giving supplementary details as to the eight parachutists mentioned in the message of June 23rd.

Missions *Soccer* and *Badminton* were sent in September and October, having as part of their object the investigation of certain aspects of the security of the Secret Army organisation and contacts. Neither of them improved the outlook, and on November 23rd, a telegram from the Dutch Legation, Berne, to Col. de Bruyne confirmed the fears entertained about penetration.

This message stated that *Chive* and *Sprout* had arrived at the Legation and had reported that they had been received by a German controlled committee. Their subsequent interrogation revealed that the Germans knew "all about our organisation", and that "for a long-time wireless contact had been maintained with England", the Germans acting as though the agents were functioning normally. They estimated that 130 men had been arrested in this way and that the whole organisation was in their hands.

By this time, deliveries to the field were held up by London, and such wireless traffic as was maintained was of a non-committal character. The Germans guessed that *Chive* and *Sprout* have probably reached the U.K. or communicated with us, and that S.O.E. were probably aware of the real estate affairs.

Early in 1944, the arrest of an S.I.S. group called Heintje revealed to them, through the interception of messages, that S.O.E. definitely knew their game. The enemy then closed down the traffic with an appropriate valedictory message.

Thus ended the German attempt to control all resistance in Holland by the application of their plan known as Nordpol.

Notes on Dutch Clandestine Organisations, 1941-1943

General: The occupation of Holland by the Germans called into being a number of indigenous bodies of people whose objects varied. Most of them carried out clandestine resistance to the Occupying Power in some form or other, whilst some were concerned with the preservation of Dutch institutions and culture against German encroachment and absorption. All were, unfortunately, permeated with political rivalries, survivals of the previous Dutch heterogeneous political system, and this was a source of considerable weakness, since much valuable time was wasted and much energy dissipated on unprofitable squabbling, the main object being often lost sight of.

Orde Dienst (O.D.)

Composition: The party nucleus was composed of the leaders of the following political parties – Anti-revolutionary party; Roman Catholic party; Socialist Democratic party; Socialist Democratic Labour party; Liberal party.

Leaders: A committee of twelve was originally formed, including prominent people such as Dr. Colijn, Schouten, Dekkers, Verschuur, Koos Vorrink, Waardi Beekman and Jolles.

Aims: Maintenance of internal order; Opposition to excesses by departing German troops; Prevention of lynching of N.S.B. members and other collaborators; Action against Communists who might take advantage of the situation to create disturbances.

Organisation: Cells were in existence in various districts but the co-ordination between them was extremely loose. It was not possible to speak of an O.D. organisation controlled from a supreme Headquarters and organised from top to bottom. A result of this was that co-ordinated action on a large scale was out of the question, the loosely knit federation precluding this.

German penetration: This was considerable. Mostly it was done in a very unobtrusive fashion, so that groups were penetrated without being aware of it. This caused the organisation to become all the more unreliable.

Strength: Estimated at about 125,000, excluding the organisation "Het Lof", the league of ex-service men, who amalgamated with O.D. in July 1941, and whose membership was estimated at 30,000.

R.V.V. (Raad van Verzet – Council of Resistance)

Formation: The event which caused serious minded Dutchmen to realise that un-co-ordinated resistance was worse than useless, was the failure of the attempted General Strike in May 1943. The Germans were able to break this due to the lack of centralised leadership. Lack of contact between the organisers of the strike and the strikers was a serious deficiency which the R.V.V. was intended to remedy.

Composition: The Council was composed of leading members of well-established illegal organisations and accordingly had a wide sphere of influence.

Aims: The co-ordination of resistance by the centralisation of the time, place and nature, as well as the methods of resistance.

Methods: The proposed plan of action envisaged the following: Passive resistance by the population to the enforced transfer of labour to Germany; Denial of food supplies to the enemy. Obstruction by all possible means of the enemy's requisitioning schemes; Denial to the enemy of essential labour in connection with communications in general. This to be accomplished by supporting workers who went underground; Destruction of public administration; Appropriation of ration papers, identity documents etc, for use of illegal workers and people in hiding; Interruption of communications by rail, telegraph, land, and water; Sabotage of industries; [and] Intimidation of co-operating officials.

German penetration: There is no doubt that there was penetration in some spheres, but it was not such as to render the whole movement useless. The rank and file were loyal and the Council could be considered sufficiently sound to be reliable and operationally efficient.

C.S.VI.

This organisation derived, its name from "Centrum van Sabotage", and the "VI" represents the sixth attempt to form such a sabotage group in Holland after five similar attempts had failed due to political differences. It was created in the summer of 1942.

Composition: Hans Katan, a student, Dr. Castijn, a medical practitioner and K. de Graaf, joined forces to establish it.

Organisation: This was in small cells, each containing three or four members at first. Subsequently it was modified to a military basis, with brigades, groups and sections. Each brigade had 240 men, divided into 8 groups of 30 each, the groups being sub-divided into five sections of six men. It was recruited from all walks of life. It co-operated with the Communists at times but claimed to be non-political.

Aims: Active acts of sabotage against population registers, labour bureau and railways. Supplying of ration cards and identity cards to Jews and others; elimination of undesirables.

Penetration: So far as is known, the organisation was sound.

The "Illegal Press"

The Underground Press was a potent weapon against the Germans, and deserves high praise for its tenacity, bold policy, and efficiency under conditions of extreme danger and difficulty.

Chief constituents: The main papers with a regular circulation were *Het Parool, Je Maintiendrai*, [and] *Trouw*.

Organisation: The editorial staffs were in the main composed of resolute men who had previously been editors of pre-war journals suppressed or nazified by the Germans. They continued a relentless campaign against the oppressor, in which ridicule played a not an inconsiderable role. Unfortunately, political currents were still strong, and journalistic hankering after "scoops" contributed toward the weakening of the combined effort. On the whole, however, the common goal was striven after with commendable perseverance. The combined effects on German morale was considerable, and the corresponding fillip to Dutch morale was notable.

Distribution: Countless means were adopted for distributing the papers produced. Special care was taken to introduce copies into German circles as a source of annoyance and a gesture of defiance. Copies were placed in letter-boxes by night and posted as commercial papers besides being circulated by couriers. The number of copies produced has been variously estimated and naturally fluctuated with the fortunes of the papers' printing facilities – often hard pressed by confiscation and destruction. It is certain that circulation figures were maintained at a remarkably high level, sufficient to be widely enough read to counteract the poison put out by the Nazis through the controlled press.

Finances: This was a difficult question. The material such as paper, ink, lead etc. was usually stolen from the Germans. The difficulty was to maintain the workers on the staffs. This was mostly done by co-operation with underground movements. Money was also donated by firms and individuals. Much support would have come from England, had our plans succeeded, as we had the right kind of man for this job, and ample supplies of the necessary material, and financial assistance, as well as a facilities for giving sound advice and the latest news of the real position in the "free" world.

Measure of success: The Germans never succeeded in suppressing the publication of these papers, which continued throughout the occupation with a buoyancy which calls for great admiration.

Operations 1943 Totals

Total "successful" sorties	37
Aircraft lost	8
Total containers	262
Stores delivered:	
H.E.	5,895 lbs.
Stens	284
T.SMG	9
LMG	58
Pistols	1,001
Grenades	4,131
Clams	135
Limpets	125

Dutch Section Financial Report, December 1940 to December 1943

Operation	Guilders
Glasshouse	3,000.
Catarrh	12,000.
Carrot	3,000.
Turnip	5,000.
Watercress	6,000.
Lettuce	17,000.
Leek	12,000.
Beetroot	12,000.
Spinach	5,000.
Marrow	100,000.
Parsnip	5,000.
Leek A	3,000.
Kale	6,000.
Mangold	4,000.
Parsley	10,000.
Parsley A	2,500.
Cauliflower	4,000.
Cabbage	5,000.
Celery	7,500.
Pumpkin	4,000.

Tomato	7,500.
Cucumber	6,500.
Broccoli	2,500.
Mustard	2,500.
Cress	2,500.
Chive	4,000.
Endive	10,000.
Radish	2,500.
Hockey	5,000.
Tennis	2,500.
Golf	3,000.
Broadbean	7,500.
Lacrosse	4,000.
Kohlrabi	4,000.
Seakale	2,500.
Sprout	2,500.
Gherkin	4,000.
Netball	2,500.
Croquet	4,000.
Squash	4,000.
Polo	4,000.
Soccer	31,000.
Badminton	1,000.
Rugger	10,000.
Gross Total	355,500.
Less amount recovered from Dutch Authorities:	128,750.
Net Total:	226,750.

Chapter 4

1944

General Situation, January and February 1944

The year 1944 opened up with a complete "impasse", no prospects of improving the situation and complete dissatisfaction in both the Dutch and S.O.E. camps.

It is obvious that if Colonel de Bruyne had had the complete confidence of his opposite numbers in the Dutch B.I., they would have been able to supply him and S.O.E. with reliable contacts on which to build up again. However, through the lack of co-operation, between the Dutch B.I., and Colonel de Bruyne's office on the one hand, and the S.I.S., Dutch Section and S.O.E. on the other hand a complete deadlock had been reached.

Colonel de Bruyne was in disfavour, and he resigned his post early in February 1944. Major Bingham had an interview with Colonel Kruls, head of the Dutch AMGOT and for whom the Dutch Minister of War had the highest regard. This meeting took place on the 9th February and during which Colonel Kruls emphasised the importance of being well-informed as to the mentality of the Dutch population in general. He also stated that circuits with which the Dutch Information Service (B.I) was in contact, could not be charged with giving a true picture of the wishes of the larger mass of the population. They apparently consisted, according to him, of a small group of politicians who wanted to revive the old game of 52 parliamentary parties, and who were already jockeying for positions in order to be in power after the liberation. He claimed that as a result, the Dutch Cabinet were in a completely false picture on which to base its attitude and that in his opinion, it was necessary to have a man with a wide view of the head of all departments, maintaining contact with the people in occupied Holland. He was extremely bitter about Major Somer, head of the

35

B.I., and considered him to be at the root of all the trouble in Dutch Government circles.

It is therefore evident that, in a sense, the Dutch Government themselves were dissatisfied at the state of things and would have welcomed a strong S.O.E., had this been possible. On the other hand, S.I.S., who are fully aware of the S.O.E. state of affairs in Holland, can hardly be blamed for not co-operating more fully at that time. Their circuits would have obviously been penetrated.

In view of Colonel de Bruyne's resignation and the general situation, S.O.E. decided also to make changes. Lord Selborne had a meeting middle February with the Netherlands Minister for War, His Excellency JHR. O.A.C. Lidthe de Jeude, to discuss the general situation, and Major General C. Mc V. Gubbins, in his letter to Lidthe de Jeude of 23rd February, stressed the urgency of building up an effective organisation in the Netherlands to implement the directives of the Supreme Commander for D-Day action and that Commander Johns, regional director for Belgium, would henceforth be responsible for all policy matters in regard to S.O.E. operations in Holland.

On the 13th March, the Netherlands Minister for War was informed that Lieutenant Col. R.I. Dobson, who had had three years' experience in the Belgian Section, vice Major Bingham, had been nominated to take charge of the Dutch Section and that S.O.E. welcomed the nomination of Major General J.W. van Oorschot as replacement for Colonel de Bruyne.

Major General van Oorschot took up his appointment on the 15th March renamed his office the B.B.O. (Bureau Bijzondere Opdrachten) and Lieutenant Col. R.I. Dobson took over from Major Bingham on 26th of February 1944.

Students in training: 20
Agents in the field: Nil

General Situation, March 1944

At H.Q. S.O.E.:

The Dutch Section, although given a new lease of life, was faced with an extremely difficult task. It not only had to live down the stigma which reared over its head but also had to tackle anew the problems of building up a new organisation in the field with apparently very little time to spare.

The S.O.E. Security Section, in good faith, considered that everything that mattered in the field had been penetrated and strongly advised against sending agents to the field but on the other hand, gave no guidance and, in fact, did everything it possibly could do to discourage further operations in Holland. This utter feeling of distrust of having anything to do with Dutch activities filtered through to the Air Operation's Section and in due course to the Air Ministry, who already having had severe losses over Holland, were extremely difficult in the selection of dropping points and would only consider "blind drops" in zones more or less selected by them.

In the field:
Although S.O.E. had no contact the following was, however, the true picture of clandestine activity in occupied Holland at that time. Many spontaneous resistance groups existed and were derived from the ex-officers' organisation which existed to aid officers who had been forced to live underground in order to avoid deportation to Germany and the student groups which were formed to assist young Dutchmen who were liable to the German Labour Laws.

Due to the needs of these groups, other groups are grown up which were concerned with acquiring false papers, accommodation and supplies for those living illegally. The Clergy were active in this respect and did splendid work in aiding Allied airman in the same way. Many people in the liberal professions formed similar groups, although a very large number of Dutch people were concerned with some clandestine activity or other in one of the following organisations:

O.D.   Intelligence. Political and Post War Planning.
R.V.V. Sabotage and "Radio Dienst" Wireless Contacts.
K.P.   Knokploegen – Refractaires.
L.O.   Landelijke Organisatie – False Papers etc.
N.S.F. National Steun Fonds – Finance.
N.C.   National Committee – Welfare and Social problems.
C.I.D. C.E., and underground telephone system.
C.P.   Clandestine Press.

Their activities have grown in a slapdash fashion through lack of guidance or directives from the U.K. They were by no means watertight and most of the leaders and organisers of different movements new each other personally. There was a semblance of security but it was not all that could be desired, added to which, there were also many minor personal and political feuds.

Enemy forces:
Much must however be said for the courage and bravery shown by the
Dutch Resisters who had survived in a very small country with little
or no natural cover. Facing them they had a formidable enemy force to
control underground activity consisting of the following units:

   The Grune Polizei.
   The G.F.P.
   S.D. and Gestapo.
   N.S.B. (Dutch Civilian Collaborators).
   Dutch and Flemish S.S.
   Feldgendarmerie.
   Landwacht.
   Wehrmacht.

Relations with Dutch Government and S.I.S.:
Major General van Oorschot, having taken office, recruited one Captain
de Graaf who had recently arrived from occupied Holland and who
had been working with a sabotage organisation called "C.S.6." and
dispensed with Colonel de Bruyne's assistants Major Lieftinck and
Lieutenant Commander Schilp.

As a first step towards closer collaboration, van Oorschot, who was
an old friend of Major Somer, called for a meeting between the four
services i.e., S.I.S., S.O.E., B.I., B.B.O., during which Commander Johns
and Lieutenant Col. Dobson expressed the wish for real co-operation
and made clear to S.I.S. and the B.I., the S.O.E. Charter and likely
functions that the Resistance Forces would be called upon to do by the
Supreme Commander.

The meeting was satisfactory and was followed up by a further
meeting with Colonel Cordeaux of the S.I.S. and Commander Johns
and Lieutenant Col. Dobson.

Our relations with the B.B.O. remained exceedingly good
throughout the whole period of relationship with them. They had very
little knowledge of the inner workings of our clandestine methods and,
apart from looking after the interests of their agents, they were satisfied
to leave the whole matter to us. We kept them fully in the picture, with
the exception of Army Plans and, have been gained their confidence,
no difficulties arose.

Having gained the confidence of the Dutch B.I., S.I.S. fell into line
and our relations with them were excellent. In fact, so good, that from
September 1944 until the German Capitulation, it was they who attended
our daily meetings at S.F. H.Q., and we who dropped practically all
their agents and stores for them to our reception committees during
that period.

Planning:
Having gone through this groundwork the Dutch Section commence planning for the three missions:

To contact the Clandestine Press, gain their confidence and through them hope to be able to contact one or more of the active Resistance groups.

Mission to contact the C.S.6., based on information brought out by Captain de Graaf.

Mission to build up an effective sabotage organisation to disrupt enemy communications on the main railway lines in Holland, leading to Germany and South to Belgium.

These missions were agreed to by the B.B.O., and S.O.E., subject to the means of infiltration being on a "blind drop" basis.

Agents in training: 20
Agents in the field: Nil

General Situation, April 1944
Developments with the Dutch:
Lieutenant Col. Klijzing, who arrived in the U.K. from Holland in March, was established in the Office of the B.B.O., as Major General van Oorschot's personal assistant. His relations with the Dutch office of the B.I. were good.

Clandestine Press:
T. Biallosterski (*Draughts*) and his wireless operator J.A. Steman (*Bezique*), were dropped on the night of the 31 March/1 April, to contact the Clandestine Press and also to obtain through them some good contacts with the active Resistance movements. The operation was successful but unfortunately their package containing the wireless transmitter, which was buried on landing, was taken away by a farmer and never traced again. *Draughts* successfully made contact with the Clandestine Press, delivered money to them and also the printing block of Queen Wilhelmina's letter to the Dutch people, which was later reproduced in the Clandestine Press and, after nominating a *Draughts 2*, returned to the U.K., on the 9th July by way of Belgium, France, Spain and Gibraltar. He arranged a dropping ground with *Bezique* to which a new transmitter would be sent. *Bezique* was however able to contact us first of all through an S.I.S. transmitter and later on by the transmitter we were able to send him.

C.S.6. and R.V.V.:
N.J. Celosse (*Faro*), A.J.M. Cnoops (*Cricket*), J.H. Seyben (*Ping Pong*), and H.A.J. Sanders (*Swale*) were dropped successfully on the night of the 31st March/1st April. *Faro* to contact the C.S.6. and *Cricket* the R.V.V. Unfortunately, a second operator *Skittles*, refused to jump, leaving only one operator to work for three organisers. This may have had some bearing on their future fate as the two teams now only had one operator necessitating the organisers to more or less keep together with the ultimate result that they were all arrested in May. *Cricket*, before his arrest, was however able to contact the R.V.V., and delivered our directives to them. They requested stores should be sent to them and also that if the R.A.F. would drop parachute flares over the Dordrecht Power Station they would attempt to sabotage it. The R.A.F. were unwilling to undertake the operation and in consequence the whole project fell through. The R.V.V. reported that as a result of a well carried out sabotage attack on the factory at Hoek Pierson, the A.S.M. of Amsterdam had been forced to cut its consumption of oxygen by half.

German controlled S.O.E. transmitter, Heck/Blue:
On the 1st April, a telegram was received from the old German controlled transmitter, reading:
"Messrs Blunt, Bingham and Succs Ltd London. In the last time you are trying to make business in the Netherlands without our assistance. Stop. We think this rather unfair in view of our long and successful co-operation as your soul agents. Stop. But never mind whenever you will come to pay a visit to the continent you may be assured that you will be received with the same care and result as all those you sent us before. Stop. So long."
    Although the S.O.E. Security Section produced this as further evidence of German penetration – especially as it coincided with dispatch of six agents on the night of the 31st March/1st April – the Dutch Section felt that there was no connection as the time factor was too short.

Agents in training: 20
Stores sent to the field: 2 packages

General Situation, May 1944
Agents sent to the field: C.M. Dekkers (*Poker*) and his wireless operator G.J. Kuenen (*Football*) were dropped on the night of the 31st May to build up a sabotage organisation to destroy enemy rail communications throughout Holland but unfortunately their aircraft was shot

Communications:

down over the Gilze-Rijen airfield. Both *Poker* and *Football* and the crew were killed.

An attempt was made to send two packages containing wireless material to *Bezique* by the same aircraft doing the *Poker/Football* operation but unfortunately these were lost when the aircraft was shot down. *Bezique* did however contact us on an S.I.S. transmitter belonging to St. Jude.

Casualties:

Faro, *Cricket*, *Swale* and *Ping Pong*, were arrested on the 19th May. *Faro* refused to talk and was subsequently shot. *Cricket* and his operator *Swale* both played the game and did not divulge their security checks with the result that we were able to play back the German controlled traffic until such time as it were deemed safe for *Cricket* and *Swale*'s security, before closing down. The fact that the R.V.V. reported the arrests through an S.I.S. transmitter was, from a security point of view, in their favour and confirming to us that they, as an organisation, were still safe.

In closing down the *Swale* traffic it was decided to send the following message to the Germans as a rebuff to their famous message of the 1st April: "With reference to your message of April First we have tried your agency once more but consider it to be so terribly inefficient as to warrant our changing for good. Stop. Please do not worry about entertainment as that matter will be in our hands and now having a detailed list of you all you may rest assured that it will hardly be pinpoints."

Poker and *Football* were killed when their aircraft was shot down on the night of the 31st/1st June.

Agents in training: 25

General Situation, June 1944

Special security meeting:

An important meeting was held in London to determine, if possible, the extent of German penetration of the R.V.V. The meeting was attended by the security sections of S.I.S. and S.O.E., the B.I., B.B.O., and ourselves. The S.O.E. Security Section had been pushing for this meeting for some time and S.I.S., on the other hand, were just as equally keen not to have it. The result was unsatisfactory and S.I.S.

felt satisfied that the R.V.V., so far as could be determined, were still sound. This did give however an opportunity to the S.O.E. Dutch Section to plan ahead.

Operational ban:
Owing to the Security ban, all operations were stopped to Holland until after D-Day. As the ban also applied to foreigners arriving in the U.K. it affected our recruiting possibilities. It also prevented the all-important *Rummy/Podex* mission, to check the security of existing organisations, from leaving the country for the field.

Agents in training:	22
Agents sent to the field:	Nil, See operational ban
Stores sent to the field:	Nil
Arrests:	Nil
Agents returned:	Nil

General Situation, July 1944

S.I.S. continued to receive requests from the R.V.V. for saboteur instructors and material. The following message was received, and the Dutch Government realised the importance and urged that special organisers should be sent to the field as soon as possible:

"OD KP and RVV again press the urgency of sending weapons on account of the total absence of suitable weapons and ammunition. Stop. Also to prevent the catastrophic destruction prepared by the enemy and in addition for the execution of sabotage projects High Command it is vital we receive weapons now. Stop. We collectively pass to the Government this great responsibility."

Agents in training:	13
Agents sent to the field:	Lieutenant L. Mulholland (*Podex*), L.A. de Goede (*Rummy*) two organisers and their wireless operator A. Van Duyn (*Cribbage*), were successfully dropped on the night of the 5th/6th July. Their mission was a real last attempt at trying to build up an active organisation in Holland. *Podex* was successful in his contact with the R.V.V. and *Rummy* in the same way was instrumental in building up the K.P. (Knonploegen) organisation. Both organisations were supplied with vast quantities of stores and, together with the O.D. (Orde Dienst), eventually amalgamated their efforts when called upon to do so by Lieut. General H.R.H. Prince Bernhard,

and became the N.B.S. (Nederlandsche Binnenlandsche Strijdkrachten).

P.J. Kwint (*Fives*), P. Verhoef (*Racquets*), J.A. Walter (*Bowls*) and J. Bockma (*Halma*), were sent on a special mission to contact the R.V.V. in the Veluwe area on the night of the 5th July but unfortunately their aircraft was shot down over the Ijsselmeer and their bodies were subsequently recovered and buried at Makkum. The Germans attempted to bluff us on the *Bowls* plan which they recovered from *Bowls'* body. Their attempts were however treated with due reserve.

Stores sent to the field:	Nil
Communications:	Nil
Casualties:	*Fives, Racquets, Bowls* and *Halma*. Aircraft shot down and all four were drowned.
Agents returned from field:	*Draughts*, who had bicycled down to France, was brought out on one of Lieutenant Col. Humphrey's escape lines to Gibraltar and arrived in the U.K. on the 9th July. Microphotographs of the Clandestine Press and information which he brought with him were encouraging and inspired the S.O.E., Dutch Section, for future action.

General Situation, August 1944

Command of the Netherlands Forces of the Interior:

On the 31st August, Lieutenant General W.B. Smith, U.S., Army Chief of Staff, on behalf of Supreme Headquarters Allied Expeditionary Force, circulated the following minute:

Now that the area of active operations is beginning to move towards the frontiers of Holland, the Supreme Commander has decided that the time has come to regard the members of the resistance movement in Holland as the "Netherlands Forces of the Interior". Lieutenant General H.R.H. Prince Bernhard has been nominated by the Netherlands Government to command the Netherlands Forces of the Interior under the command of General Eisenhower. These measures will take effect forthwith.

The Supreme Commander's directives on the action required by the Netherlands Forces of the Interior will be issued from time to time to H.R.H. Prince Bernhard, who, assisted by a small staff, will continue to operate through the agency of Commander Special Forces. It has been agreed that this change in command will not necessitate any change in the organisation or location of the staff of Special Force Headquarters.

Agents sent to the field:

S. Postma (*Sculling*) and his operator H.G. Reisiger (*Turniquoits*), were successfully dropped in Holland on the night of the 7th August to build up an active organisation through the L.O. (Landelijke Organisatie). They started successfully in the wooded area of the Veluwe but eventually retired to the Utrecht area where they were instrumental in building up an extremely valuable resistance movement. Unfortunately, they were both eventually arrested. *Sculling* was caught and shot in November and *Turniquoits* was arrested in December and is still missing. Their good work was however carried on by *Cubbing*, who had gone to Utrecht from Rotterdam prior to *Sculling's* arrest, right up to the time of the German capitulation in May 1945.

F.L.J. Hamilton (*Rowing*) and his sister A.M.F. Hamilton (*Tiddleywinks*) were dropped on the night of the 9th August together with wireless equipment for *Bezique*, money for the Clandestine Press and a special photograph and caption signed by H.M. the Queen of the Netherlands. *Tiddleywinks*, on landing, broke her ankle and remained in the hands of hospitals and doctors until the German capitulation. *Rowing* successfully delivered the wireless equipment to *Bezique* but owing to nerves following on *Tiddleywink's* accident threw away the propaganda material and which was never recovered. He did an extremely good job however in North Holland later, and through *Draughts 2*, linked up with *Draughts 1*, when he went to the field in September, and instructed a large number of potential instructors in sabotage and reception committee work.

J.H. Luykenaar (*Shooting*), J.R. Hinderink (*Hunting*) and their wireless operator J. Beekman (*Charades*), were successfully dropped on the night of the 28th August to build up the resistance organisations in the Veluwe area. A message confirming their safe arrival was received through an S.I.S. channel on the 30th August. Owing to the hectic conditions prevailing after the Arnhem Airborne Operation, they were unable to remain in the area – *Shooting* went to Rotterdam to work with the R.V.V. as an instructor – *Hunting* and the operator *Charades* went East of the River Ijssel and worked in the Overijssel area. *Shooting* did a magnificent job instructing resistance members in the Rotterdam area but owing to the eventual difficult situation there, he was obliged to come out through the lines on the 16th March 1945. *Hunting*, in spite of his tender years, instructed a vast number of resistance members in Overijssel and assisted with a Eureka at several dropping operations.

Charades carried on as wireless operator and eventually acted as second operator to *Dudley* and, on his death, continued in this capacity for Evert and Herman, both of the Salland area. He was a moody operator and his morale suffered in accordance with local conditions, but he proved to be invaluable and carried on until his release by the Allies in April 1945.

J.M. Van de Meer (*Stalking*), K. Buitendijk (*Fishing*) and their wireless operator G. Kroon (*Skating*), were dropped on the night of the 28th August in the Eindhoven area to build up the resistance there and to arrange delivery of stores. Their aircraft was hit by flak and had to make a forced landing. *Stalking* and *Fishing* managed to escape and after a short interlude with the resistance in the area came through the lines on the 10th November. *Skating*, who must have been injured in the crash, was caught and eventually died from his injuries or ill treatment on the 2nd May 1945.

Stores sent to the field: Although urgent requests were received from the field for material, normal air operations were limited as Bomber Command was unable to agree to Tempsford based aircraft operating to Holland during the non-moon period – 38 Group were tied up with the forthcoming airborne commitments. Our Dutch opposite numbers and ourselves were very disturbed at the state of affairs as morale in the field was suffering considerably from the lack of operations and stores. H.R.H. Prince Bernhard, who was now taking an active interest in our

	activities, personally urged the Air Ministry to do everything possible to deliver material to Holland.
Sabotage activities:	A special B.B.C. message was broadcast requesting the Resistance to dislocate railway traffic in Holland.
Casualties:	G. Kroon (*Skating*) as explained above.
Agents returned from field:	Nil
Agents in training:	13

General Situation, September 1944

H.R.H. Prince Bernhard:

Prince Bernhard left for the Continent on the 9th September accompanied by Captain A.G. Knight of the S.O.E. Dutch Section, Captain de Jongh of the B.I. and two S.O.E. wireless operators Sergeants Spence and Hannaford. His H.Q. was established in Brussels and his wireless contact with us was on plan Northaw. Henceforth Prince Bernhard worked in close liaison with No's 1, 2 and 3 S.F. Detachments and 30 Corps Rear H.Q. In early 1945, a second H.Q. was established in Breda until a final H.Q. was formed in Apeldoorn, at the Royal Palace, later. He became actively engaged in arming reliable Resistance Groups in liberated Holland, South of the Rivers, for the maintenance of law and order, also to assist Allied troops in their requirements. For this purpose, some 50 tons of arms were flown by Tempsford in Hudson aircraft to Brussels from where they were transported by road to Eindhoven.

Resistance activities:

Although each service maintained its own links with the field, the S.I.S. and S.O.E. wireless channels were from now on more or less pooled and put at the disposal of Prince Bernhard. This caused some confusion in the beginning as the Prince also used the S.I.S. Internal wireless net at Eindhoven and replies to his messages sent on this net would very often come in on the U.K. channels, necessitating re-transmission to the Prince on the Northaw channel. Owing to the fight for supremacy between the O.D., R.V.V., and K.P., Prince Bernhard called for unity and the first step towards this end was the forming of the Driehoek (Triangle) which ultimately became the D.C. (Delta Centrum), staff to the C.B.S. Although a certain amount of internal opposition existed between the organisations, they were at any rate combined in their efforts against the Germans.

Arnhem Airborne Operation "Market":
This took place on the 17th of September and one Jedburgh Team was
attached to each of the following units:

Airborne Corps HQ. Team "Edward".
Captain Staal. Dutch.
Captain Sollenberger. U.S.
Captain Mills. British.
2/Lieutenant Willmott. British.
Sergeant Billingsley. U.S.

I Air Transported Division. Team "Claude".
Captain Groenewoud. Dutch.
Lieutenant KnottenbeLieutenant Dutch.
Lieutenant Todd. U.S.
Sergeant Scott. U.S.

82 Div. (U.S.). Team "Clarence".
Captain Bestebreurtje. Dutch.
Lieutenant Verhaeghe. U.S.
Sergeant Beynon. U.S.

101 Div. (U.S.). Team "Daniel".
Major Wilson. British.
Lieutenant du Bois. Dutch.
Sergeant Fokker. Dutch.
Sergeant Mason. British.

Concurrent with this Arnhem Airborne Operation, secret wireless
messages were transmitted to the Resistance by S.O.E., and S.I.S. the
text read:
"Parachute troops have landed on the bridges at Arnhem Nijmegen
and Grave. Stop. Reinforcements will follow quickly. Stop. Give every
possible assistance to these Allied troops so that the bridges over the
Rhine Neder Rhine and the Maas Canal are not rpt not destroyed.
Stop. Resistance Groups inside the area should only provide guides
give intelligence information and provide labour. Stop. Resistance
outside the area but within twenty kms will give the same assistance
but also try to prevent enemy troops approaching the area. Stop.
Resistance outside the twenty kms radius should interfere with enemy
movements towards and from the area but protect and preserve petrol
dumps. Stop. Put into action immediately the Intelligence Plan with
the password telephone as per our previous instructions. Stop. Special
trained Allied Resistance Teams in uniform have landed in the area

with parachute troops and can be contacted daily at the entrance to the Oudenhof between Bessen and Bemmel at 0900 hours. Stop. Password is Ik Zoek Jan Blom and the reply is U Wilt Zeggen Van Utrecht. Stop. Give them all the help and information you can regarding the Northern and North Eastern and Eastern parts of Holland. Stop."

Of the airborne operation itself, little more need be told. Of the four Jedburgh Teams, the team "Edward" was the only one to maintain wireless contact with the U.K. The first message was transmitted by them at 2000 hours on the 17th September. The teams put up an exceedingly good show and were able to act as liaison between the Airborne Forces and the Dutch local resistance forces, arranging for labour for the building of air strips, guides, guards and collection of intelligence. They were commended by the Airborne Force Commander for their valuable work. It is unfortunate, however, that up to the time of the airborne landing no weapons had been dropped in the area and, in fact, only some 700 weapons in all had been despatched to Holland up to that time.

Railway strike:
Concurrent with the Arnhem operation and at the suggestion of the field, special wireless broadcasts were made to the railway personnel in Holland, requesting them to go on strike and into hiding. This they promptly did and upset the whole of the railway traffic in Holland with the exception of such lines which the Germans put back into commission with their army personnel. The result of this strike, although not then apparent, not only impeded the Germans but eventually rebounded on the Dutch population themselves and prevented the transport of food from the better stocked larders of Eastern Holland to the poorer ones in Western Holland. This eventually led up to the terrible famine in Central and Western Holland and the ultimate dropping of food in daylight to the stricken areas by the Allies.

Russians working for Wehrmacht:
Of some 50,000 Russian Georgians and Turkestans captured by the Germans on the Eastern front, the bulk of whom were starved to death or murdered, about 2/3000 were forced into submission and eventually put on German uniform and worked for the Germans as a labour corps in Holland. They were stationed on the West coast of Holland on general defence duties and, being anti-German at heart, eventually came into contact with the Resistance movements and expressed their willingness to mutiny and kill their German officers. A pre-arranged B.B.C. message was broadcast to reassure them but

owing to subsequent events and international policy, the action message was never broadcast.

Special daily meeting:
Although relations were extremely good with S.I.S. and both the Dutch offices of the B.B.O. and the B.I., it was generally felt that, owing to the pressure of work and the need for prompt and collective action, a daily Conference should be held to study messages from the field and ensure complete unity vis-à-vis the field, the Dutch Government, Prince Bernhard's H.Q., and army requirements. This procedure was agreed to and from September 1944 until May 1945, a daily conference was held between the four services S.I.S., S.O.E., B.B.O., and B.I., in Lieutenant Col. R.I. Dobson's room at S.F. H.Q.

Agents sent to the field:
T. Biallosterski (*Draughts I*) and his wireless operator P. de Vos (*Backgammon*), were dropped on the night of the 8th September to build up resistance in the Amsterdam and North Holland areas. This was *Draughts'* second mission. The operation was successful, and they both put up a magnificent show. The whole of the central executive of the N.B.S., was built up through the *Draughts* liaison. Vast quantities of stores were dropped which found their way down to Amsterdam by a motor barge having a specially constructed double bottom. *Draughts* was unfortunately arrested by chance on the 10th February when returning from a dropping operation. He was fatally wounded whilst trying to escape and died later in Scheveningen prison. *Backgammon* faithfully carried on his work with Dr. X – *Draughts* successor – until the German capitulation in May 1945. The ingenious methods he employed for transmitting his messages to the U.K. were instrumental in maintaining vital communications with Dr. X. and the C.B.S. (Commander Binnenlandsche Strijdkrachten) appointed by Prince Bernhard to lead the N.B.S. in Holland.

Major Brinkgreve (*Dudley*), Major Olmsted U.S. and their wireless operator, Sergeant Austin, three Jedburgh trained men, were dropped in Eastern Holland on the night of the 8th September in order to build Resistance in the Veluwe area. Conditions there were unsatisfactory – *Dudley* and his team returned to the Overijssel area where they were able to build up a first-class resistance movement under the command of the Zone Commander Eduard. A number of dropping operations took place in their area and its Resistance Forces put up a very good show when the Allies push the enemy back in April 45 through Overijssel into the Northern provinces of Drenthe, Friesland and Groningen.

Sergeant Austin was unfortunately arrested in December 1944 and shot later together with other prisoners for the attack on Rauter. *Dudley* however maintained contacts through the W/T operator *Charades* and Eduard's operator *Squeak* until he was shot while trying to escape from a house search on March the 5th 45.

W.H. Hoogewerff (*Coursing*), P. Polak (*Boating*), M. Cieremans (*Cubbing*) and G. de Stoppelaar (*Monopoly*), three sabotage instructors and the wireless operator *Boating* were dropped to the Rotterdam area on the night of the 15th September. At their own request they dropped in uniform but had to revert to civilian clothing soon after their arrival. A number of containers were subsequently dropped to them through their reception committees. *Coursing* and *Monopoly* settled down in the area and did very good work. *Coursing* was however arrested in February 45 and subsequently shot. *Cubbing* went to the Utrecht area and linked up with *Sculling* and carried on *Sculling's* work after he was caught and shot. *Boating* at his own request, joined *Draughts I* and *Backgammon* as a second wireless operator to the Amsterdam Group.

S.A.S. Party "Regan"

S.A.S. wishing to liven up resistance activities dropped a party of four men in uniform in the Drenthe area. As movement in allied uniform was impossible, they reverted to civilian clothing. They were instrumental in arranging the delivery of a few consignments of containers. The security of these S.A.S. men and of the resistance members in the area was not good and eventually numerous arrests and the seizing of arms dumps took place. The party split up and eventually return through the lines.

Stores sent to the field:

During the month of September, there were 86 Air sorties over Holland of which 42 were successful. In all some 765 containers and 71 packages were dropped.

Sabotage activities:

Reports which came through were encouraging and the following activities were reported:

The K.P. effectively carried out sabotage on the railways. Directive of 27th Aug 44. This was confirmed by messages received by S.I.S. reporting that the line Roosendaal/Breda/Tilburg/s'Hertogenbosch was seriously affected – railway traffic in South and Southeastern Holland was at a standstill and that lines in Eastern Holland were being cut nightly.

Lines cut between Veenendaal and Rhenen, Amersfoort and Apeldoorn, Amersfoort to the South. Sabotage carried out on the railway bridges over the Dedemsvaart and Zwolle-Meppel.

The three blockade ships the *Borneo*, *Westerdijk* and *Axenfels* had been sunk by Resistance in the Port of Rotterdam.

Acting upon intelligence received from the field, some successful air attacks were carried out on rocket sites North of the Hague.

Casualties:	Captain Groenewoud – killed at Arnhem
Agents returned from field:	Nil
Agents in training:	16

Daily Summary, 25 September 1944
Northaw Mission. H.R.H. Prince Bernard and staff:

The mission says that: They are in touch with Tromp (S.I.S.), are reliably informed that there are at least 4,000 partly armed men available in Beilen, who are well-led and prepared even for a push against the rear of the Ijssel line. He contacts them through Mickey (S.I.S.). Deliveries to this group are advocated. Telephone communication through Albrecht is successful.

Their contacts with Amsterdam have been broken, and they ask for a message to be sent to their S.O.E representative in Amsterdam arranging for schedules so that contact can be re-established.

Karel (S.I.S.) should be told that orders for local and regional Driehoek were not given by Northaw and should not have been given by Karel.

The Mission has been informed that the following commanders have been appointed:

RVV. Afdeeling 1.	Karel	Veluwe. Utrecht. Rotterdam.
RVV. Afdeeling 2.	Van Dam Arnhem.	
K.P.	Frank	Rotterdam.
Utrecht Brigade.	Scholberg.	
Amsterdam Brigade.	Ed.	
Rotterdam Brigade.	Maarten.	
Hellendoorn Brigade.	Evert.	
Ermelo.	Piet.	

Karel says that he has no contact with the Achterhoek (area N.E. of Arnhem) and Bethuwe (area between the Rhine and Maas) brigades. He also says that he has taken his seat in the Driehoek.

Kor (S.I.S.) is in Breda and has been asked with what organisation he has contact.

Fock (B.I.) states that broadcast announcements of the work of Resistance in preventing the enemy from looting, aggravates the position in the occupied territories.

Albrecht (S.I.S.) reports that Eduard is in telephone contact with S.I.S. at Eindhoven.

R.V.V. report that internal communications are working between Utrecht, Eindhoven, Rotterdam, the Hague and Deventer. That between Twenthe and Amsterdam is under repair.

Podex has been asked whether the sinking by sabotage of the block ships *Westerdam, Borneo, Axenfels* at Rotterdam which has been reported by the Brigade Commander Rotterdam, is his work.

Draughts reports that the provincial commandant of the North Holland Northern quarter is Lieutenant Col. J. Wastenecker, who belongs to the Netherlands Indies Army. He has 500 well trained storm troopers who need arms and ammunition.

Draughts also reports that there are 1050 Mongols who are willing to fight with us in the area Schagen.

Jedburgh Edward was near Driel on 24 September in order to contact Claude, who is in Arnhem. He is trying to contact Daniel and says Clarence is all right.

S.A.S. Brutus reports that 24 September Dutch Resistance Groups and 21 Army Group have temporarily telephone communication from Maastricht and Eindhoven to Roermond, Venlo, Breda and Arnhem, via a water and electric works private telephone system. There is, however, no information of any system working further to the North.

S.A.S. Regan reports 24 Sept that R.V.V. and K.P. are well organised and efficient, but not trained and only 5% armed. He has 300 men waiting to be armed.

S.A.S. Regan also reports that R.V.V. 1, wishes a small party in civilian dress to be sent to each RVV Brigade with wireless equipment to perform liaison and intelligence missions.

Total figures to date of controllable resistance strength is 3,820 men.

Daily Summary, 26 September 1944
Northaw Mission:

The mission agrees that Jedburgh Edward should return and that he should undertake a mission to Northeast Holland.

The mission says that the contact committee should be told that the Driehoek ordered by the Mission is only to be transformed on a high level, and not on local or regional level. Locally and regionally one commander should be appointed by agreement, this man should be appointed by a high level Driehoek and should be a man with experience of Resistance.

Karel (S.I.S.) is to be instructed that all special orders to brigades and only general measures to high level groups.

Podex. A message from *Podex* indicates that it was his group which sank the block ships at Rotterdam.

Edward reports that a member of K.P. Utrecht has arrived at his H.Q. and supplied information on the enemy. K.P. Utrecht is active having 60 members and has arms and explosives. Instructions are being passed to disrupt enemy rail communications.

Edward is sending a member of the mission to Oss to try to re-establish contact. He is getting in touch with Northaw mission for instructions on railway sabotage, and in the meantime will try to obtain information on the enemy in the Deventer area. He hopes to hear *Dudley's* reaction soon.

Edward contacted Daniel at Veghel, where they are doing good work, mainly collecting intelligence from the civilian population. Daniel's resistance contacts are very few.

Edward has contacted three members of KP Kesteren who have brought valuable information on enemy dispositions at Tiel. The KP Kesteren strength is 25 men, all instructed to work on intelligence work only. Rail traffic in the Betuwe area has been stopped completely.

No. 3 SF Det, answering the enquiry put to them on Edward's statement that he considers his mission finished, asks that Edward be instructed to report to No. 2 SF Det (*Varicose*). *Varicose* will investigate whether Clarence and Daniel still serve a useful purpose: a decision on Claude will be given later.

S.A.S. Regan 25 Sept reports that Resistance has cut the railway Veenendaal-Rhenen over a sector of 100 metres.

Jedburgh Clarence reports 26 Sept that he has two companies available for military duties but who need arms badly.

Daily Summary, 27 September 1944
Jedburgh Edward reports 26 Sept that Jedburgh Claude is missing. Lieut. Knottenbelt, who accompanied Claude, was last seen on the night 25 Sept on the North bank of the Rhine having been wounded slightly. Edward will check his arrival in Nijmegen and will inform S.F. H.Q.

Edward reports having met, at a meeting in Oss, the district leader of the East Brabant OD, the Oss leader, and the leaders are two independent KP groups. Co-ordination of resistance activities was arranged. The KP groups, numbering 40 men, were sent for harassing action in the Maas and Waal areas; these men are armed with captured enemy arms. Strength in Oss is 100 men partly armed.

Edward further reports that before his arrival resistance was generally organised in small bodies. After his arrival, the organisation was greatly enlarged and organised to meet immediate military needs. He says that fewer arms have been received from S.F. H.Q., than from captured German stocks. In view of the non-combatant use of Resistance he suggests that arms are not of primary importance.

Edward advises S.F. H.Q., that he will return to Brussels as soon as possible after clearing up his commitments. He will find out from Clarence and Daniel how many are returning and inform S.F. H.Q. of the total.

Daily Summary, 28 September 1944
Northaw Mission:

The mission was informed by the Dutch Section on the 27 September that, OD reports that the Burgemaster of the Hague has already made preparations several months ago with OD for the maintenance of order after the liberation of the Hague. The Burgemaster considers that it is essential that only OD will assist the police in this. However, some groups have joined OD and relations with R.V.V. and K.P. are well established.

Marinier (S.I.S.) reports that the railway yards at Hertogenbosch are destroyed and that the railway bridge over Dedemsvaart Zwolle Meppel (East of Zwolle) has been sabotaged by railway personnel.

Vanveen an S.I.S. organiser, reports that there is a group called Paul, numbering 1,000 men in the area between Dordrecht and Rotterdam. This group is in close relation with the provincial K.P. and has detailed plans for the protection of bridges at Zwijndrecht, Barendrecht, Alblasserdam, Sliedrecht and Spijkenisse.

Driehoek reports that lines of roadblocks are being prepared outside built-up areas: Around the end of the Afsluitdijk at Makkum, Wons and Zurig, on the line Groote Brekken, Koevoordermeer, Sneekermeer, Wijde-Ee, Bergumermeer, Lauwerszee, paying special attention to main roads going West to East. They await orders before embarking on these plans.

A message dated 28 Sept from Northaw gives instructions that Radio Oranje broadcast that all captured weapons in liberated or unliberated districts should be placed at the disposal of the members of Resistance.

S.A.S. Regan states 27 Sept that Resistance has cut both tracks of the railway Amersfoort to Apeldoorn and made them unusable for 36 hours.

He also reports 25 Sept that a Jedburgh in Twenthe has been captured by the enemy. His source is not stated. The Jedburgh may be *Dudley*.

Jedburgh Edward reached *Varicose* 27 Sept proposing to return to U.K.

Communication has been established with S.A.S. Portia, who was sent to the field on the night of the 26/27.

Arnold (S.I.S.) says that there are still difficulties in obtaining unity of command of resistance, and OD Rotterdam appear to be concentrating on post liberation plans for maintenance of order, as a result of which Arnold considers of the protection of vital installations is now doubtful.

A report states that Resistance has sunk the *Arensfeld* which was under construction at the Rotterdam shipyards and was about to be removed to Hamburg by the enemy. Resistance have also sabotaged a tramway in Rotterdam.

Daily Summary, 29 September 1944

Sculling. A message has been received from the W/T operator to *Sculling* from whom nothing has been heard for some time, saying that *Sculling* is safe but had lost his code. They intended to leave for Apeldoorn and will transmit from there in two days.

Draughts reports 28 Sept that the railway strike is now general, and the inland traffic is entirely held up excepting only Wehrmacht trains carrying German personnel.

Dudley has been in further W/T touch with SF HQ on 28 September It is considered that he is safe and has not been captured as previously thought.

S.A.S. Regan state that they are not in permanent contact with Resistance but work through couriers. They are in enemy country 12 miles from dropping ground Bertus.

S.A.S. Portia report that their location is V 328779. Resistance is well organised.

S.A.S. Regan also reports that beginning at 1100 hours, German munition transport was held up on the road at E 4589 for at least 5 hrs., and that the railway from Amersfoort to the South was cut by Resistance for one day.

Daily Summary, 30 September 1944

Northaw Mission states that they are getting hundreds of volunteers from Eindhoven and Maastricht, for whom directives are required. They also say that Resistance forces are required for guard and other duties after liberation.

Podex states that he is planning attacks on the Schiehaven and Jobshaven at Rotterdam. He states that a "commando" is trying to protect these harbours, meaning it is believed, that the Germans are trying to protect them before they put their port scorching into effect. Owing to the departure of German warships the attack will probably take place on the morning of 2 or 3 Oct.

An S.I.S. report, reliability unknown, states that the RVV Brigade Commander Rotterdam says that underground fighters, owing to lack of weapons, cannot oppose the German port scorching which has already started in the Mass and Rijn Harbours. Attacks by Resistance now would lead to reprisals against the civilian population without accomplishing anything unless help came quickly.

Draughts asks for the bombing of the H.Q. in Amsterdam of the Sicherheitsdienst. He says that the SD are increasing their activity and destruction of the H.Q. is necessary to prevent them from dealing Resistance a severe blow.

A message through S.I.S. channels, reliability unknown, says that an RVV representative will leave Rotterdam on 30 Sept for Eindhoven, with maps of fortifications and reinforcements in the Rotterdam district.

Dudley gives details of the measures being taken to ascertain whether their grounds are secure.

No. 3. SF. Det is trying to trace Jedburgh Claude, but from little information they have at present are not very hopeful.

Jedburghs Edward and Daniel have returned to the U.K.

It is proposed to re-supply Regan on 2/3 Oct and to reinforce them with a party of 7 all ranks.

S.A.S. Brutus is at Eindhoven and says that S.A.S. Regan has established wireless contact with Second Army.

S.A.S. Portia has been instructed to send the German defence plans which they have acquired through the lines by selected local Resistance.

General Situation October 1944

Although there were still some differences of opinion between the O.D. on the one hand and the R.V.V. and K.P. on the other hand, this was mostly amongst the heads juggling for position. The active members, however, continued their good work under extremely difficult conditions. The Rotterdam area reported that about 1000 men had been armed and, although they called for active resistance, they were instructed to remain clandestine until instructed to do otherwise. Working conditions had become difficult added to which the Germans started their famous Razzias. Reports that some 2000 resistance men were available in the Friesland area were encouraging.

Railway Strike:
Owing to the extreme discomfort the civilians were suffering, London was asked by the field if it was still necessary to carry on with the railway strike. However, as the strike was serving a useful purpose to the allies and, if the railway men were to return to work, they would only be arrested or deported to Germany, so the field was asked by broadcast to carry on with the good work.

Blockade Ships Rotterdam:
Rotterdam Resistance were asked to do everything possible to prevent blockade ships being sunk in the River Maas.

Airborne Evaders:
Various resistance organisations were successful in arranging the exfiltration of some Airborne Troops through the Tiel area. This route was however later penetrated and further escapes were arranged further West through the Biesbosch and across the Maas.

Agents Infiltrated:
Portia II. An S.A.S. party of four Dutch Commandos was dropped on the night of the 9th October in the Drenthe area to act as weapon instructors to the Resistance Forces. Their mission on the whole was not very successful and owing to the arrests in the area, they eventually split up and came out through the lines.

S.I.S. Two S.I.S. agents were dropped to a Dudley reception committee in the Overijssel area. Both landed safely and were passed on to the S.I.S. circuit.

Stores sent to the Field:
130 Air sorties took place during the month of October of which 47 were successful. Containers dropped totalled 996 plus 108 packages. In addition, 6 packages were dropped for S.I.S. and 4 for S.A.S.

Sabotage Activities:
The following information was received:

Dudley reported on the 4th October that since the 10th September, thirty rail tracks had been cut and five major canals put out of action.

Shooting reported that his men had cut the railway between Amersfoort and Apeldoorn, derailing a train and causing two days delay on the line. A railway bridge two miles South of Amersfoort was blown up by the Resistance on 13/14th October. The line between Amersfoort and Zwolle was cut in four places on the night 20/21st October 1944.

S.I.S. reported that the railway bridge between Rijswijk and Delft had been sabotaged.

Podex reported the sinking of the *Schoenfeld* at her berth in the Wiltonhaven, Rotterdam.

K.P. attacked the lift bridge at Wijk Bij Duurstede, causing damage to the lifting machinery.

A message received through S.I.S. channels gave a good idea as to the intensity of sabotage and harassing being done:

"Railway lines, bridges, viaducts have been continually blown up and troop trains derailed. Stop. Locomotives and munition trucks have been destroyed, telephone cables cut and tyre bursters strewn over the main roads. Stop. Enemy patrols and cars have been attacked and a considerable number of Germans killed valuable information has been seized. Stop. Transport has been considerably hindered not only by direct attack but also by the sabotage of records connected with the requisitioning. Stop. There was considerable cutting of railway lines in the Achterhoek and Betuwe when the Arnhem landing took place. Stop. Telephone lines and switch station put out of action thereby interfering with supply to the Ruhr. Stop. Explosive charges under the bridge at Rhenen were removed but bridge was destroyed by R.A.F. later."

Casualties:	Nil
Agents Returned:	Nil
Agents in Training:	11

Daily Summary, 1 October 1944

Northaw Mission has put to 21 Army Group the proposal of *Podex* to attack the Germans at the Rotterdam harbours. *Podex* stated that the demolition of these ports cannot be prevented, but can be held up for a few days, and that counter measures against reprisals will not be possible. His opinion was that the success of the attack is the prime consideration, and that Resistance can hold out a certain time until

Army help arrives. 21 Army Group have decided that the Field should be instructed not to carry out the project.

Podex also states that he is planning to capture a German General and two men of his staff, and that reprisal on this account can be countered for a certain time. Instructions were sent to him not to carry out this project.

The Field is instructed to make preparations to preserve the bridges to avoid premature action, and not to act before orders are sent. Similar instructions are to be sent with regard to the roadblocks.

Draughts reports that there are many indications of extension of German measures to break the railway strike. The food and coal position is growing worse.

Northaw Mission was asked by the Dutch War Minister to find out if 21 Army Group considered that the continuation of the railway strike was still of military importance. If not, it was intended to inform the field to make the best possible arrangements to try to maintain the food supply in the cities. In reply 21 Army Group stated they wished the strike to continue East of the line Apeldoorn-Arnhem.

S.A.S. Regan reports that on 30 Sept Resistance cut the railway between Ede and Barnevel.

S.A.S. Brutus who has telephoned Utrecht from Nijmegen wished Regan to be told to contact:

An OD group 2,000 strong in the Utrecht area which is in touch with the power company's telephone.

An OD group in the Bennekom area where there is a telephone terminal and a small maquis with 50 airborne refugees.

Brutus says that the telephone has not so far been tapped, but that tapping must eventually occur. The Nijmegen terminal is manned by 21 Army Group personnel 24 hrs. a day.

Daily Summary, 2 October 1944

Northaw Mission are informed by the Dutch section that they have conferred with S.A.S. on the suggestion that the two S.A.S. teams be dropped, one to Hilversum and one to Deventer. The Dutch suggests that S.A.S. undertake one party to Deventer and that the Dutch Section suggests one Jedburgh to Blaricum. Northaw's approval is asked for.

R.V.V. requests arrangements to be made for the transportation to England from Holland of representatives of the Resistance. These have been called for to give the Queen the latest information. People for this are being chosen.

Boating has been sent a message 1 Oct suggesting that he go to Amsterdam to work there with Driehoek or to any other place they think important.

Jedburgh Dudley states that Resistance in the Zwolle area urgently needs weapons for 600 men and gives a ground in the N.E. Polder.

S.A.S. Portia reports strength of Resistance at Drenthe is 1,500 and Groningen 1,800. Morale is good but there are no weapons.

Daily Summary, 3 October 1944

Varicose has sent an S-phone operator and courier through the lines S.E. of Tilburg, and established contact on 1 Oct.

Northaw Mission has been told of the Dutch Government's decision to continue the railway strike, as it is impossible to divide the country into areas for the purpose of the strike. Northaw considers that the continuation of the strike is the best solution as to re-start work partially or even totally would result in large scale murder of personnel now underground. They suggest that the railway workers opinion be obtained.

Draughts states that a notice appeared in the Amersfoort newspaper on 30 Sept threatening stern reprisals against railway strikers from 2 Oct. The reprisals appear to consist of taking hostages, and if no one is in the house, of removing furniture. Most of the railway personnel is at present at home. The necessary arrangements are being made with regard to money and accommodation so that the strike can continue.

Sculling says that he has been chased from his H.Q. and is living in the woods near Elspeet and that the Germans have killed many civilians in Apeldoorn. Inland communications are very difficult.

Jedburgh Dudley reports that communications, including canals, are cut nightly. When Allied troops arrive, he will have 3,500-5,000 men under arms if arming continues as at present.

Daily Summary, 4 October 1944

Northaw Mission has been informed that on further consideration the view of S.F. H.Q., is that the Hilversum area is not suitable for Jedburgh work. The area can be covered by *Draughts* and arms can be dropped in the normal way. The proposal is now to send a strong Jedburgh team to Drenthe or the Friesland area, where they could have more freedom of action.

Sculling states that conditions in his area are difficuLieutenant Until a few days ago his men destroyed railway communications nightly, but now whenever any sabotage is effected the Germans burn down the whole of the nearest village, and murder the people they believe may be responsible.

Jedburgh Clarence. It is planned that Jedburgh Clarence should be made available to Northaw Mission for work based on Eindhoven.

Daily Summary, 5 October 1944
Regan reports 4 Oct that Flight Sergeant T. Wood is en route to Wijk and Oss with a film of the waterway to Rotterdam showing depth of channels.

In reference to the scheme for sending representatives of resistance to the U.K. to report to the Queen (see summary 2nd October), *Draughts* complains 5 Oct that the most suitable people for this can be spared only with great difficulty at this time.

In reference to a request by *Draughts* for the bombing of a Gestapo H.Q. Amsterdam 9 Sep, SIS reports 2 Oct. that Gestapo activity is considerable in Amsterdam in preparation for action against railway personnel and resistance and that action will start soon.

Dudley 4 Oct reports that the Groen Polizei are still in great strength in his area and are very active. He reports many shootings and also that the population of fifteen hundred was moved to Germany and the village demolished for reprisal. He also reports at least thirty railway lines cut since 10 September plus five major canals.

Uppermost (3 S.F. Det) reports 4 Oct that Jedburgh Clarence has seen Prince Bernhard who has decided to keep the team intact temporarily for work in the area Nijmegen. Meanwhile the team is available for future operations at a few days' notice.

Sculling reports 4 Oct that the Germans burnt down 50 houses in the village of Putten and arrested 1200 including women and children, in reprisal for the disappearance of 2 SS Police Officers. Active resistance has, therefore, ceased temporarily, and an information service has been organised.

Daily Summary, 6 October 1944
1 SF Det reports that they are having successful contact with the S-phone infiltrated through the enemy lines.

Podex reports that the Grune Polizei have partly burned down the village of Berkel, owing to the discovery that air operations were taking place in the neighbourhood. Ground Whisky, near Hoorn, is the ground concerned.

Draughts reports the arrest of Professor Muysken of Delft University, who had connections with the resistance. *Draughts* says that the professor's behaviour at his trial was disappointing.

Draughts also says that Ground Dora, (2 miles West of Brandsburen), has not been used owing to some prejudicial statements contained in a broadcast on Radio Oranje.

On 2 October a meeting of the Sicherheitsdienst took place at their HQ at Westerbork with the object of increasing activity in the Hague.

Draughts has been sent a message in which it is stated that Rogers (SIS) reports that he has been appointed Driehoek leader but that some of the organisations do not accept his authority. *Draughts* is asked for clarification of the position, and for which area and Driehoek, Rogers is working.

S.A.S. Portia has been asked whether operational parties (of S.A.S.) can ever work in his area.

On the night 5/6 October one wireless set was dropped to Portia.

Daily Summary, 7 October 1944

Varicose has received a message from OD Middelburg asking urgently for the dropping of weapons for resistance groups on Walcheren and Zuid Beveland to harass the retreating enemy.

Stanley (ex-Clarence) reports that he is in Nijmegen where he is carrying out his new mission to arm Resistance behind our own lines. He has some small groups for use by the Army.

Brutus reports that enemy infiltration into the Albrecht intelligence group is feared. This is unconfirmed.

Sculling states, he has several men who are willing to be dropped in uniform behind German lines to do demolitions. etc.

He has been asked if he can contact groups in Utrecht and Het Gooi (the area North of Hilversum).

Regan reports that he is living in a farm. His party is still in uniform and is keeping indoors. RVV has appointed a Dutchman to act as liaison officer and he brings reports from local observers twice daily. Regan is in touch with RVV 1 by courier, but it takes time, so making it impossible to organise receptions for them.

In a later message Regan says Resistance id highly organised and very keen, but badly need weapons and explosives for demolition and to harass convoys.

Daily Summary, 8 October 1944

Brutus suggests that the Dutchman who is Regan's liaison with Resistance, may have been followed from Amsterdam, and that Regan should move his location at once.

Stanley (ex-Clarence) reports two organised groups:

Dreugel – Fust – Alphen – Oyen – Lithijen.

Apel – Leeuwen.

Using English and German arms, these groups every night engage the enemy who cross the river to burn villages.

Regan fears that telephone connections with the Second Army are liable to break down soon and asks for a W/T set with a fifteen-mile range for ranging military artillery fire.

Portia reports 1500 men of Resistance in Friesland who require arms.

Rummy, who is in Rotterdam, reports that KP now has about 400 armed men. They are completing their training and will be ready to receive orders next week.

An S.I.S. report states that only the electricity station has been demolished at Ijmuiden. This station served the North Sea Canal, which, however, was already useless having been filled with sand. Booby traps have also been placed along the canal.

Daily Summary, 9 October 1944

In a cable to Northaw it is stated that the situation regarding the central command of Resistance is not at all clear. *Draughts* has said that he commands the Groote Advies Commissie Illegaliteit (GAC) or Delta Centrum (Triangle for North Holland) which however, Rogers says is commanded by a regular officer (whose name is being conveyed by courier). The GAC has appointed the Top Driehoek, which Rogers says is commanded by him. The Dutch section considers that it is very unlikely that either *Draughts* or Rogers are acting as commanders. *Draughts* was appointed liaison officer between Northaw and Resistance, and it seems logical that Rogers should not be accepted as Commander by RVV, OD and KP. The field has been asked to clarify the position.

An S.I.S. message states that Putten was set on fire after a fight between Resistance Groups and the Germans, 600 men were shut in a church and brought to Amersfoort, 30 bodies labelled with the word "Terrorist" were lying about the roads in Apeldoorn. These will be cleared away when 4,000 men have volunteered for work. In the previous call up only 8 men appeared. It is stated that there are now no men in Apeldoorn.

S.A.S. Regan reports that Divisional Commander RVV 1, is moving his H.Q. East of the Ijssel. He wants a liaison party there.

No operational parties are now required for Portia

A message from Regan on behalf of RVV states that Ground Bertus is unsafe and gives an alternative.

Daily Summary, 10 October 1944
Coursing reports that he has been giving a thorough training to 60 men taken from 10 KP groups. These men in turn will instruct the members of their respective groups. *Coursing* expects 290 armed and trained KP men will be ready for use in Rotterdam by 12 Oct. *Coursing* is now starting RVV training.

Draughts reports thatRogers is handling OD liaison with London.

DC is the cover name of the commander of Driehoek. He is an ex regular army officer and is also functioning as the commander of the Delta Centrum.

Draughts is DC's liaison officer, and any contact must be through *Draughts*.

Podex reports that the *Schoenfeld* at Wiltonhaven in Rotterdam has been sunk by saboteurs.

Jedburgh Stanley reports that he has telephone communication with large towns still in enemy hands. These lines have been used for informational use only, not operational.

RVV in Utrecht states that Resistance members, when captured, are tortured and murdered by the Germans. The civilian population also frequently suffers savage reprisals.

Daily Summary, 11 October 1944
Commander RVV reports that the order given to his troops to take no prisoners is still in effect, and that the wounded are left by the roadside. The number of troops has increased and although there is now a greater number of them, they have respected the order. Now that counter measures are allowed, high officers are being seized as hostages. The Commanders ask for permission to execute these hostages if the enemy reprisals continue, or if this does not help, to kill all Germans who fall into their hands.

The Albrecht group has submitted a plan for bombing the dykes in order to impede the German retreat from the Island of Dordrecht. This plan involves the inundation of Oude Beer Polder, Nieuwe Beer Polder, and some of the small polders to the South of the latter. These proposals have been sent to Northaw.

Van Ven reports that at Rotterdam unified command of Resistance has been achieved. RVV, OD and KP have given command to Inspector of Police Staal, alias Van Rijn, who has been underground since 1941.

An S.I.S. report states that by the exercise of extreme care, the food supply will last about another fortnight. Sabotage by the Germans is now added to transport difficulties, industrial troubles, and considerable destruction.

Draughts reports that nearly 200 men were arrested at Amsterdam on 5th and 6th Oct.

Dudley reports that activity is becoming very difficult due to the fact that the top members of the OD in Apeldoorn, Groningen and the Drenthe area have either been killed or captured. The top members of the Landelijke KP at Apeldoorn, however, managed to escape at the last minute. There have also been rumours either of leakage or of treason in the top ranks of the RVV. However, *Dudley* will contact RVV upon arrival in Overijssel if possible. He further adds that casualties in his own HQ group have been heavy, and they are now working entirely as agents.

Stanley reports that men from Druten are reinforcing the South bank of the Waal.

S.A.S. – 4 Arms Instructors were sent to SAS Portia 9/10 Oct. They were dropped on Ground Rhododendrun, 4 miles WSW of Veenhuizen.

Daily Summary, 12 October 1944

In a message to Northaw the Dutch War Minister says that he considers that if Resistance Groups are given authorisation to execute hostages the consequence will be the greatest possible reprisals against the population, and that RGs should be left to act as circumstances arise.

In reply the Northaw Mission wishes the field to be told that only important hostages are worth while taking and that the others, unless in great number, should not be taken.

The Northaw Mission on 9 Oct reported the arrival of special Knokploeg people in the area of Achterhoek, Bennekom, Wageningen and Ede who stated that they were under the direct command of General Eisenhower and not of Prince Bernhard and were giving counter orders to the latter's troops. Northaw has no knowledge of these people whose obscure identity is being checked with 12 Army Group. The field has been warned to break contact with them until further checks have been made.

Draughts has given instructions to the local and district commanders to hamper enemy rail traffic as much as possible. He is afraid that if a strike were called on road and water transport, the Germans would profit considerably as far as their military traffic is concerned, and would be in a position to steal goods. Also, the only result of a strike would be that all means of transport for the Netherland population would cease.

S.I.S. Agent Marinier at Amsterdam is now reporting under another name.

S.A.S. Regan reports that the telephone terminal is being moved on 12 Oct to Ede. He does not state which terminal this is.

Daily Summary, 13 October 1944

Dudley, *Draughts* and *Podex* have been informed that the Germans are planning to send trained agent provocateurs to large cities and farms, who will attempt to penetrate underground groups by pretending to be British or other parachutists. They will probably have identity papers belonging to soldiers of the Dutch Brigade Irene, who have been killed or captured. These men are being trained by SD school at Hoogeveen in Drenthe.

Northaw agrees to *Draughts'* instructions issued to the District Commanders regarding the hampering of rail traffic, and also that a strike should not be called on road and water transport.

Draughts reports that on the night of 10/11 Oct a fight took place between Resistance and Landwacht on the Ground Lobster, 9½ km NW of Hoorn.

Draughts also reports for Delta Centrum, a great drive by the enemy against men of 15 to 50 years old from Utrecht, Zeist and Amersfoort. They are taken in groups of 1000 as prisoners to Visserhaven, Huizen and thence over the Ijsselmeer in barges.

Rummy reports that an unknown number of Grune Polizei arrived in Rotterdam on Oct 13th.

Stanley has been told that it is very difficult to drop food and medical supplies North of Arnhem, but if dropping grounds can be arranged the matter will be pressed.

Dutch Intelligence states that apparently civilians are not allowed to evacuate Walcheren and that Middelburg is overcrowded with civilian evacuees from outlying villages.

Daily Summary, 14 October 1944

Draughts reports that on the morning of the 7 Oct the enemy attacked a section of his men near Rustenburg. Resistance lost 2 men killed and 2 wounded. Their arms store was attacked, and arms were lost to the Germans, who have threatened to burn the village of Ursem.

Shooting reports that some 3 weeks ago his men cut the railway Amersfoort to Apeldoorn derailing a train and causing two days delay.

Daily Summary, 15 October 1944

Regan reports that on 30 September 5 men of Resistance and a sergeant of 10 Parachute Battalion ambushed a German Staff car. 2 German Air Force officers were killed and 1 wounded. In reprisals the Germans burned houses in Putten.

Regan reports that the railway bridge two miles South of Amersfoort was blown up by resistance on the night 13/14 Oct.

Varicose reports that 2 Dutch artillerymen were infiltrated 14 Oct through the line with S-phones. Their mission is to spot targets for corps artillery in the area Rhenan – Wageningen. An s-phone is also with the C.B.O., thereby enabling the whole corps of artillery to engage the targets if necessary.

Daily Summary, 16 October 1944
Owing to publicity among 21 Army Group formations, with effect from 0001 hrs 17 Oct, codename Regan is replaced by Fabian and codename Portia by Gobbo.

S.I.S. reports (reliability not known) that a meeting was held between key personnel of the Luftwaffe, the S.D., and the W.H. which was presided over by Seyss Inquart. Measures to bring the railway strike to an end were discussed, and it was decided to starve the cities of Amsterdam and Rotterdam in order to provoke armed Resistance by the population. The Germans would then have an excuse to bomb both towns.

Draughts has been informed that the Government shares his opinion and does not desire a general transportation strike.

Rummy reports that:

The activity of the S.D. and the Gestapo is even greater than usual.

A great many ships with victuals for Resistance are hidden among the waterways of the Biesbosch area. *Rummy* requests that firing on these ships stop.

Daily Summary, 17 October 1944
Northaw reports that Montagne and Lijbenga have arrived at the Mission's H.Q., from Friesland. They report that there are 2,000 men available in Resistance activity in Friesland, but only 70 men (KP) are armed. Montagne and Lijbenga are in contact with Macbeth and his men.

Charades reports that there is considerable control activity by "rascals" from the "cursed camp" at Ommen. They surround suspects' houses at night and make arrests.

The following message should be broadcast to the Dutch people:

"Guard your tongue, even among your own family, as to what you may hear by chance, or see, about underground organisations. At the same time, report names of traitors or suspects to these organisations."

From an S.I.S. channel comes a report that because Germans shoot at groups of more than 5 people, hospitals receive large numbers of people, including children, suffering from bullet wounds. Also, in the country, children are being fired upon while gathering firewood or berries, and 2 were killed recently in Uddel.

Daily Summary, 18 October 1944
Northaw states that instead of sending food to Amsterdam, which is near starvation, the Germans confiscate food and take it by ships to Germany via Ijsselmeer.

S.A.S. Fabian is now equipped with an s-phone.

A message from S.A.A. HQ., to Major Hardwicke (SAS Liaison 21 Army Group) instructs him to ascertain from Lieutenant Col. Dobie (an Airborne Div evader who Fabian reports is on his way back), whether 1 Airborne Div evaders who are in Fabian's area can stay in enemy occupied Holland. These evaders want to work with Resistance and harass the retreating Germans. Unless this work is of great value and the retreat is likely to be early, G.O.C.1 Airborne Div want the men back in order to reconstitute the Division. The danger of personnel working in civilian clothes and thereby compromising wounded who are still at large is emphasised.

Podex confirms that the block ships *Borneo, Westerdam, Axenfels* and *Schoenfels* at Rotterdam were sunk by sabotage.

Daily Summary, 19 October 1944
The field have been instructed that they should under no circumstances let themselves be provoked into taking armed action without express orders from S.F. HQ. and should restrain the population.

Draughts reports that telephone contact between Utrecht and Nijmegen has been cut, and that Delta Centrum asked him to send all messages destined for Allied HQ in Nijmegen. He has been informed that transmission of these messages is not his official job, and that this HQ is asking the intelligence service to try to arrange something, possibly through an internal wireless network.

Dudley reports that big razzias in Rijssen, Holten and Nijverdal make it impossible for him to use Ground Coos until 25 Oct.

An S.I.S. report states that the KP attacked the lift bridge at Wijk-Bij-Duurstede, damaging the lifting machinery.

From S.I.S. channels comes a report that it was unfortunate that adequate delivery of arms to resistance groups could not have been effected some months ago, as arming of resistance groups at present is extremely difficult owing to difficulty of communications, strict control and requisitioning of all land and water transport, and the increasing number of German troops everywhere.

The chief of SIS contacts in Holland suggests that, since reception of weapons depends mainly on withdrawal of troops and AA guns and since he is familiar with such developments, arrangements for deliveries should be made through him.

Referring to the arrival of men to KP saying that they were from Gen. Eisenhower, North Mission says that they know only of one man who this might be, namely one Van Der Valk who has gone through the lines with a W/T set without authority. The man is said to be a deserter and should be arrested.

A message from Major Hardwick to SAS states that it is considered that the use of evaders in a harassing role is unlikely to be required, and that he is to discuss the matter with Northaw. *Uppermost* (3. S.F. Det.) sends a message to the same effect, adding that possibly a small number of instructors might be left with Resistance.

Major Hardwick also asks that Fabian be warned that the Tiel organisation is blown and many Dutch have been arrested. No attempt should be made to move evaders until further orders.

Daily Summary, 20 October 1944
Referring to the message received from Northaw on 18 October, Northaw has been told that it has been found that Van Der Valk is not a deserter, and asked what further action is required.

Podex states in answer to an enquiry from this H.Q., that the name of one of the block ships sunk in Rotterdam should be *Westerdam* and not *Zuiderdam*. The *Westerdam* has been salvaged, and *Podex* asks for further stores. The *Borneo* can be salvaged within 3 or 4 days, but that they will do their utmost to cause heavier damage.

S.A.S. A message from Brigadier McLeod to Fabian states that there are indications that the escape route in the Tiel area has been blown and that a general attack is taking place on Dutch Intelligence Services. He strongly advises Fabian to change his location and temporarily to sever all but his surest contacts and says that all evaders should be dispersed and evasion be stopped.

Fabian says that he is shortly moving.

Brutus reports that Lieutenant Colonel Dobie has crossed the lines. It is understood that the evaders in the Ede area now number 200.

Daily Summary, 21 October 1944
Draughts reports for Delta Centrum that Dutch underground troops are fighting the Germans in NW Brabant. There are two Allied Pilot Officers with the underground troops. Arms and stores are needed.

Draughts also reports that the German SD has ordered great activity in Amsterdam against underground forces, which it is expected, will start on 23 Oct. He again asks for bombing.

In a response to a request from Northaw, the field has been warned that the Germans are infiltrating agents and Dutch provocateurs who claim to come from other areas and ask to join the local organisations, or to be helped through the lines.

Rummy has been told that his request not to bomb food ships in the Biesbosch area has been passed to the Air Ministry, who will do what they can, but no further details of the ships and their approx. locations in view of possible other enemy activity in the area.

Draughts says that some large motor car makers have asked him to arrange for a strike of concerns which are repairing German cars. According to the Government Department in charge the distribution of food to the Dutch people would not be affected. The strikes of large firms would cause a gradual strike to other producing concerns and a gradual stoppage of the very meagre Dutch motor traffic, and *Draughts* recommends the strike. He asks for consideration of this project and that the strike should be proclaimed by the Dutch Government over Radio Oranje rather than by him on the ground, so that reprisals would not be so severe.

Daily Summary, 22 October 1944
Draughts reports that the telephone line between Amsterdam and Utrecht is not working.

Dudley reports that 17 of his men have driven back an enemy patrol near Wamel, killed 3 and taken one prisoner.

Dudley also states that the RVV leader Evert who was only a contact for the rural part of Overijssel is causing trouble by refusing to co-operate and claiming to have been nominated head of Resistance in Overijssel by Prince Bernhard's HQ via radio contact Maurits (*Charades*). The HQ of Overijssel which is extending into Drenthe and Achterhoek was formed some weeks ago with a Colonel (ex-leader of OD in Overijssel) in command. The HQ is divided into 4 districts, two of which are commanded by former KP chiefs, and two by RVV men of which Evert is one.

S.A.S. Fabian reports that the railway line between Amersfoort and Zwolle was cut in 4 places by Resistance on the night 20/21 October.

Daily Summary, 23 October 1944
Stanley reports that Harry has gone to Eindhoven to meet various underground chiefs.

Dudley states that he now has detailed defence plans of Zwolle and he has asked instructions as to their disposition.

Northaw has agreed to *Draughts* request that Radio Oranje should order a strike in those concerns engaged in repairing German cars.

H.Q. Airborne Forces have requested that no publicity be given to evacuation of evaders.

Daily Summary, 24 October 1944
The following report, via S.I.S. channels, was dated 7 Oct, but was received at our H.Q., 23 October:

Twenthe District:
Railway lines, bridges and viaducts, as well as dyke machinery, have been repeatedly sabotaged. A troop train was derailed; 3 locomotives were destroyed, and 4 ammunition trucks were blown up, causing delays of several hours to several days. All District and German telephone cables, as well as lines in the frontier area, are constantly cut.
　　The canal Almelo – Coevorden is constantly emptied.
　　Records of the Landwacht have been captured, and 2 traitors were killed and 8 prisoners taken. (In reprisal for this action the Germans took 7 hostages at Laren and 9 at Corssel). Resistance lost 11 men and had 1 arrested.
　　A Jedburgh (probably *Dudley*) was looked after by SIS personnel.

Veluwe District:
Activity similar to that in Twenthe.
　　Leads of the fuses on the Rhenen bridge (since destroyed by the R.A.F.) were cut.
　　Tyre bursters were strewn along main roads, and many attacks were made on cars and patrols. On one such attack 30 of a column of 60 Germans were killed.
　　Transport was not only greatly hindered by direct sabotage, but also by sabotage of requisitioning records.
　　An S.A.S. party (probably Fabian ex Regan) was cared for.

Betuwe District and Achterhoek:
When the Arnhem attack took place, many railways were cut and telephone lines and switch gear were either cut or destroyed, thus interrupting the supply to the Ruhr.
　　50 buses and a drawbridge were destroyed.
　　S.I.S. source also report that the enemy will shortly make false broadcasts on various wave lengths to Resistance inciting them to premature action. S.I.S. requests that warning against these broadcasts be sent to the field.
　　Draughts states that air raids on railway targets at Deventer, Hengelo, Zutphen and Utrecht have had little military results but many civilian

casualties, and he requests, is possible, that such attacks on towns be stopped.

Centrum RVV 2 reports that the contact address of the internal net at Apeldoorn has been cancelled. A new address will be sent.

Dudley has been informed that this HQ is definitely interested in the defence plans of Zwolle.

Daily Summary, 25 October 1944

With regard to the request to bomb the Sicherheitsdienst HQ at Amsterdam, the Dutch Prime Minister, Gerbrandy, stated that before the Government agrees to the target, it would like to know from Northaw whether the Mission has any new facts which would justify the inevitable killing of numerous civilians.

Northaw replied that strong pressure for this bombing had been applied by Resistance and stated that if the bombing was delayed or cancelled, thereby resulting in mass arrests and shootings, it must be done on the Prime Minister's responsibility, and he must so inform Resistance.

Draughts reports that the RVV W/T operator in Amsterdam is in contact with Eindhoven and the OD.

Draughts also reports that since the beginning of September he has been in contact with:

1100 Georgians living in the area of Noordwijkerhout and Zuiderpier Ijmuiden. There are 350 Germans in these Georgian units.

1250 Turkestans whose units contain 250 Germans in the area Hergen Aan Zee-Grooteketen.

Both these groups are prepared upon instruction from this HQ to annihilate their German members.

Draughts has been asked to pass on two requests to the Delta Centrum:

To find out, if possible, the whereabouts or the HQ of Field Marshal Model who is reported personally to be issuing orders for savage reprisals on the Dutch population.

To send a report on the practical experience in actual resistance work of leaders in each area.

Rummy has also been asked by Prince Bernhard whether the question and position of OD leadership has improved and whether the professional OD Commanders are individually unsuitable for their present responsibilities.

Rummy reports that Resistance is ready to sabotage all railway lines in the province of Utrecht. This is necessary due to daily transport of German munitions on these lines and due to unsuccessful RAF attempts to bomb the line North of the town of Utrecht. Resistance is waiting for permission to undertake this sabotage.

Dudley reports that, although still in Veluwe, the RVV HQ is about to move to Drenthe.

Daily Summary, 26 October 1944

Draughts I has been informed that the matter of the Georgians and Turkestans is being examined, but that in view of the international complications, he is not to take any action unless advised to do so by SF HQ.

Draughts I has been asked to inform Delta Centrum that precision bombing of the SD HQ is impossible. In view of the probable loss of civilian life by normal bombing methods, *Draughts'* opinion is requested before a final decision is reached.

In the same connection, Northaw has sent a message to the Dutch Prime Minister, stating that pressure has been brought to bear for the bombing by Resistance because Military operations were expected to go much faster than they did. Because of this expectation, Resistance was armed and has been exposed to great dangers which will be increased if the SD HQ is not bombed, since the enemy may be able to eradicate the Resistance Movement, Prince Bernhard feels that the value of this bombing would justify the loss of civilian life.

Northaw reports that De Beer of Begonia Straat, Hillergesberg, the first contact of *Podex* and *Rummy*, has arrived at Prince Bernhard's HQ with important information. It is most important that he return as soon as possible. Since sending him through the lines is too dangerous, he must be dropped by parachute to the Rotterdam area.

RVV has been instructed, via *Podex*, to put plan Mars (sabotage of telephone communications) into action immediately, but only on the lines East of the Ijssel. He will be advised later if further action is necessary in the area West of the Ijssel and North of the Neder Rijn. SF HQ is to be informed when action is taken and assumes that the execution of Plan Mars will not interfere with any of the Resistance secret telephone networks.

Draughts has sent special contact addresses for 2 SF Det.

Daily Summary, 27 October 1944

Delta Centrum, replying to the information that precision bombing of the SD HQ is impossible gives details of the movements of the Staff of the HQ, and says that if no precision bombing is possible, then normal bombing is urgently required, even though serious losses will be incurred. This has been sent to Northaw.

Rummy has been told that he can proceed with his project to sabotage railway lines in the province of Utrecht but that no major demolitions which might take Allied troops long to repair should be attempted.

Daily Summary, 28 October 1944

S.H.A.E.F. has agreed to *Draughts'* project for the mutiny of the Georgians and Turkestans. BBC messages to this effect will be broadcast on the German programme was from 28 Oct. *Draughts* is to be informed that this measure does not imply recognition of these Russians as allied troops. Action messages will not be sent until Army Group and SHAEF have given their approval.

A further message has been sent to *Draughts* on a matter of the bombing of the SD HQ. It originally appeared that the object of the attack was to destroy SD records, but from further telegrams in which *Draughts* recommended the timing of the arrack, it would appear that the object is the destruction of personnel. *Draughts* is asked to state what other object than the deaths of SD personnel is contemplated.

S.I.S. source reports that Resistance groups are unable to attack troop trains on the Zwolle-Deventer line, or munition trucks at Olst, owing to the danger of bloody reprisals.

Daily Summary, 29 October 1944

Draughts II reported on 25 Oct that a proclamation by the German High Command requisitioning blankets and winter clothing, was shortly to be issued, to apply only apparently to the well to do people. The proclamation appeared on 26 Oct in the Northern part of the Hague, but the officials concerned with the collection, several of whom are N.S.B.'s (collaborators) decline to co-operate. The public show no signs of complying with the order, even though a search of the houses is to be made by the military while delivery of the clothing is proceeding. The matter is now in the hands of the Grune Polizei.

Podex reports that Resistance has been watching for several weeks for an opportunity to sabotage the blockship *Westerdam* which was sunk in Rotterdam harbour, but later salvaged by the Germans. The project was, however, found to be impossible as the area around the ship is heavily mined.

Dudley reports that there is to be a big razzia in the Wierden area, beginning the week of 30 October.

Dudley requests funds to finance measures to save the N.E. Polder from inundation by the Germans. He also states that he has enough money with which to pay the railway strikers in Overijssel until 1 Dec.

Sculling reports that the Germans plan to finish all civilian traffic on 31 Oct, giving this as the reason for the urgency of immediate operations to him.

Daily Summary, 30 October 1944

Draughts reports that the Resistance Commander of North Holland is preparing to plan to hamper the German retreat over the North Sea Canal towards the Afsluitdijk (the causeway which links the provinces of North Holland and Friesland). He suggests occupying, if possible, the bridge at Hembrug when allied troops are in the neighbourhood but not before. He also plans to barricade the roads in North Holland especially near the approach to Afsluidijk and is awaiting permission from SF HQ to carry out his scheme.

Draughts II now reports that people are standing in queues at the offices for the delivery of clothes, owing to measures taken by the Germans to ensure that their order is carried out. People must either stay at home for 3 days or else display a certificate proving they have given up their clothes.

He also states that many of the farmers are now only willing to deliver food in return for watches or jewellery, and requests a BBC message rebuking them, but at the same time commending the farmers who have remained patriotic.

Northaw has been informed that:

Delta Centrum has stated that the request for the bombing of the SD HQ visualised, apart from the deaths of SD personnel, the destruction of records which involve people of the underground movement who are still free. As precision bombing is impossible, Delta Centrum are dropping their request for the time being.

Draughts considers the bombing necessary but will accept responsibility for civilian casualties only if the possible range of damage is about 150 metre radius.

Northaw is asked to consider the matter further.

Daily Summary, 31 October 1944

Podex has been asked to do everything possible to prevent the remaining block ships leaving Rotterdam, including a large vessel in Merwehaven. As the width of the channel off Maas Sluis is now only 325 feet, any one vessel can block the Nieuw Waterweg.

Cribbage states that the Germans are carrying out intensive DF work in the Rotterdam area, making wireless work increasingly difficult.

Dudley has been told that the Dutch Government agree with his measures to save the N.E. Polder, and that money will be sent to him.

Dudley's plans were made by an inspector and engineer of the N.E. Polder, and he says that his chances of success are good.

Dudley asks for information about a man calling himself Johan, leader at Deventer, who claims to be in wireless touch with London, and who says that 450 Communists in Deventer partly armed by SF HQ, plan to take over the town after its liberation. Johan wants to stop this with his own group of 300 men.

The identity of Johan is being investigated by SF HQ.

SAS HQ has heard nothing from Gobbo since 23 Oct.

General Situation November 1944

Recruiting reports were exceedingly encouraging but were damped by the Razzias which took place in Rotterdam and Amsterdam and it is estimated that about 50,000 men were taken in Rotterdam area alone for work in Germany or building defences on the Ijsselline. The O.D., and R.V.V. suffered severe losses but the K.P. only suffered slightly. Through the arrest of a courier, some 12 district commanders of the province of Utrecht, together with *Sculling*, were arrested at a meeting. *Cubbing* and *Turniquoits* managed to escape. Arrests also took place in the area of Groningen and Friesland. In view of the razzias and arrests the field was instructed to reduce activities to a minimum.

T.A.F. Co-operation:
Two S.D. (Sicherheitsdienst) targets submitted by *Draughts* and *Rummy* in Amsterdam and Rotterdam respectively, were attacked and, although not 100% successful, these attacks scared the S.D. and boosted the morale of the Resistance members. A certain number of Germans were killed and some records destroyed in the Amsterdam raid. Rotterdam reported that 11 prisoners were able to escape during the attack.

Special Planning Conference:
Owing to the delay in the Allied advance across the Waal and Neder Rhine and the rapid growth of the Resistance Forces in Holland, it was decided to hold a special planning meeting in London. This was held on the 27th, 28th and 29th November and was attended by the Commanding Officers of No's. 1, 2 and 3 S.F. Detachments who came especially from the Continent for it. As a result of this Conference two directives were drawn up on 3 Dec 44:

Agents Infiltrated:
P. Tazelaar (*Necking*) with his wireless operator L. Faber (*Bobsleigh*) were dropped in North East Holland to build up the resistance groups in Friesland. Owing to the arrests in Drenthe and Groningen areas, *Necking* was instructed to remain in Friesland. His mission was very successful, and he was able to supply 2000 men with arms sent from

this country. These later gave a very good account of themselves when called to Overt Action and gave great assistance to the Canadian troops when these were pushing the Germans out of North East Holland in April 1945.

R. Barme (*Trapping*) was dropped to a K.P. reception committee in the Rotterdam area on the night of the 1st November, to act as a second wireless operator to the Resistance forces in that region. He nobly carried on his work under very difficult conditions until he was caught and shot in February 1945.

P. De Beer (*Snooker*) who had come out of Holland through the lines, was dropped on the night of the 10th November to a K.P. reception committee North of Rotterdam with special instructions from Prince Bernhard and a wireless plan for direct contact between Rotterdam and 2 S.F. Det, to be used only in connection with an Allied advance in that direction. His mission was not very successful in that he became involved in political disputes and lost faith with *Rummy* and other leaders. He eventually returned through the lines at the end of January 1945 and arrived in the U.K. on the 2nd February 45.

Foxtrot. This Belgian Verstrepen operator was infiltrated across the Maas and into occupied Holland by Mr Boot (*Captain Boot*). Foxtrot commenced transmitting tactical information from the Dordrecht area and then eventually moved to the area South East of Gouda. He was instrumental in transmitting messages relating to the escape of some of the Airborne evaders across the rivers, and eventually returned through the lines himself shortly before the German capitulation.

Stores Sent to the Field:
During the month of November there were 83 sorties of which 40 were successful. 834 containers were successfully dropped together with one container for S.I.S. and 6 for S.A.S. 83 packages were dropped plus 4 for S.I.S. and 4 for S.A.S.

Sabotage Activities:
The following actions were reported:

Train derailed at Heerde-Eppe.
Demolition of a small railway bridge at Coor, Delden, resulting in the engine falling into the water.
German troop train derailed at Budel and Weert – several Germans killed and wounded.
Both tracks on the Groesbeek-Nijmegen line blown up.
Several wagons on the Maarssen-Bruekelen line derailed.

Railway line Meppel-Zwolle sabotaged.
Railway line Zwolle-Marienberg sabotaged.
Derailment of one locomotive and 20 wagons at Ede De Klomp.
Raid on the Wehrmacht bank at Almelo – 46,000,000 – Guilders were lifted.

Casualties:	*Podex*. Caught as an ordinary civilian in the Rotterdam Razzia of Nov 44. He was sent to Germany to work on the railway and where he continued to sabotage until liberated by the Americans.
	Sculling. Caught in November 44 during a meeting with other resistance commanders at Utrecht. Was shot shortly afterwards together with the others.
Agents Returned from the Field:	*Fishing* and *Stalking*, escaped through the lines and returned to the U.K. on 10 November 44.
Students in Training:	15

Directive on the Employment and Development of Resistance in Holland

Military Possibilities:
No major Allied attack in Holland is contemplated before the end of December. This attack, if launched, would most likely be confined to the provinces of Utrecht, Gelderland, Overijssel. An Allied advance into the provinces of North and South Holland, Friesland, Drenthe and Groningen is not at present contemplated.

Zone Divisions:
Unliberated Holland will be divided, for the purpose of developing and executing the plans contained in this directive, and as far as possible for other purposes connected with Resistance, into the following zones:

I   Friesland, Groningen, Drenthe.
II   Overijssel and Achterhoek.
III Veluwe, up to and including River Ijssel, province of Utrecht and Het Gooi.
IV   Betuwe.
V   Province of South Holland and the Regions of Haarlem and Amsterdam.
VI   Holland, Noorde Kwartier.

Role of Resistance until D-Day:
The arming, equipping and building up of Resistance will continue with a view to bringing resistance organisations to a pitch where they can afford the maximum assistance to the Allied assault. Current sabotage and counter-scorching tasks will be continued in such a manner as will not prejudice the security of Resistance.

Role of Resistance after D-Day:

Zones II and III	On receipt of orders from London, Resistance Groups in these regions will be prepared to undertake action against the Germans on the following lines: Widespread railway sabotage, limited to damage capable of repair in eight days. General harassing of road movement. Sabotage of telecommunications. Attack on isolated headquarters and detachments. Provision of tactical intelligence and local guides to the Allied forces. Prevention of enemy demolition. Prevention of removal to Germany of plant, machinery, railway stock and other material vital to Allied interests. Preparation will also be made for Dutch Resistance leaders, specialists and technicians to be available to assist the Allied forces after liberation. These preparations may involve certain personnel requiring special protection.
Zones I, V and VI	Resistance in these Zones will remain underground. Activities will be confined to: The provision of tactical intelligence to the Allied forces; Such interference with enemy movements on specific routes as may be called for; On the enemy's starting to withdraw, the prevention of enemy demolitions; The prevention of removal to Germany of plant, machinery, railway stock and other material vital to Allied interests.
Target Date:	For planning purposes, the target date will be 1 Jan 45.

NOTES ON POSSIBLE PLANS

Introductory:

The following are notes of the discussion of possible SAS plans, based upon information contained in No. 3 S.F. Det's signal, GO.350 dated 27 Nov 44, which summarised discussions held recently by Comd. SAS Brigade at HQ 21 Army Group.

Possible Plans:
The following plans are under consideration: The despatch at an early stage in the Allied offensive of about 60 Belgian SAS to wooded area covering coast road Nijdkerk-Zwolle to carry out harassing tasks; At a later stage in the Allied offensive the despatch of a coup-de-main party to an area in Northeast Holland. Task not certain but would probably be increased later to work with Resistance.

Planning and Timing:
Plans to be worked out with SF HQ and Army HQ concerned as military plans become more firm.

Recce:
Recce party for plan A. to go to Fabian in near future.

Existing Parties:
Fabian – To be recalled after recce party has been dropped to him if he wants to come out.
Gobbo – To remain.

Directive for the Operation of Basic and Specific Plans

Orders for Action on D-Day:
Orders for Action will be issued in accordance with the table below by BBC code phrase or W/T order from London:

Zone No. and Area.	I.	II.	III.	IV.	V.	VI.
Rlys and Roads.	√	√	√	-		
Telecoms.		√	√	-	√	
Harassing Attacks.		√	√	-		
Exfiltration.		√	√	-	√	
Prevention of Demolitions.			√	-	√	√
Essential Personnel.		√	√	-		

Open broadcast by Voice of SHAEF and/or HRH Prince Bernhard. Details of this to be arranged with PWD.

Orders for Action after D-Day:
As the battle develops, further code messages will require to be sent out to Regions to call for additional action.

Directive on Supplies for Dutch Resistance, 1 December 44 to 1 February 45 Priorities:
   The following are the air priorities as between zones:
   Zone II.
   Zone III.
   Zone I, V and VI.

Target figures:
The following table shows the strengths of Resistance armed and to be armed, by regions:

Zone.	Present armed strength.	Ceiling strength.	Balance to be armed.
1. Friesland Groningen Drenthe	3,000	5,200	2,200
2. Overijssel Achterhoek	2,300	5,000	2,700
3. Veluwe, up to and including River Ijssel, Province of Utrecht and Het Gooi.	2,400	6,000	3,600
4. Betuwe	-	-	-
5. Province of South Holland and Regions of Haarlem and Amsterdam	3,500	4,000	500
6. Holland, Noorde Kwartier	500	1,500	1,000
Totals	11,700	21,700	10,000

Special Requirements:
The following are the special requirements of zones, in addition to normal loads:

Explosives	Zones I, II and III.
Bazookas	Zones I, II and III.
Brens	Zones II and III.
Tyre Bursters or	
75 Grenades	Zones I, II and III.
Welrods	Zones V and VI. (2 Packages each.)
M.C.R.s	Zones I, II, III, V and VI. (1 package per sortie).

Directive to Nederlands Section on the Employment and Development of Resistance in Holland following 1 December 1944

Military Possibilities:
Apart from the operations in the Venlo district, the Allied advance into Holland has stabilised, and at present a period of comparative lull prevails.

Zone Divisions:
Unliberated Holland will be divided for the purpose of developing and executing the plans contained in this directive, and as far as possible for other purposes connected with Resistance, into the following Zones:

I.   Friesland, Groningen, Drenthe.
II.   Overijssel and Achterhoek.
III. Veluwe, up to and including River Ijssel, province of Utrecht and Het Gooi.
IV.   Betuwe.
V.   Province of South Holland and the Regions of Haarlem and Amsterdam.
VI.   Holland, Noorde Kwartier.

Resistance Activity in Holland

During period of lull:
Resistance North of the Lek and Rhine is still underground and has not yet been called out. It is essential it should remain clandestine and retain its integrity until the time comes for it to undertake intensified activity.

The policy for Dutch resistance during the present period of lull will therefore be as follows:

To continue the supply of arms and equipment.

To maintain satisfactory W/T communications between Holland and the UK, and to make preparations for rapid reinforcement or replacement of such communications in case of need.

To refrain from any activity likely to lead to reprisals or the penetration of Resistance.

To prepare plans for action against the enemy in support of Allied military operations.

To continue to harass the enemy and lower his morale wherever this can be done without prejudice to the security of Resistance Groups.

To prepare plans for the prevention of demolitions, and in particular port demolitions.

When the time comes for Intensified Activity:
Resistance will be so organised as to be able to undertake the following types of activity,

Widespread railway sabotage, limited to damage capable of repair in eight days.

General Harassing of road movement.

Sabotage of telecommunications.

Attacks on isolated headquarters and detachments.

Provision of tactical intelligence and local guides to the Allied forces.

Prevention of enemy demolitions.

Prevention of removal to Germany of plant, machinery, railway stock and other material vital to Allied interests.

Preparations will also be made for Dutch Resistance leaders, specialists and technicians to be available to assist the Allied forces after liberation. These preparations may involve certain personnel requiring special protection.

Plans for these activities will be capable of being put into effect region by region and in accordance with separate code instructions. All instructions for action by Resistance will be issued in accordance with the requirements of Allied military authorities. It will be essential for Resistance in areas which do not receive instructions for action to retain their discipline and remain underground.

Immediately Upon Liberation:
Resistance groups will be ready to assist Allied forces liberating their respective areas of operation by placing their organisations at their disposal for the purpose:
Of supporting forward troops, as may be required.
Of maintaining order and keeping the roads clear.
Of repairing war damage.
Of providing labour and technical services.
Of providing guides.
Of providing such information as the intelligence authorities may require.

Wherever possible local leaders will make the Stadhuis their rendezvous with forward commanders.

Instructions to Resistance:
General instructions will be issued to Resistance in accordance with the terms of this directive as soon as possible. The detailed plans necessary to enable Resistance activity to be set in motion in accordance with the Allied military authorities' requirements will be worked out and transmitted to the appropriate Resistance Groups as soon as possible.

Specific Plans:
They will be put into execution on receipt of special instructions, except in cases where they can be incorporated into the Basic Plan.

Supplies for Resistance:
Resistance will be supplied as necessary in order to implement the plans contained in this directive.

Communications:
Every effort will be made to maintain at least one W/T link with each region. Where necessary, reserve operators will be despatched to the field to lie low until it is necessary for them to be called into action. Highest importance will be attached to the maintenance of communications with those zones which are nearest to the Allied front line, namely II, III, and V.

Security:
In the employment and development of Dutch Resistance, the following principles will be strictly observed:
    No indication will be given to the field of the nature, location or timing of planned or likely military operations. AD/E will, therefore, be previously consulted in regard to all dealings with the field likely to have a bearing upon military operations, proposed or otherwise.
    Wherever there is evidence that Resistance is penetrated by the enemy, every effort will at once be made to limit the penetration and to seal off that portion of Resistance affected by it.
    No written instructions will be sent to the field.
    Operational instructions will be sent direct to regional leaders although the outline of regional plans may be referred to the Delta Centrum. Details relating to the machinery for putting them into operation should not be passed outside zones. Particular care should be taken to prevent collateral communication between zones of the

details of their respective plans. These restrictions apply particularly to BBC messages and code phrases.

The field will be advised that on no account should messages of operational matters be sent over the internal W / T or telephone networks.

All W / T sets sent to the field will be camouflaged as necessary.

No more agents will be sent to the field with code names on the "Pastime" system.

Reserves:
No reserves will be despatched without reference to AD / E.

Basic Resistance Plans for Regions
The following basic plans will be prepared for each zone. They will be capable of being set in operation zone by zone, and plan by plan.

Railway Sabotage:
The railway system will be attacked with the object of causing the maximum interference with enemy movement, and to prevent the removal to Germany of plant, machinery, railway stock, and other material vital to Allied interests. No damage should be caused which is liable to take more than eight days to repair. Special priority will be given to the attacking of routes passing through Eastern Holland.

Sabotage and Destruction of Road Communications:
Enemy road transport will be delayed, destroyed and obstructed to the maximum extent. Ambushes will be employed wherever consistent with security and road signs will be altered or removed. Full use will be made of improvised road blocks, and such arms, explosives and mines as can be supplied to Resistance. Bridge demolition will be avoided.

Sabotage of Telecommunications:
Civilian and military telecommunications will be attacked as widely and repeatedly as possible once the order for action has been given. Exchanges and repeater stations being attacked will not be damaged so as to be incapable of repair by the Allies within a reasonable time. Whenever possible, essential parts or duplicates will be removed and held by local resistance in readiness to return to their positions on the arrival of the Allies.

Attacks on Isolated Headquarters and Detachments:

Whenever opportunity offers, resistance will be prepared to attack isolated Headquarters and detachments, and to mop up small bodies of the enemy operating in front of, or on the flanks of, the Allied forces.

Passing of Intelligence and Provision of Local Guides:
In addition to sending tactical intelligence by W/T, Resistance will set up machinery whereby couriers and local guides can be exfiltrated into the Allied lines with up-to-date tactical intelligence.

Prevention of Demolitions:=
Once the enemy has begun to withdraw from a region, every effort will be made to protect port facilities, industrial and public utility plants and other material vital to Allied interests. A general scheme of protecting road and rail bridges and waterways will be included in each regional plan.

Although every effort will be made by London to advise resistance when to put this plan into operation, local conditions may be such as to make this impossible. Local Commanders, therefore, will use their discretion and put this plan into effect if they are satisfied that, although no order has been received from London, the moment for action has come.

Protection of Essential Personnel:
Specialist in public utilities, and other technicians, will be warned to lie low until liberated. After liberation they will immediately report to the Allied authorities.

Execution of Plans:
Except for the plan for the prevention of demolitions, no plan will be put into effect until receipt of orders by BBC or W/T. from London.

Orders to put plans into effect will be sent to zones by means of BBC broadcast code messages supplemented as necessary by W/T.

Discipline:
Effective support for military operations can only be achieved if strict discipline is maintained, and action taken only upon receipt of instructions. In no circumstances should plans be put into execution in one region because of information that similar action has been called for in another region.

Notes on the Machinery to be set up for the Exfiltration of Couriers and Local Guides

Type of Exfiltrees required:
Exfiltrees will be of two types. Couriers who will be sent by Resistance groups into the Allied lines, as requested, bearing tactical intelligence on enemy concentration, movements, etc, not in the immediate neighbourhood of the Allied front lines.

Members of Resistance who will remain in situ, until they are approached by the Allied forces, when they will exfiltrate into the Allied lines with local tactical intelligence and act as guides.

Information Required:
Information of the following types is particularly required:

Concentration of troops, particularly in villages, with information as to whether these concentrations include wireless masts.

Location of minefields and field works.

Areas completely free of enemy troops.

Signs and symbols on vehicles.

Reliefs and movements of troops.

In all cases time, date and source of information will be given.

Place of reporting:
Exfiltrees should report to the Intelligence Officers at Brigades.

Password:
It is suggested that the following system be employed.

Two passwords will be used:

A one-word password common to all exfiltrees which will be known to forward Allied troops and the giving of which will enable exfiltrees to contact Brigade Headquarters.

A password varying according to the year in which the exfiltree was born, and which he would give to the Intelligence Officer at the Brigade Headquarters to which he reported. The system would work as follows:

The resistance organiser would ask the recruit, among other questions, for the year of his birth.

If he was born in 1929, the password would be any word beginning with the letter 'A'.

If he was born in 1928, any word beginning with the letter 'B', and so on until the letter 'Z', which would be the initial letter of a word for a person born in 1904.

A person born in 1903 would be given a word beginning with the letter 'A', and so on through the alphabet again.

The Brigade Intelligence Officer would ask the exfiltree for his password, and, discreetly, for his age, and would make sure they tallied.

It would be essential, in order that this system be of any value, that the organiser should not reveal to the exfiltree the system by which the password is chosen.

Summary of Specific Plans at Present Prepared or in course of Preparation by Dutch Resistance Telecommunications:
Plan 'Bang' – cutting of German communications.

At the request of 21 Army Group, the field was asked, on 25th October 44, to put this plan into action, but only in the area East of the Ijssel in order to interfere with the Germans in that area.

Interference with withdrawal:
Plan 'Thud'.

The organiser in Amsterdam has put forward Plan 'Thud' to interfere with possible German retreat through Noord Holland. The Plan is in preparation to hinder German retreat over the Afsluitdyk-Zuider Zee causeway, particularly at its western bridges by mines and road barricades and to occupy the bridge at Hembrug (Y92) – his last bridge. The field was told that the plan may be most valuable at a later stage but that no action was to be taken at present.

Preservation of Bridges:
Plan 'Screech' – areas Rotterdam, Dordrecht, Zwijndrecht, Barendrecht Alblassendam, Sleidrecht and Spijkenisse.

They could be protected for a maximum period of 2 hours, but the field would like to have some information, in due course, on impending routes in order that more men can be concentrated at vital points.

Plan 'Wail' – preservation of bridges on the main roads and railway routes between Rotterdam and Utrecht, with special attention to bridges at Gouda and on West side of Utrecht. Also, road and railway bridges over the River Ijssel at Deventer and Zutphen.

The field have been told, in general terms, to consider protection of bridges but, for obvious reasons, routes have not been indicated. Our agent in the Utrecht area has suggested that paratroopers could be dropped to his reception committees, hidden and eventually brought forward to protect the bridge at Vianen in co-ordination with the advancing Allied troops.

Road Blocks:
Plan 'Cry' – to prevent or hinder German troop movements, particularly West to East at the Eastern exits from the Zuider Zee causeway by creating a series of road blocks forming two barrier lines:
First Line – end of the Arsluit-Dijk at Hakkum, Wons and Zurig.
Second Line – on the line of lakes Groote Brekken, Koevordermeer, Sneekermeer, Wijdsee, Bergumermeer, and Lauwersz.
Special action BBC messages have been tied up with the field.

Russian Mutiny:
Plan 'Cheep'.
Our agent in the Amsterdam area reported that approximately 2,350 Russians and Georgians located in the Ijmuiden, Bergen-aan-Zee and Groote-Keten districts were prepared to mutiny against their German comrades on a signal from us by broadcast. Recognition messages have been broadcast, but, at the request of 21 Army Group, the field were informed that no mutiny was to take place until requested by us.

Railways:
Plan 'Whine'.
Although instructions had been passed to the field for the cutting of railways, the Germans have been able to repair the main line running East and West through Utrecht, and as Allied bombing has since not been effective our agent at Rotterdam had suggested re-attacking all the railway lines in the province of Utrecht:
To prevent German troop movements, and
To prevent liquid oxygen containers for the rockets being fired in the West of Holland from being transported by rail.
In accordance with the agreement with 21 Army Group, action signals were broadcast on 6 Nov with instructions that no major demolitions should be attempted which would take the Allies too long to repair.

Infiltration of Allied Troops:
Plan 'Ring' – infiltration of Allied troops from the Brabantsche Biesbosch across to the Tong Plaat and the Zuid Hollandsche Biesbosch.
A contact at Rotterdam reports that the Resistance could ferry about 2000/3000 Allied troops across to the mainland South of Dordrecht. He has been asked to submit further particulars of this plan.
The above plans will be put into action as follows:
Plans Bang, Thud, Wail, Cry and Whine will be incorporated in the Basic Plan, in those zones to which they relate.

Plan Cheep will be put into action by special BBC code phrase or W/T order from London as and when required.

Resistance will be instructed to put Plan Screech into operation at their discretion.

Plan Ring will be shelved.

Clandestine Communications

SF HQ W/T Operators in the field:
The policy with regard to W/T communications between SF HQ and the field will be as follows:

There should be at least one W/T link with each region other than IV. Wherever possible, alternative links should be provided.

Spare W/T sets should be sent to the field in order to obviate the necessity for the operator's having to carry his set from place to place.

Reserve operators should be established in the field with instructions to remain dormant until called upon – Zone order of priority to be II, III, I, VI and V.

SIS W/T Operators in the field:
Traffic should not be passed through SIS channels, from or to the U.K., except in an emergency or where there is no SF HQ operator available.

The Eindhoven Links:
The following is the policy with regard to the Eindhoven links:

These links should not be used by the Resistance in the field except for the passing of intelligence.

No messages will be sent to the field through these links except in case of emergency. Such messages will be approved by HRH Prince Bernhard and one of the following:

Lieutenant Col. M.A.W. Rowlandson.
Lieutenant Col. M.L. de Rome.
Lieut. H. Hooper.
Captain A.G. Knight.

Internal Networks:
During the period of lull, minimum use will be made of internal networks.

Couriers:
Couriers will not work direct into or from Eindhoven. Arrangements have been made whereby they report to, or are sent out by, the I(b) authorities at Army Headquarters and Lieutenant Col. de Rome.

Care will be taken not to prejudice, by excessive traffic, the security of lines through the Biesbosch area.

BBC Messages:
N will keep D/Sigs informed of the number of operational messages to be sent out by the BBC.

MCRs:
Up to 400 MCRs will be supplied to the field. The question of the possibility of using crystal sets in the field will be investigated.

S-phones and Walkie-Talkie:
The following is the policy with regard to S-phones and Walkie-Talkie:
    There will be no infiltration of S-phones.
    No S-phone operators will be dropped to the field until the results of the present experiment have been examined.
    Two further S-phone operators will be trained, but will not be sent to the field without the sanction of AD/E.
    Walkie-Talkie will not be employed.

Summary of Reserves of Personnel
The following is the position with regard to reserves of personnel in the U.K.:

Jedburghs:	One team available (Edward, employed on *Market*).
W/T Operators:	Three ready on 2 Dec 44.
	Three ready on 6 Dec 44.
Organisers and Instructors:	One ready.
	One ready on 6 Dec 44.
	One ready at the end of December 1944.
Additional:	Eight men are in process of being recruited.

General Situation December 1944

As the field had been instructed to reduce activity and the excitement of possible immediate military activity had died down, the Resistance forces and the Dutch population in general, became more concerned with the difficult food situation. This was becoming critical in the West but still fairly good in the Eastern provinces. In consequence, children were being sent from Western Holland to Eastern Holland. *Draughts* asked us to request the Air Ministry to stop the shooting at night of shipping on the Ijsselmeer engaged in the transport of food Westwards and the transport of children Eastwards.

Frank, the K.P. leader in Rotterdam was arrested and murdered whilst on a reconnaissance for the attempt to release prisoners in the prison at Amersfoort.

A successful raid on the prison at Leeuwarden resulted in the release of some 50 resistance and political prisoners.

Owing to the continued reports of disunity amongst the top Resistance men, Prince Bernhard sent a message to *Rummy* suggesting that unless this quarrelling ceased, he would be obliged to send an officer to take over the command of all active Resistance.

German Atrocities:
Cubbing reported that after the most inhuman treatment, 30 political prisoners were murdered by the Germans in Apeldoorn. As in previous occurrences, 12 almost unidentifiable bodies were thrown out into the street from a lorry. This was followed by a Razzia. The train carrying several hundred men taken during the razzia was attacked by Allied planes near Bocholt in Western Germany; it is estimated that 40% of the victims were shot by the Germans whilst trying to escape or shelter from the raiding planes.

Planning:
In accordance with the planning directives the field was informed that for security reasons Resistance should be decentralised and advised of the boundaries of the 6 zones. Outlines of the directive were also communicated to them.

Agents sent to the Field:	On the night of the 30th December two S.I.S. agents *James I* and *II* and one S.A.S. agent *Yodel* were successfully dropped. The wireless material of the two S.I.S. agents was unfortunately smashed on landing.
Stores sent to the Field:	During the month of December there were 22 air sorties of which 13 were successful. 231 containers were dropped plus 4 for S.I.S. and 22 for S.A.S. In addition, 25 packages were dropped plus 3 for S.I.S. and 4 for S.A.S.
Sabotage Activities.	Nothing to report but a special rubber boat and a supply of limpets was dropped to the Rotterdam K.P. for a further attempt to sink the *Westerdam*, the last blockade ship.
Casualties:	Sgt Austin. Was arrested in December and shot later with other political prisoners for the attack on Rauter.

Cribbage. Was arrested on the 20th December but was released later shortly before the German capitulation.

Turniquoits. Arrested on the 27th December whilst transmitting. He is still missing.

Agents Returned from Field: Nil.
Students in Training: 21

Chapter 5

1945

General Situation January 1945

Lieutenant Colonel R.I. Dobson paid Prince Bernhard's H.Q., and 3 S.F. Det. at Brussels a visit on the 14th January and then proceeded to 2 S.F. Det at Tilburg to discuss several resistance matters. He also paid a special visit to the S.I.S. unit (2 I.U.) and Major Somer of the B.I. at Eindhoven. The object of this latter visit was to obtain full co-operation from the B.I. in regard to documents and intelligence required by S.O.E. German Directorate for their infiltrations behind enemy lines. Although the German Directorate had sent Lieut. Laming R.N. on two occasions to clear this matter he had met with little success. Lieutenant Col. Dobson had no difficulty however and future operations remained unhampered.

Deception Plan "Fortitude":
In order to assist S.H.A.E.F. in its deception plan Fortitude (intended to make the Germans think that an Allied crossing of the Rivers South of Rotterdam was about to take place and in consequence persuade them to hasten to that area as opposed to retaining them in Eastern Holland) an increased number of innocent B.B.C., messages were broadcast on programs known by the Germans to be listened to by Resistance movements for action messages or messages indicating operations. It was later reported that the deception plan was successful.

Growing Difficulties in the Field:
Occupied Holland was much perturbed by the new German regulation calling up for forced labour all men from 16 to 40 years of age. The situation was in fact a difficult one. Men who were unable to obtain food for their families were more or less obliged to report to support

their wives and children. The Resistance forces, however, did manage to feed most of their men from carefully kept stocks and very few of their men did actually report for forced labour.

Draughts I asked for considerable quantities of medical supplies which were extremely short or non-existent in Holland. He also asked for 200,000 blank Identity Cards for the underground workers who were in danger of being roped in owing to new Ausweiss regulation issued by the Germans.

The situation in Rotterdam was becoming precarious – an arms dump was seized by the Germans and *Rummy* received an ultimatum from them to either stop all further activities or a large number of prisoners would be shot. *Rummy* ignored the threat.

Owing to the S.D. activity and in order not to endanger the resistance fighting elements who were being reserved for overt action later, the Delta Centrum was asked to instruct all Regional Commanders to ensure that their sabotage groups were segregated from the fighting elements.

Personnel Infiltrated:	S. Sjoerdsma (*Squeak*), a wireless operator was dropped on the night of 5/6th January to an Evert reception committee in Overijssel. He remained in the area for a short while and then acted as operator to Eduard, Regional Commander for Overijssel. He did an extremely good job and remained with Eduard until overrun by the Canadian troops in April 45.
Stores sent to the Field:	10 Air sorties were made of which 3 were successful. 53 containers and 14 packages were dropped.
Sabotage Activities:	A report was received on a successful attack on the blockade ship *Westerdam* at her berth in Rotterdam and also the sinking of the Titan – 180 ton floating crane to prevent its departure to Germany.
	Draughts I reported a successful attack on the Atlanta building, Amsterdam, which contained registers of personnel due for labour service in Germany. Similar attacks were carried out on another building on the 5th January. Another registration building in the Paseerdergracht, Amsterdam, was also destroyed on the 7th January and various registers of the population brought to a place of safety. *Draughts I* also asked for tear gas bombs for further attempts but owing to the Chemical Warfare aspect, smoke bombs were sent instead.

Casualties: Nil.

Agents Returned: Rob (*Scrape*), District Commander of the N.B.S.
                                     Rotterdam, arrived in liberated territory for the
                                     first time on the night of the 8/9th Jan, having
                                     crossed the River Maas at Lage Zwaluwe. He
                                     confirmed that the K.P., R.V.V., and the O.D.,
                                     had now co-ordinated their efforts in Zuid
                                     Holland and had at least some 3825 active men
                                     at their disposal. Detailed plans were brought
                                     out by Rob showing certain targets which they
                                     wanted bombed in order to assist them in their
                                     plans for the protection of port installations
                                     not already damaged, Water Works, Electric
                                     Power Stations, Gasworks, Maas Tunnels, Maas
                                     Bridges and numerous other bridges and locks
                                     in the Rotterdam and Dordrecht areas.

Agents in Training: 22.

General Situation February 1945 Amsterdam:

Draughts I reported arrests amongst the Delta Centrum and feared for
the security of the organisation. The central depot of the S.I.S. internal
wireless net between Amsterdam and Eindhoven was raided by the
S.D. and all equipment lost. *Draughts* himself was caught returning
from a dropping operation in North Holland, was wounded and
subsequently died of his wounds in captivity. *Rowing* was instructed
to take over *Draughts'* work, but the field refused to accept him because
Dr. X, who had unbeknown to us already been working for *Draughts I*,
was more suited to the work. We agreed to this, and Dr. X then carried
on the good work right up to the time of the German capitulation.

Rotterdam:

Reported the arrest of *Coursing, Trapping* and Lorenz, an R.V.V. wireless
operator who had from time to time transmitted messages for *Shooting*
on the Raad wireless plan. An innocent letter had been received by
them from *Podex* in Germany who was then doing forced labour on
the railways. We too had received an innocent letter from him via
Switzerland asking for a wireless operator to be sent to him and giving
special B.B.C. message to be broadcast on the German programs if we
wished him to carry on sabotage on the railways in Germany. After
consultation with the German directorate it was decided to send him
an operator and to broadcast the special B.B.C. messages. An organiser
and an operator were subsequently dropped but never linked up
with *Podex*.

Utrecht:
Cubbing requested permission to come out through the lines but as it was felt impossible to lose him in the Utrecht area he was requested to remain and carry on the good work.

Overijssel:
Evert was killed whilst trying to escape after his arrest at Wierden and was succeeded by Herman of Salland, right up to the time of liberation by the Canadian forces in April 1945.

Groningen:
Necking reported that important arrests had taken place in Groningen. The regional Commander, however, managed to escape.

Passing of Tactical Information:
Owing to the lack of tactical information, four Belgian Verstrepen Wireless Operators were infiltrated by "Capt" Boot into Regions 5, 6, and 8. They were instrumental in passing excellent tactical information direct by wireless to S.F. Det. Owing to their nationality there was some misgivings as to whether or not they would fit into the picture but, as a precaution, a special message was sent to the field pointing out the nationality and mission of these operators. They did an excellent job and were eventually liberated by the Canadian Forces.

Personnel Infiltrated:	Hein, an S.I.S. agent was successfully dropped in the Overijssel area on the night of the 24/25th February.
	M. Van Der Stoep (*Scrape*). As *Rummy* had returned from the field with very pessimistic views on the general situation in Rotterdam, it was decided not to drop *Scrape* to a reception committee but to drop him "blind" so as to enable him to make the necessary investigations. He was dropped on the night of the 27th February, a few kms, North East of Rotterdam – the aircraft also threw some bombs out a small distance away as cover for his landing. His Mission was an important one and the final plans for the protection of installations and for Overt action had been discussed with him. From the Dutch side he had been specially briefed by Prince Bernhard to co-ordinate the Rotterdam activities with those of Amsterdam, if this was found necessary. There had been some differences of

opinion between the two areas and *Scrape* was told that his men must recognise the authority of the C.B.S. This matter was thrashed out at a special meeting in London at which Prince Bernhard, Lieutenant Col. Dobson and Richard (one of the Vertrouwensmannen – Political advisors to the Queen who had come through the lines from occupied territory) were present. *Scrape* landed safely and found the security of his men intact. The field reported its pleasure at his return and the final Rotterdam plans were completed. Unfortunately *Scrape* himself assisted at an attack on an S.D. H.Q., was shot through the head and died on the 11th April. His work was carried on by one Ferdinand right up to the time of the German capitulation in May 45.

Stores sent to the Field:	During the month of February there were 18 air sorties, 4 of which were successful. 62 containers were dropped plus 10 for S.I.S. In addition, 14 packages were safely received.
Sabotage Activities:	*Draughts I* reported that transformers supplying current to German Naval establishments and important factories working for the German War Industry, had been sabotaged.

Rotterdam reported the sinking of a newly launched 3000-ton vessel.

Utrecht reported the sinking of four barges loaded with 180,000 litres of oil.

5 H.E. charges were placed in the S.D. office at the Singel, Dordrecht – 16 S.D. personnel being killed.

Casualties:	*Trapping.* Arrested in February and executed later.

Coursing. Arrested in February and executed later.

Draughts I. Arrested on 10 Feb and wounded whilst escaping. Died of his wounds later.

Bezique. Arrested in February but later released through Resistance intervention.

Agents Returned to field:	*Snooker.* Returned through the lines on 2 Feb 45.

Rummy. Returned through the lines on 21st Feb 45.

Agents in training:	22.

General Situation March 1945

Following up on the Planning Conference of November and its subsequent directives, a further Conference was held in London on the 19/20th March 45 to discuss the:

NOTES FOR PLANNING CONFERENCE ON DUTCH RESISTANCE

Those in attendance were:

Brigadier Mockler-Ferryman.
  Commander Johns.
  Lieutenant Col. Saunders.
  Lieutenant Col. Gable (U.S.).
  Lieutenant Col. Rowlandson.
  Lieutenant Col. de Rome.
  Lieutenant Col. Thynne.
  Lieutenant Col. Dobson.
  Major Drake.

Action Messages:
In accordance with the Pencil Plan and concurrent with the Allied advance into Southern and Eastern Holland, action messages were broadcast on the 24/25th March for:

  Zone 2.
  Railway and Road sabotage.
  Passing Intelligence.
  Protection of Technical Personnel.

All zones were ordered to commence sabotage of overhead lines used by the enemy but to preserve all repeater station records. Technical personnel were ordered to go into hiding. This was more successful in Eastern Holland than in Western Holland where the resistance made considerable use of telecommunications for their own use and for tapping German intelligence reports. If the lines had been sabotaged in Central Holland the Resistance would have been unable to pass information through the enemy lines to the Canadians situated East and West of the River Ijssel.

Zone 2 was ordered to sabotage road and rail communications and to prevent bridge demolition wherever possible without engaging in stand-up fights with the enemy to hold same.

The Resistance Forces did extremely well but complained that had they received the action messages earlier they might have been able to do considerably better. However, owing to the Army security aspect and the delay incurred before we received the word "go" from the

Army authorities through either 3 or 2 S.F. Det., this was impossible. There was also the aspect of trying to prevent too great a loss of life amongst the Resistance ranks. Zone 2 was also instructed to send their couriers with tactical information through the lines. No. 2 S.F. Det. reported that valuable intelligence matter was received in this manner by them.

Whilst this activity was going on in Eastern Holland and, in view of the Armies' intention to go East and Northeast into Germany, it was important that the Resistance Forces in Central and Western Holland should remain as quiet as possible in order to avoid German reprisals and subsequent Dutch Government pressure for our troops to go West to the assistance of the population. They did however behave extremely well and kept to their instructions. Very few incidents occurred.

Personnel Infiltrated:

R.L. Bangma (*Whimper*) and his operator J. Van Der Weyden (*Snort*) were dropped in the Veluwe area on the night of the 2nd March in order to arrange supply of arms to the resistance forces in that area under the command of Piet Van Arnhem, the regional commander. Their package containing the wireless equipment was however lost on landing and it proved impossible to replace this before April. They were only able to arrange two deliveries before being overrun by the Canadian Forces shortly after.

Miss B.J. Gemmeke (*Cackle*), owing to the urgent need for a line through which to infiltrate agents into Germany it was decided to send this agent to try to organise one through North East Holland. She was dropped on the night of the 10th March but owing to the rapid advance of the Allies the scheme was no longer possible. She was liberated with *Draughts* 2 in the Hague.

A.M.J. Gehrels (*Grunt*) and his operator W. Pleysier (*Rumble*) owing to the possibility of an early advance over the Rhine into South East Holland, this organiser and wireless operator were dropped in the Achterhoek on the night of the 17th March to arrange supply of arms to the Resistance in that area. They were installed rather late and succeeded only in arranging one delivery of containers before being overrun by the Canadian Forces.

Major J.J.F. Borghouts (*Swish*), owing to the urgent need for the C.B.S. to have an assistant, it was decided to send this agent who had already worked in the field under the alias Peter Zuid. As he had been working on Prince Bernhard's staff, he was also conversant with the Prince's wishes and was dropped on the night of the 17th March. He successfully contacted the C.B.S. and, having previously worked in the Rotterdam area, successfully co-ordinated all future activities. He, and the C.B.S., played an important role on behalf of the Resistance Forces in Western Holland at special meetings which took place with the German Commanders immediately preceding and on the German capitulation in May 1945.

J. Ten Broek (*Ping*) was dropped on the night of the 17th March to a K.P. reception committee in the Rotterdam area to replace the wireless operator *Trapping* who had been arrested. *Ping* remained active in Rotterdam until the German capitulation in May 45.

S.I.S.:
An S.I.S. agent *Gremlin* was dropped to a K.P. reception committee on the night of the 27th March.

J.J. Weve (*Hoot*), owing to the death of *Scrape*, it was felt that another U.K. trained agent should be sent to assist Ferdinand in the Rotterdam area. *Hoot* was dropped on the night of 30th March, North of Rotterdam. He successfully contacted Ferdinand and remained in the area until liberated in May 1945.

Stores Sent to the Field:	There were 40 air sorties during the month of March of which 27 were successful. 514 containers were delivered plus 74 for S.I.S. In addition, 92 packages were dropped plus 7 for S.I.S.
Sabotage Activities.	Overijssel reported the blowing up of a viaduct between Zwolle and Almelo, causing a derailment and a traffic hold up.
	Utrecht reported the cutting of all railways from Amersfoort to the East to impede the transport of political prisoners to Germany.
Casualties:	*Dudley* – Was arrested and killed whilst escaping on March the 5th.
Agents Returned from Field:	*Shooting*. Escaped through the lines on the 16th of March.
Agents in Training:	29.

NOTES FOR PLANNING CONFERENCE ON DUTCH RESISTANCE TO BE HELD AT SF HQ ON 19 AND 20 MARCH 45.

General:
The Pencil Directives, issued as a result of the Planning Conference held at SF HQ on 27, 28, 29 Nov 44, and subsequently amended from

time to time, have not been materially affected by the circumstances which have arisen during the 4 months since November.

The object of these notes is to summarise the present situation of Resistance and of Resistance planning in Holland, and in particular to draw attention to points still outstanding.

Specific Plans:
Action messages for Plans Bang, Wail and Whine have been tied up with the field.

Voice of SHAEF:
Broadcasts by the Voice of SHAEF and/or HRH Prince Bernhard will have to be prepared.

Supplies to Resistance:
Deliveries of MCR's since 1 September 44 are as follows:

Zone I	16
Zone II	22
Zone III	9
Zone IV	-
Zone V	71
Zone VI	24
Total	142

It has not yet proved possible to deliver the Weldrods to Zones V and VI.

Additional Points for Discussion:
The situation with regard to the establishment of a stock of arms for liberated resistance requires clarification.

It is necessary to decide what, if any, direct communications should exist between ME 27, after its establishment in Holland, and No.3 SF Detachment.

Liaison groups from 1 and 2 SF Detachments.

Bombing support by TAF for the counter-searching operations in Rotterdam.

Command, West Holland District.

Resistance Situation in Holland
The following is a resume of the resistance situation in Occupied Holland, detailed by the individual zones.

Zone I

Zone I Includes the provinces of Friesland, Drenthe and Groningen.

SF Agents:

Necking and *Bobsleigh*.

The SF Liaison officer for this Zone is *Necking*, working with a W/T operator *Bobsleigh*. Another operator is being trained locally but has not yet become active. Both these agents are working satisfactorily and there is no reason to doubt their security.

Resistance Situation:

The situation throughout the Zone appears to be precarious. In both Drenthe and Groningen, recent drives by the Germans against Resistance appear to have been widespread and successful. At the end of January, arrests took place in the HQ of the NBS in Drenthe, and more recently the NBS in Groningen lost all the members of their Headquarters with the exception of the Commandant.

In Friesland, the only one of the three provinces in which *Necking* has been engaged, the Germans appear to have been less active, although a recent report states that the operations leader for Friesland has been arrested; this has led to the discovery of the files relating to the past activities and future intentions of the Resistance.

Political Situation:

Resistance is organised on an NBS basis, and, so far as is known, there is no political strife in the Zone.

Arms Supplied:

The following arms have been sent since August 1944:

Stens	2,164
Brens	74
Bazookas	60
P.I.A.Ts	4
Rifles	1,263
Carbines	150
Pistols	165
	3,880

In addition, 2,706 grenades have been sent to Zone I. Approximately 85% of these arms have been sent to Friesland, 15% to Drenthe and none to Groningen.

Conclusion:
Resistance appears to be in a fairly healthy condition in Friesland. SF HQ has liaison with the local organisation, and, at a conservative estimate, it can be expected that at least 3,000 Resistants are armed.

On the other hand, Resistance in Groningen and Drenthe must be regarded as negligible and likely to remain so until liaison has been established with these provinces and substantial deliveries of arms have been sent to them.

Zone II
Zone II includes the N.E. Polder, Overijssel and Achterhoek.

SF Agents:
Edouard and *Squeak*.

The organiser for Zone II is *Edouard*. He is not, properly speaking, an SF HQ agent as he has never been to this country. He is, however, in direct contact with his headquarters through his W/T operator, *Squeak*. Most of *Edouard's* work has been in Overijssel, but he has recently gone to the Achterhoek, with a view to organising resistance in that area.

Herman and *Charades*.

Herman, another local organiser, works under *Edouard* as the sub-commander of the Salland district of Overijssel. His predecessor, Evert (killed) had been until recently in constant contact with his Headquarters through his W/T operator *Charades*. For the time being, however, *Charades* is in hiding and will only operate in case of emergency.

Hunting.

Edouard has an SF HQ sabotage instructor, *Hunting*, with him. *Edouard* does not, unfortunately consider *Hunting* to be sufficiently experienced to be of much value.

Grunt and *Rumble*.

Grunt an organiser, and his W/T operator, *Rumble* were dropped to the Achterhoek on the night of 17/18 Mar.

Bock.

There is a Verstrepen operator, Bock, in the Achterhoek.

Resistance Situation:
There is good reason to suppose that Resistance in the Overijssel is well organised. *Dudley* was active in the NE Polder, until his death

at the beginning of March. Little is known of the state of Resistance in the Achterhoek, but a report can be expected from *Edouard* in the near future.

Political Situation:
Resistance is organised on the NBS basis. Reports were received from *Dudley* at the end of January that the KP and the LO were both trying to cut adrift from the NBS, but this was not confirmed by the DC, who had no knowledge of any political differences. There appears to be an independent RVV organisation in the Achterhoek.

Arms Supplied:
The following arms have been sent since August 1944:

Stens	2,588
Brens	48
Bazookas	48
P.I.A.T.s	3
Rifles	333
Carbines	210
Pistols	454
	3,654

In addition, 3,588 grenades have been sent to Zone II.

The majority of these arms have been sent to Overijssel, but some of them are known to have been distributed in the NE Polder and in the Achterhoek.

Conclusion:
Allowing for losses, it can be estimated that there are at least 2,500 armed Resistants in the area. *Edouard* appears to be a capable organiser, and there are three W/T operators, two of which are active. Provided, therefore, that no further arrests take place, there are reasonable expectations of Resistance giving a good account of itself in Zone II. The 200 Evaders in the Overijssel should prove of considerable value in support of the Resistance.

Zones III and IV

Zone III includes the Veluwe and the province of Utrecht. Zone IV is the Betuwe, which will be called into action at the same time as Zone III.

SF Agents:
Cubbing and *Bob*.

The principal SF HQ liaison officer in this area is *Cubbing*, who works through his locally recruited W/T operator, *Bob*. *Cubbing* works principally in the province of Utrecht.

Whimper and *Snort*.

Whimper, with his operator *Snort*, were sent to the Veluwe at the beginning of March. News has been received of their safe arrival, but they have not yet contacted this Headquarters.

Gueuze.

A Verstrepen operator, Gueuze, is working in the Apeldoorn area, and is in touch with Piet Von Arnhem, Commander of the Veluwe.

Foxtrot and Kriek.

Verstrepen operators, working in the province of Utrecht.

Fabian.

Exfiltrated, 15 Mar 45.

Resistance Situation:

There have been numerous arrests in this Zone during the last few months, and many local leaders have been lost. There is reason, however, to hope that the rank and file of Resistance is more or less intact.

Political Situation:

Resistance is organised on an NBS basis, but there have been repeated reports from *Cubbing* of political disunity. *Cubbing* appears, however, to be a somewhat unreliable witness, and it may well be that his reports are exaggerated and have their source in jealousy and rivalry which appears to be an inherent characteristic of para-military and resistance organisations in all occupied (and some un-occupied) countries.

Arms Supplied:

The following arms have been supplied:

Stens	2,089
Brens	56
Bazookas	28
P.I.A.T.s	2
Rifles	378
Carbines	105
Pistols	405
	3063

3,236 grenades have been sent to this Zone.

Conclusion:

There are known to be strong resistance groups in this Zone, of which about 2,000 may be assumed to be armed. The presence of 5 W/T operators in what is a relatively small area, should ensure that orders are passed rapidly to the field. There seems no reason to doubt that Resistance, assisted and strengthened by some 80 Evaders, who as seasoned British troops should prove invaluable in forming cadres, will give a good account of itself in the Veluwe and in Utrecht.

Zone V

Zone V includes the province of South Holland, the city of Amsterdam, and that part of the province in North Holland that lies South of the North Holland Canal.

SF Agents:

Draughts II.

Draughts II is the SF liaison officer at the Hague, working through the W/T operators in Amsterdam. *Draughts II* is principally concerned with the activities of the clandestine press but has recently been taking a more active part in Resistance and has assisted in the infiltration of agents to Germany.

Scrape, Cor and *Ping.*

Scrape, alias Rob, working through his W/T operator, *Cor*, is in charge of Resistance in Rotterdam, where he has recently returned from this country. Communications with *Scrape* are at the moment very unsatisfactory but a new W/T operator, *Ping*, was dropped on the night of 17/18 Mar. He will work with *Scrape*.

There is also a sabotage instructor, *Monopoly*, in Rotterdam. He is however, ill.

Doctor X, *Rowing, Boating* and Backgammon.

On the arrest of *Draught I, Rowing*, a sabotage instructor, was instructed to take over *Draughts I's* job as principal liaison officer to the DC in Amsterdam. On representations from *Draughts II*, who stated that *Rowing* was incompetent, Doctor X, a local Resistance leader, was appointed, with *Rowing* to act as technical adviser. *Boating* and *Backgammon* are the W/T operators for Amsterdam. There is also a female courier, *Tiddleywinks*, in this area, who has been more or less incapacitated with a broken leg ever since she was dropped in Holland some months age. She is now reported to be working.

Swish.

Swish (alias Pieter Zuid) was dropped on the night of 17/18 Mar. He will act as second in command of the CNBS and will operate between Rotterdam and Amsterdam.

Resistance Situation:
There have been many arrests throughout the Zone during the last few months, and most of the principal SF Liaison officers and W/T operators have been lost. Now, however, the situation seems to have improved, and there is reason to believe that the rank and file of Resistance is intact and reasonably well armed.

Political Situation:
Generally speaking, the RVV, OD and KP are working together satisfactorily in South Holland, and there have been no reports of serious political differences, although alleged communist activity is causing HRH Prince Bernhard some anxiety. In Amsterdam itself, there appears to be a considerable amount of intrigue in and about the DC, but it should be remembered that the DC is largely a political set-up, and that the disputes are of a government rather than a purely Resistance nature.

Arms Supplied:

Stens	4,062
Brens	102
Bazookas	76
PI.A.T.s	4
Rifles	549
Carbines	255
Pistols	772
	5,820

In addition, 5,745 grenades have been sent to this Zone.

Conclusion:
Resistance has been considerably weakened in this Zone, through recent arrests and difficulties of food supply. There are at the moment only 3 W/T operators, but the arrival of *Scrape's* operator will improve the communications situation. As in the other Zones, it is hoped and believed that the rank and file of Resistance is safe. Of these, some 5,000 should be armed, taking into account the arms that have been dropped to Zone VI and distributed in Zone V.

Zone VI

Zone VI includes the part of North Holland that lies to the North of the North Holland Canal.

SF Agents:
There are no SF Agents in this Zone, which is administered from Amsterdam.

Arms Supplied:

Stens	3,471
Brens	82
Bazookas	74
P.I.A.T.s	1
Rifles	405
Carbines	45
Pistols	379
	4,457

4,810 grenades have been sent to this Zone. The bulk of these arms are believed to have been delivered to Resistance Groups in Zone V.

Conclusion:
Little is known about the strength of Resistance in this Zone, in which there are no large towns, and it is not believed that there are more than 1,000 armed Resistants. The question of sending a sabotage instructor, and possibly a W/T operator to Zone VI, is under consideration.

Resume:
In spite of recent drives by the Germans against Resistants, numerous arrests and deportations and an extremely precarious food situation, the position of Resistance throughout Holland is by no means unsatisfactory and should be considered improved by the arrival of the agents who are due to leave in the immediate future.

More arms are needed everywhere, and in particular Groningen and Drenthe will need agents and considerable deliveries of supplies before any assistance in the liberation of Holland can be expected from Resistance in those provinces.

It would seem that in Holland there are some 12,500 armed Resistants, but it is probable that when Resistance is called into action, many hundreds if not thousands of men will be found to be in possession of some sort of weapon, and will come out into the open to assist in the liberation of their country.

SAS Operations in Holland Fabian.
This officer, together with his W/T operator and three Evaders came through the lines 14/15 Mar 45.

Gobbo.
Reported by Fabian to be safe at Barnvelt on his way out.

Keystone.
The scope of this operation will depend upon that of Anger. If 1st Canadian Army considers that there will be sufficient ground forces available to clear up the South bank of the Zuider Zee, SAS Troops will be dropped as far North as the road Amersfoort-Zwolle. If 1st Canadian Army intend only to hold a bridgehead at Arnhem and so make use of the roads to the South East on the North side of the Rhine, SAS Troops will be used in smaller numbers and will probably not be dropped North of the road Amersfoort-Apeldoorn. This whole operation may yet be altered if German troops are found to be less numerous than expected. In any case, Keystone will not now be mounted until two weeks after Plunder.

Action Messages
The position for action messages according to the Pencil Directive in Holland is as follows:

Zone I
On account of the arrests of various Resistance leaders in this area, the original action messages are known to the S.D. Fresh action messages, cancelling the old ones, were sent to *Necking* on 9 Mar 45, with instructions to pass these on to the Regional Commanders, together with the information that the messages should be made known only to the minimum number of persons necessary to mobilise their men for action 36 hours after the messages are heard.

Confirmation from *Necking* that these messages have been passed on to the Commanders was received on 14 Mar 45. He has passed the messages to the Commander of Friesland and is trying to send them to Groningen and Drenthe.

Zone II
Originally, different action messages were sent to Evert and *Edouard*. After the raid on *Edouard's* Headquarters, he was asked whether the S.D. could possibly know the action messages. His first reply was that the S.D. did not know the messages but, on 13 Mar 45, he stated that it would be advisable to change them.

Fresh action messages were sent to him on 13 Mar with instructions to confirm that they were all understood, at the same time pointing out that these messages would cancel all previous ones, (this also cancelled Evert's previous ones). These have not yet been acknowledged.

Zone III

Action messages were sent to *Cubbing* on 22 Dec 44. They were acknowledged by him and have not since been altered. On 13 Mar 45, the Commandant of Utrecht was asked whether there was any reason to suppose that the messages for his zone were known to the S.D. No reply has been received so far.

Zone IV

Action messages for this zone are the same as for Zone III.

Zone V

On account of the arrest of *Draughts I*, the possibility exists that the action messages originally sent for this zone might be known to the enemy. Fresh messages were, therefore, sent to the D.C. on 10 Mar 45. No acknowledgement has been received yet.

The D.C. has also been told that these messages are only to be made known to the limited number of persons necessary to mobilise Resistance for action 36 hours after the messages are heard.

Zone VI

Since the arrests in Rotterdam, it has been found necessary to send fresh action messages for this zone. These were passed to the D.C. on 10 Mar 45, with instructions to inform the Regional Commanders of Zone VI.

There is no confirmation yet that these have been received.

TABLE SHOWING QUANTITY OF STORES DELIVERED TO HOLLAND AS AT 14 Mar 45.

Zone	I	II	III	IV	V	VI	Totals
H.E. lbs.	2,985	3,393	2,476	-	5,520	6,531	20,905
Stens	2,164	2,558	2,089	-	4,062	3,471	14,344
9mm. ammo	1,003,900	1,085,100	902,550	-	1,680,355	1,371,289	6,043,194
Rifles	1,263	333	378	-	549	405	2,928
•303 ammo	190,350	49,950	56,700	-	82,350	60,750	440,100

Carbines	150	210	105	-	255	45	765
•30 ammo	64,500	109,500	66,750	-	107,250	27,750	375,750
Pistols							
various	165	454	405	-	772	379	2,175
Ammo							
various	8,250	22,750	20,230	-	43,100	18,725	113,075
Grenades	2,706	3,468	3,176	-	5,025	4,450	18,825
Hawkins							
grenades	-	120	60	-	720	360	1,260
Brens	74	48	56	-	102	82	362
•303 ammo	185,596	118,832	137,504	-	244,509	169,852	856,293
Bazookas	60	48	28	-	76	74	286
Rockets	840	752	392	-	1,236	1,236	4,456
PIAT	4	3	2	-	4	1	14

2,913 Containers and 342 Packages delivered to Holland as at 14 Mar 45.

Summary of Reserves of Personnel.

The following personnel are ready to proceed to the field:

W/T Operators:
[Name redacted]   Earmarked for the Achterhoek
[Name redacted]   Earmarked for Rotterdam.
Dekker   Spare.
Stuvel   In hospital.

Organisers:
[Name redacted]   Earmarked for the Achterhoek.
Pieter Zuid   Earmarked for Rotterdam and Amsterdam.
Gans Spare.

Sabotage Instructors:
Christiaansen   Earmarked for the Overijssel.
Den Dekker   Earmarked for the Overijssel.
Nijdam   Earmarked for North Holland.
Weve   Earmarked for Rotterdam.

The following personnel are in training:

W/T Operators.
Seven started training 13 Mar 45.
One due to start training 25 Mar 45.

Organisers/Instructors.
Two ready on 25 Mar 45.
Four ready on 4 Apr 45.
One started training on 6 Mar 45.
Four started training on 13 Mar 45.
Two due to start training on 25 Mar 45.

There are two Jedburgh teams in preparation.

MINUTES OF PLANNING CONFERENCE ON DUTCH RESISTANCE HELD AT SF HQ ON 19/20 MARCH 45.

Present:

Brigadier Mockler-Ferryman.
Commander Johns.
Lieutenant Col. Saunders.
Lieutenant Col. Gable.
Lieutenant Col. Rowlandson.
Lieutenant Col. de Rome.
Lieutenant Col. Thynne.
Lieutenant Col. Dobson.
Major Drake.

General:
A meeting was held at SF HQ on 19 and 20 Mar to plan the co-ordination of Resistance activity in Holland with future military operations. The following is a summary of the decisions reached.

Action to be taken immediately:
Helmsman Missions.

Lieutenant Col. Dobson:
A password is to be chosen for each zone, to be given by the exfiltree to the Brigade Intelligence Officer when he reaches the Allied lines.

The cover password, "Toulouse", common to all zones, will be given by the exfiltree to the Germans, if he is compelled by them to talk under interrogation.

Lieutenant Cols. Dobson and Thynne.

These passwords will be sent to the SF Detachments.

SF Dets.

The SF Detachments will inform the Brigade I.O.s of the passwords, and of the machinery of the Helmsman Missions.

The same passwords will be used by the Resistance personnel who are left in hiding, with the object of furnishing intelligence when they are overrun by the Allies.

The Voice of SHAEF:

Major Drake.

Ops "C" SHAEF will be asked whether G-5 have prepared a broadcast to follow the opening of Plunder.

Lieutenant Colonel Rowlandson.

Lieutenant Colonel Rowlandson will enquire in Brussels whether arrangements have been made for a broadcast by HRH Prince Bernhard. If not, Lieutenant Col. Rowlandson will make the necessary arrangements with the Prince.

Lieutenant Colonel Saunders.

Subject to the above, PWD will be asked to prepare suitable broadcasts.

SAS and Jedburghs:

Brigadier Mockler-Ferryman.

Brigadier Mockler-Ferryman undertook to maintain close liaison with SAS to ensure that SAS operations are tied up with those of Resistance and of the Jedburgh teams.

Signals:

Captain Heffer.

Jedburgh traffic will be received in London and passed immediately after recording to No. 2 SF Detachment. In addition, Signals are arranging one sked per Jedburgh per day direct to No. 2 SF Detachment (Verstrepen base station). Signals will be issuing special plans and instructions to cover these arrangements.

Upon the entry of the Allied troops into Zone III and IV, No. 2 SF Detachment will become responsible for the activities of Resistance in that zone. It will be necessary therefore to make arrangements for copies of all signals received from agents in Zones III and IV to be passed by Signals to No. 2 SF Detachment.

A member of the Dutch Resistance pictured in 1945. From 1944, the various elements of the Dutch Resistance were officially called the Binnenlandse Strijdkrachten, or Domestic Armed Forces, by the Dutch government. (Unknown/Alkmaar Regional Archives/1011524)

Members of the Binnenlandse Strijdkrachten on the platform of the railway station at Bergen in May 1945. (Unknown/Alkmaar Regional Archives/FO206828)

A portrait of Georges Louis Jambroes, an agent assigned to Special Operations Executive Dutch Section. Born in Amsterdam on 22 May 1905, Jambroes was dropped into The Netherlands on 26 June 1942. He was arrested the very same day. Jambroes was executed in Mauthausen Concentration Camp on 7 September 1944.

Members of the Binnenlandse Strijdkrachten guarding the entrance to their headquarters, the former tax office on Kennemerstraatweg in Alkmaar, May 1945. (Bosman, PJ/Alkmaar Regional Archives/FO1300128)

Members of the Binnenlandse Strijdkrachten form a guard of honour at an unknown location in The Netherlands, April 1945. (Dutch National Archives)

A despatch rider from the Dutch Resistance pictured in front of a former German post office in April 1945. (Dutch National Archives)

Men of the Dutch Resistance shelter in the Beurspoortje during the shooting on Dam Square, Amsterdam, during which German soldiers opened fire on the celebrating crowd, 7 May 1945. (Dutch National Archives)

A member of the Dutch Resistance, armed with a Sten, is pictured in the Dam Square during the moment when German soldiers opened fire on 7 May 1945. (NARA)

Members of the Dutch Resistanec march along Koorstraat, in Alkmaar, on 8 May 1945, the day that Canadian troops liberated the city. (Bosman, PJ/ Alkmaar Regional Archives/ FO1300055)

The funeral of two members of the Binnenlandse Strijdkrachten, or Domestic Armed Forces, killed in May 1945. The two men were part of a three-man patrol on duty in the centre of Alkmaar when they were fired upon by drunken German personnel on the night of 6 May 1945. Johannes Smit (aged 29), a furniture maker living on the Lindengracht, and Johannes Jacobus Baas (19 years old), were killed. The third member of the patrol, Piet Sijm, was badly injured but survived. Baas and Smit were buried with full military honours on 12 May 1945. (Bosman, PJ/Alkmaar Regional Archives/FO1300175)

Members of the Binnenlandse Strijdkrachten arresting German
personnel in the Mauritskade, Amsterdam, in May 1945.
(Amsterdam City Archives)

SS-Schutzhaftlagerführer Karl Peter Berg,
the Commandant of Kamp Amersfoort
Concentration Camp, in the centre wearing
his cap, is escorted by members of the
Dutch Resistance following his capture.
Sentenced to death for War Crimes,
Berg was executed, by firing squad, on
22 November 1949. (Dutch National
Archives)

Members of the Binnenlandse Strijdkrachten guard the crew of a Kriegsmarine vessel as the latter are ordered to unload ammunition in Amsterdam port, May 1945. (Dutch National Archives)

Members of the Dutch Resistance having arrested Willem van der Vegte, who can be seen with his hands on his head. Van der Vegte was a civil servant who was a prominent member of the Dutch Nazi Party. (Dutch National Archives)

Members of the Binnenlandse Strijdkrachten pictured outside houses
in Toussaintstraat in Alkmaar, May 1945. They are searching for people
suspected of collaboration with the Germans, participating in the black
market, and so on. (Bosman, PJ/Alkmaar Regional Archives/FO1300116)

Volunteers from the Dutch Resistance parade down the Gedempte Gracht
in the city of Schagen following its liberation in May 1945. (Unknown/
Alkmaar Regional Archives/1010906)

Verstrepens:
2 SF Det.

A Verstrepen operator will be infiltrated as soon as possible to work in the Veluwe and to stand by to supplement Gueuze as and when required.

The remaining Verstrepen operator and signal plan will be kept in reserve.

Stadhuis:
Lieutenant Colonel Dobson.

Messages will be sent to all zones informing them that, as and when towns and villages are liberated, Allied representatives will be present at the local Stadhuis to meet the leader of the local Resistance; the leader will be expected to produce all the necessary local contacts.

Action to be taken after the start of the Plunder.
3 SF Det and Lieutenant Col. Dobson.

Provided that a message is not received by 1800 hours on D-Day from 3 SF Det, warning SF HQ to take no immediate action, messages will be sent to the field by the BBC and clandestine means with instructions to take action.

Telecommunications:
Lieutenant Colonel Dobson.

Messages will be sent by clandestine means to all zones, giving them the following instructions:

Overhead lines to be sabotaged.

Records of exchange and repeater stations to be removed and hidden, together with records of sabotage carried out.

The following personnel of each exchange and repeater station to be instructed to go into hiding:

The man in charge of the exchange or repeater station.

The man in charge of the external repair service.

The man in charge of test desk duties.

Two external maintenance engineers.

All telecommunications personnel to report back to their posts immediately following liberation.

The BBC action messages will not be used for the above.

Lieutenant Colonel Rowlandson.

This plan will be cleared by Lieutenant Colonel Rowlandson with 2 I.U.

Intelligence:

Lieutenant Colonel Dobson.

Messages will be sent to all agents instructing them to send information of the German reactions to Plunder, and in particular the following:

Direction of movements and identification of bodies of troops of 500 men or over.

Concentration of large bodies of troops, not easily visible from the air.

Areas evacuated by the Germans.

Important defence systems being prepared by the Germans.

The source, time, date and pinpoints should be given. Agents will be instructed that the passing of intelligence is not to interfere with operational traffic.

Helmsman Missions:

Lieutenant Colonel Dobson and 2 SF. Det.

The passwords will be sent by W/T to all operators in Zone II, who will also be informed that the BBC message for the Helmsman plan will be broadcast immediately.

Lieutenant Colonel Dobson.

The BBC message for putting into effect the Helmsman plan in Zone II will be broadcast not less than 24 hours after the despatch of the messages.

SF. Dets and Lieutenant Colonel Dobson.

The SF Detachments will report on the success or otherwise of the Helmsman plan. If it does not work satisfactorily, a Helmsman organiser will be despatched to Zone II.

Railways and Roads:

Lieutenant Colonel Dobson.

The BBC action message for attacks on railways and roads in Zone II will be broadcast. This will be confirmed by messages to all W/T operators in Zone II.

Protection of valuable Technical Personnel:

Lieutenant Colonel Dobson.

The BBC action message for Zone II instructing valuable technical personnel to lie low will be broadcast. This will be confirmed by messages to all W/T operators in Zone II.

Action to be taken after the Entry of Allied Troops into Zones III and IV:

On the entry of Allied Troops into Zone III the responsibility for the organisation of resistance will pass from SF HQ to No. 2 SF Detachment. All signals from W/T operators in Zones III and IV will therefore be repeated by Signals to 2 SF Detachment.

Helmsman Missions:
Lieutenant Colonel Dobson and 2 SF Det.

The passwords will be sent by W/T to all operators in Zones III and IV, who will also be informed that the BBC messages for the Helmsman plan will be broadcast immediately.

Lieutenant Col. Dobson.

The BBC messages for putting into effect the Helmsman plan in Zones III and IV will be broadcast not less than 24 hours after the despatch of the messages referred to above.

Protection of valuable Technical Personnel:
Lieutenant Col. Dobson.

The BBC action message for Zones III and IV instructing valuable technical personnel to lie low will be broadcast.

This will be confirmed by messages to all W/T operators in Zones III and IV.

Jedburghs and Harassing Attacks:
Lieutenant Col. Dobson.

In accordance with plans to be co-ordinated with SAS, two Jedburgh teams will be despatched to Region 6 of Zone III.

Lieutenant Col. Dobson and 2 SF Det.

By the Jedburgh and SAS parties and by all available W/T operators in Region 6, Resistance will be called upon to carry out maximum harassing activity in Region 6. All operators in Zones III and IV will be clearly instructed that harassing activity is not to be carried out in Regions 7, 8 or 9.

2 SF Det:
Lieutenant Col. Dobson and 2 SF Det.

All W/T operators in Zones III and IV will be informed of the arrival and tasks of the Jedburghs and SAS parties.

No BBC message for harassing attacks will be broadcast to Zones III and IV.

3 SF Det.

The BBC message for harassing attacks to be carried out in Zone II will be sent out, as directed by 21 Army Group.

Armenians:
2 SF Det and Lieutenant Col. Saunders.

The position with regard to the Armenians will be watched; orders for their employment will be sent as circumstances may demand.

Zone V :
Lieutenant Col. Dobson.

Messages will be sent to all W/T operators in Zone V, instructing Resistance to take no action, except to watch events closely and to send information.

Action to be taken after the entry of Allied troops into Zone V
As envisaged at present the principal tasks of Resistance in Zone V, will be as follows:
Counter-Scorching.
Containing enemy reduits.
The Helmsman plan.

Administration and Liaison:
SF representation with the advancing Allied forces will be the responsibility of the SF Detachments.

General Situation April 1945
The Canadian Forces had by now advanced Westwards and consolidated themselves East of the Grebbe Line. The Germans threatened to do wholesale flooding of Western Holland should the Allies come further West. Rumours of a possible German capitulation commenced to seep through and in view of S.H.A.E.F.'s plan, for the dropping of food to the Dutch population, being well advanced, we stopped all arms' dropping as from the 24th April in order to avoid clashes between Germans and resistance members and to ensure the smooth operation of the food dropping.

No 2. SF Det. reported good results in Eastern Holland by the Resistance Forces. The following are some extracts of Liaison Officers' reports:

Up to date resistance has been useful in giving information on military and resistance matters by means of exfiltrees and secret telegrams.

In nearly all the towns and villages, order has been maintained after liberation by the Resistance leaders taking over. This appears to have gone very smoothly.

Resistance groups have undoubtedly played an important part in mopping up isolated Germans, and there has been some hard fighting by resistance groups.

The use of Resistance for guarding of bridges and perimeter defences of H.Q. has been reported.

A German Luftwaffe Colonel captured on April 16th, stated that he had more casualties from the Resistance than from the Canadian Forces.

Resistance successfully defended bridges at Augustinusga, Drogeham and Schuilenberg.

Very good show by resistance at Dieren, who had rebuilt roads ready for allied forward troops.

Brigadier Smith, 1 Canadian Infantry Division, congratulated the resistance forces for the high quality of military information passed to him and for keen co-operation of Resistance elements in his area.

Action Messages:
In accordance with the Pencil plan and, concurrent with the Allied Army advance into Eastern and Northeast Holland, the following B.B.C. action messages were broadcast:

Zone 2:
3rd April – Prevention of Demolition of Bridges.

7/8th April – Harassing attacks. Prevention of demolitions and protection of Bridges.

Zone 1:
7/8th April – Railway and road sabotage. Passing Intelligence. Protection of Technical Personnel.

15th April – Harassing attacks. Prevention of Demolition and Protection of Bridges.

Zone 3:
11/12th April–Passing of Intelligence. Protection of Technical Personnel.

N.B. Protection of Technical Personnel:
The Resistance reaction to this order for technical personnel to go into hiding was not favourable and in fact only occurred in actual fighting areas. The reason for this being that whilst on the job, men could watch the interests of the factory or other installation whereas, if they went into hiding, the Germans would only replace them and the output would only be greater than if passive resistance methods were employed.

High Level Conferences:
After a conference with Lieutenant Gen. W.B. Smith on April 30 about the provisioning of Western Holland with food, Lieutenant Gen.

Foulkes, commanding First Canadian Corps, had several discussions with General Reichelt, Chief of Staff of General Blaskowitz, about the possibility of the German forces in Holland and about the necessary arrangement to ensure safe transport of the food provided by S.H.A.E.F. into and through Western Holland by road.

While these discussions between General Foulkes and General Reichelt were going on, the C.B.S. (Commanding Officer of Resistance Forces in Holland) Major General Koot, had discussions also with General Reichelt about conditions of surrender etc., General Reichelt informed him that the German Forces would recognise the Interior Forces and would consider surrender to them. General Koot made several further suggestions in order to ensure that the Interior Forces should have a definite task during this German capitulation, as their original task of fighting the Germans had ceased after the Conference of April 30. These suggestions from Major General Koot were passed on to Prince Bernhard and Lieutenant Gen. Foulkes with the request that the Interior Forces should be used to the fullest extent during this capitulation. General Foulkes noted these suggestions and promised to see whether it were possible to use them.

Personnel Infiltrated:	Gambling. A Jedburgh team consisting of Major Clutton, Captain Knottenbelt and wireless operator (Sergeant Somers) together with a team of three S.A.S. Officers.

In view of an imminent crossing of the River Ijssel by the Canadians, East to West, it was felt necessary to drop army personnel to co-ordinate the activities between Resistance Forces and the Canadians in the Veluwe area. At first the S.A.S. wished to drop large numbers of their troops "willy nilly" throughout the area but after pointing out the dangers of this and resultant difficulties which would arise, S.A.S. agreed to limit the operation to two joint S.A.S/S.O.E. teams. Two teams left on the night of the 3rd April but owing to German activity on the ground, the reception committee for the second team were unable to operate. The Gambling team however landed safely N.W. of Apeldoorn and made contact with the Resistance leader Piet Van Arnhem. Wireless contact was established with us and 2 S.F. Det. The team had dropped in uniform but owing to the density of Germans in the same area some of them were obliged to put on civilian clothing. Stores were dropped to them, and they made reconnaissances of bridges North of Apeldoorn which they, with the help of the resistance, intended holding for the Canadian troops to cross over the Apeldoorn Canal. A telephone link with the Canadians was established but in spite of the fact that Gambling informed them that they were holding the bridges, the Canadians never made use of them but remained immediately East of Apeldoorn. The Germans pulled out of Apeldoorn unbeknown to the Canadians and Gambling on his telephone link, was able to warn them and avoid the shelling of Apeldoorn. This team did extremely well under difficult circumstances and were eventually overrun by the Canadian forces.

J.M. Christiaansen (*Hiss*) and his wireless operator C. Den Dekker (*Rap*), were dropped in Western Holland on the night of the 3rd April to organise deliveries of arms in North Western Holland. They contacted the resistance forces safely but by the time wireless contact had been made the food dropping plan was well under way and it became too late to send them stores. They were both liberated when the Germans capitulated.

Orval. This Belgian Verstrepen wireless operator was dropped into the Utrecht area on the night of the 4th April to pass out tactical information direct to 2. S.F. Det. and, in the event of a German withdrawal, to continue his mission from Western or North West Holland. He passed several messages and was liberated when the Germans capitulated.

Dicing. Jedburgh Team consisting of: Major Harcourt, Captain Bestebreurtje, Captain Ruys Van Duchteren and wireless operator Sergeant Menzies. In order to accelerate their advance into Northeast Holland, the Canadian Force planned to drop Airborne Troops in the Drenthe area in the region of Assen. We were asked to supply liaison officers to co-ordinate the activities of the Resistance forces. The team together with the airborne force was dropped on the night of the 7th April. Captain Bestebreurtje broke his ankle,

Major Harcourt was taken prisoner, leaving Captain Ruys Van Duchteren and his operator. They managed to contact the resistance force leader, arranged one delivery of arms by air and successfully co-ordinated the resistance activities with the requirements of the Airborne Force. They were overrun by the Canadian Forces a few days later.

J. Greydanus (*Jingle*) and his operator F. Decker (*Whistle*), together with an S.I.S. operator were dropped on the night of the 11th April, South of Hilversum. Unfortunately *Jingle* and the S.I.S. operator fell into the lake at Loosdrecht and were both drowned. *Whistle* dropped on the edge of the lake and was fished out by the reception committee. He contacted *Swish*, but owing to the loss of his equipment was only able send a few messages at a later date after this had been resupplied.

W.S. Bisschop (*Howl*) and H. Geysen (*Scream*), two saboteur instructors were dropped in the Rotterdam area on the night of the 11th April. They remained in the area until liberated in the month of May.

S. Sjoerdsma (*Squeak 2*), this operator who had already worked in the Overijssel area with Eduard, was re-dropped to the Rotterdam circuit on the night of the 11th April to assist with their wireless communications. *Ping* was not proving too successful, hence the need for *Squeak*. He remained with the resistance forces there until liberated in May 45.

A.M.J. Gehrels (*Grunt*) and F.J. Stuvel (*Fizz*). Owing to the repeated requests for arms to be dropped to the Hague area, this organiser and operator, were dropped on the night of the 23rd April to a *Draughts 2* reception committee. Owing to the political intrigue which was going on in the Hague and the eventual German capitulation, their mission was not very successful. No material was dropped to them and *Grunt* felt extremely disgruntled.

Lieutenant Pleysier (*Rumble*), W. Bouma (*Gurgle*), W. Dinger (*Grind*), Van Der Putt (*Splash*) and B.J.A. Nijdam (*Yelp*). These organisers and operators were dropped on the night of the 23rd

	April to assist the resistance in the Gooi and Amsterdam areas. They did what they could but owing the food dropping and the German capitulation their mission was short lived.
Stores sent to the Field:	During the month of April there were 79 air sorties of which 53 were successful. 1179 containers plus 48 for S.I.S. were dropped to Resistance together with 190 packages plus 8 for S.I.S.
Casualties:	*Scrape* – Killed during an attack on an S.D. H.Q. at Rotterdam on 11th April.
Agents in Training:	22

General Situation May, June and July 1945

On Thursday, May 3, the situation was that General Reichelt had informed General Foulkes that the German troops would surrender at once if they got an assurance that they would not be sent to Russia as prisoners of war. General Foulkes passed this matter on to the 21st Army Group, but before the answer to this question arrived, General Montgomery received, and signed, the official capitulation of all German forces in Northern Europe, excluding Norway, but including Holland. This naturally ended all the direct arrangements between General Foulkes and General Reichelt of surrender of the German forces in Holland as the conditions laid down by General Montgomery were now valid for these forces also.

One of these conditions was that the German forces should be concentrated in certain areas to be designated by General Foulkes, and to proceed to these areas after Allied troops had occupied Western Holland, and especially that they were allowed to retain their arms until this had taken place. This immediately put a stop to the possibility of the German forces surrendering to the Forces of the Interior, whose task now became even more limited.

On Saturday, May 5, at 1000 hours, a meeting to which Prince Bernhard was invited, took place between General Foulkes and General Reichelt to discuss the capitulation and the necessary measures to be taken.

This was followed by a meeting in the afternoon of May 5 with General Blaskowitz. General Blaskowitz was told that the Forces of the Interior had to be recognised and they would, as from now, appear armed in public. He was further informed that the 49th Division would march into Western Holland on Sunday May 6, and that he would be held responsible for any incidents or any disorders which might interfere with the smooth settlement of everything. General Blaskowitz pointed out that German communications were extremely bad and that

in order to give the necessary orders to all his troops he asked General
Foulkes whether he could possibly consider postponing the entry of
the 49th Division by 24 hours, as otherwise it would be practically
impossible for him to prevent incidents and he thought that this was
rather unfair. General Foulkes agreed that, if German communications
were so bad, he would postpone the entry of the 49th Division by 24
hours. General Blaskowitz then pointed out that if the Interior Forces
appeared armed in the streets while his troops had not been informed
of the true state of affairs, and in view of the very high feeling of the
Dutch population against the Germans, this would certainly lead to
incidents, as his troops would have to protect themselves by making
use of their arms. He again inquired whether General Foulkes and
Prince Bernhard would consider ordering the Resistance Groups not
to carry arms until such time as First Corps had taken full charge and
German troops were disarmed as, if he was to be held responsible for
any incidents, this would be an almost impossible task for him.

General Foulkes and Prince Bernhard agreed that this situation
might lead to great disturbances, which had to be avoided at all costs
and Prince Bernhard agreed to order all Resistance Forces not to carry
arms in public until further notice.

On Sunday May 6, Prince Bernhard telephoned to Major General
Koot and asked him about the effect of this order. Prince Bernhard was
informed that the troops of the Resistance Forces would be bitterly
disappointed not to be able to be of any service and the fact that they
would not be allowed to carry arms would be a blow to their morale.
It was decided to issue an order of the day, pointing out the necessity
to obey this order strictly. In effect this order was issued on Monday,
May 7.

On Sunday afternoon, May 6, General Foulkes had another
conference with General Blaskowitz, to which Prince Bernhard was
invited, to sign the official capitulation. Several small incidents had
occurred which were discussed between the interested parties, and it
was agreed that they should be settled on the spot between General
Reichelt and Major General Koot. It was also agreed that it was almost
impossible to decide who had started these incidents, and the least
said about it the better. (Casualties were small and about even on
both sides).

The Corps Commander, General Foulkes, then promised Prince
Bernhard to allow the Interior Forces to carry arms at the earliest
possible moment. On Monday morning, May 7, General Koot informed
Prince Bernhard by telephone that in several places in Western
Holland the German Commanders had asked Resistance troops to

carry arms and help them to ensure law and order. General Koot was informed that the decision already arrived at should not be interfered with as the German Commanders still carried full responsibility but that if they took it upon themselves to ask resistance troops to go out armed, it would be up to them to make sure that nothing happened. This arrangement was put into practice in several places during the following week and caused no trouble anywhere.

On the same day, however, Brigadier General Spalding, of 1st Corps drove through Amsterdam under German safe custody, with one German car in front and two German cars behind and was fired upon. Several people in his car were wounded, and the bullets found were from British Sten guns.

General Foulkes informed Prince Bernhard of this in the evening of Monday, May 7, and said that he did not want to lose the life of one single more Canadian soldier and, if Resistance troops were undisciplined, he would have to proclaim martial law; in the meantime, he would issue an order to shoot on sight at any civilian carrying arms.

Prince Bernhard pointed out to the General that a great many German Gestapo personnel, and even German Army personnel, were armed with British Sten guns which they carried even in public, and that moreover certain extremist groups had been armed with British material by the Germans after September 1944. Prince Bernhard also pointed out to General Foulkes that he had foreseen this and that, to avoid such instances by either German provocateurs or extremist groups he had, several months ago, issued orders that all Resistance troops should be concentrated in companies, immediately after Liberation, and be provided, if possible, with uniforms; if this were not possible they should be provided with arm bands which could not be imitated easily. In view of the situation that had arisen, however, he had not been able to carry out these ideas, not had the Resistance commanders been able to do so. He had intended to make the carrying of arms illegal by anyone except those in uniform or wearing the authorised arm band.

General Foulkes finally agreed that it was most unlikely that Resistance personnel had been the cause of the above mentioned incident, but in order to eliminate those elements which might create trouble, Prince Bernhard agreed that he would telephone immediately to Amsterdam to issue orders that in the three towns of Amsterdam, the Hague and Rotterdam, as from Tuesday, May 8, 0700 hours, all Resistance troops should carry no arms, as those seen on the streets carrying arms would not be authorised Resistance personnel. At the same time General Foulkes said that, in order to ensure that these people would be able to carry arms again as soon as possible, he would provide uniform arm bands from Amry sources, to be issued to personnel assisting 1st Corps.

On Tuesday, May 8, Prince Bernhard again telephoned to General Koot at Amsterdam. The necessary orders had been passed out during the night but General Koot pointed out that the local Allied commander had asked Resistance personnel to carry arms in the Hague in order to help him. Prince Bernhard agreed that this private arrangement should not be interfered with, as local commanders must be allowed to use their own judgement.

On the evening of Tuesday, May 8, Prince Bernhard was informed by 1st Corps that General Foulkes was going to issue enough arm bands to arm all Resistance personnel in Western Holland that would be needed by 1st Corps, and that he would, at the same time, issue an order that no other type of arm bands would authorise the wearer to carry arms. Prince Bernhard agreed that this was a very logical solution and hoped that it would be carried out satisfactorily everywhere.

On Wednesday, May 9, Prince Bernhard passed through Amersfoort, Utrecht, Rotterdam, the Hague and Amsterdam. He noticed that the above mentioned order had not yet been carried out anywhere, and that armed Resistance troops were on duty at several places, sometimes together with German armed personnel on guard duty. They wore different sorts of arm bands but not a single one provided by 1st Corps. However, on first sight, everybody seemed to be content – at least those he saw. He also saw a great number of Resistance personnel not carrying arms.

During the evening of May 9, Prince Bernhard had a meeting in a house near Amsterdam with General Koot and his junior commanders, where he discussed the whole situation and its possibilities. It was agreed there was very little they could do at the moment and that, as it was a very bitter disappointment for the Resistance Troops to be standing idle after waiting four years for this moment, the best that could be done was to give them something to do as soon as it could possibly be arranged.

On Thursday, May 10, Prince Bernhard telephoned to General Foulkes to inform him of several authorisations that S.H.A.E.F. had given regarding the employment of German prisoners, and several requests from the Dutch Government regarding material used by the Germans and which was previously Dutch property. General Foulkes informed Prince Bernhard that everything was going very well, that he had a great number of arm bands now available which would be issued and that everything should continue to be quite satisfactory.

On Friday, May 11, several reports came in from Prince Bernhard's liaison officers from Western Holland. According to these reports there were cases of the public getting out of hand because the Interior Forces could not ensure law and order because, not having armbands, they could not be armed. There were cases of individuals who should have been arrested but were still free and this was also causing unrest amongst the civilian population. In some places arrests were carried out by the civilians themselves. There were other serious instances but too numerous to raise.

Prince Bernhard therefore decided to send Major Meynen and Major Boekkooi, both of his staff, to 1st Corps to make sure that the issue of arm bands, which authorized the carrying of arms would be taken in hand at once, as more delay would cause greater confusion and having a lasting influence on Dutch internal affairs.

The two officers were informed by Brigadier Kitching, Chief of Staff 1st Corps, that everything was well in hand and that the Corps Commander would personally issue a proclamation to the Interior Forces to the effect that he would issue the necessary arm bands for all personnel requiring arms to carry out their duties.

In the afternoon Lieutenant Colonel de Rome, O.C., 2 S.F. Det, who had been attached to 1st Corps came to see Prince Bernhard and Major Frowein and the different problems that had arisen out of the confusion of carrying arms and armbands was discussed. Lieutenant Col. de Rome promised to discuss the matter with 1st Corps the same evening and where he hoped that their wishes would be met with full sympathy and dealt with.

Lieutenant Col. de Rome was especially asked to point out to the Corps Commander that the Interior Forces had already shown discipline by carrying out orders strictly – orders, which under the circumstances, made discipline most difficult indeed.

On Saturday, May 12, Prince Bernhard flew to S.H.A.E.F. to discuss with Lieutenant General Bedell Smith the raising of battalions from Resistance forces, and to hear their views on the employment of the resistance during these days and in the near future. He was informed that the Interior Forces of the Netherlands was still directly under General Eisenhower's command, and that if Prince Bernhard as their commander, wanted any additional equipment for them, General Foulkes, who would then hold all German equipment, was naturally authorized to issue as much as he considered necessary for the duties of the Interior Forces, either for the Allies or for the Dutch themselves.

As things were running quite smoothly now, General Foulkes agreed that armbands and arms should also be handed out for purely Dutch requirements, i.e., for arrests, maintenance of law and order, and so on.

On Sunday, May 17, General Foulkes visited Prince Bernhard's H.Q., together with Lieutenant Col. de Rome, for a final conference and informed Prince Bernhard that he had more than 20,000 arm bands i.e., the number needed for Canadian and Netherlands' requirements. Lieutenant Col. de Rome was made responsible for handing out these arm bands and it was agreed that the Regional Commanders should be held responsible for distributing them to those people that they could vouch for.

Hence the procedure to receive arm bands for each region was as follows: the Regional Commander would inform the Prince's Liaison Officer or the 2 S.F. Liaison Officer as to the numbers required for Army duties and numbers for civilian duties. These in turn ordered the necessary number through Lieutenant Col. de Rome at 1st Corps.

The next few days the country was toured to make sure that this arrangement was being carried out satisfactorily.

Summing up the whole situation it can be definitely stated that under the circumstances the discipline of the Interior Forces was extraordinarily good and, although provocations from the German side were not lacking, no serious incidents occurred again.

The following are personal notes by H.R.H. Prince Bernhard on the problems which had to be coped with:

I realized from the start that it was an impossible thing to ask the Resistance Forces to leave their arms at home, not so much in view of the Germans still being armed, but of the Gestapo, S.D., collaborators etc. They would feel completely powerless, which would be too much for a man who had been a good Dutchman.

In view of the fact that it was reliably reported that S.D. Agents and Landwacht were using orange armbands and possibly the same as Resistance, measures had to be taken in order to ensure that the confusion should not become greater. Therefore, new arm bands were the only logical solution, and we naturally complied with the Corps' Commander's wishes in this matter.

I realized that many of the Resistance personnel would perhaps not understand any these difficulties, neither would they understand my position. They should realise, however, that as soldiers they, as well as I, had to carry out orders issued to us, however unpleasant they might be.

All my Staff Officers and myself have taken every available opportunity to make clear to the Allied Commanders the psychologically different situation in which the Interior Forces found themselves. This was fully understood by these Commanders.

O.C.M.E.27 (Special Force Mission Netherlands) Proceeds Overseas.

In view of the general situation, Lieutenant Colonel Dobson proceeded overseas on the 4th May 45 and temporarily joined 2 S.F. Det., then situated at Harskamp, Southwest of Apeldoorn, with a view to establishing the Mission when this became possible.

At that time the situation was still rather hectic, food had been dropped to the famine-stricken areas and, by special arrangement with the Germans, lorries containing food were being driven through the Grebbe Line into Western Holland. Some of these lorries were attacked, it is believed by Dutch S.S. Some German elements were still in a dangerous mood and reports of continued flooding came through. In the meantime, the C.B.S. and *Swish* had made an agreement with the German S.D. that if further sabotage etc., were stopped, they would stop all further executions and political prisoners would be released.

The instruction to the Resistance Forces forbidding them to carry arms in the streets was well adhered to and there were very few incidents. The Resistance Forces were eventually issued with proper military arm bands which entitled them to be armed if on special duties appointed by the Canadian Force Commanders. These duties consisted of maintaining law and order, rounding up German stragglers, undertaking guard and point duty, arresting collaborators and guarding bridges.

The first main task was the guarding of the Grebbe Line, from the Ijsselmeer to the Neder Rhine, in order to prevent the population from the East streaming over into the Western provinces where food was very scarce and to prevent possible sickness spreading back to the Eastern provinces. Special Guards were also placed on the bridges over the Ijssel river to prevent Germans or collaborators escaping back to Germany in civilian clothing. It is estimated that some 20/30,000 resistance personnel were employed by the Canadians in some form or other.

When the 1st Canadian Corps set up its H.Q. at Hilversum, 2. S.F. Det moved into Utrecht on Thursday, May 10, and M.E. 27 set up its Mission on 12th May 1945, at Utrecht.

The Mission consisted of the following officers:

Lieutenant Col. R.I. Dobson. O.C.
Major W.A. Murphy. G.S.O.2.
Captain A.G. Knight. G.S.O.3.
Captain Olink. G.S.O.3.
Captain Tivey. G.S.O.3.
Captain W.E. Mills. G.S.O.3.
Lieut. Gardiner. Staff Lieutenant,

plus Sergeant Spence, the Missions wireless operator and 12 Other Ranks. Major Olmsted and Captain Mortlock, two O.S.S. U.S.A. Officers were also attached to the Mission.

Captain Hooper and Sergeant Hannaford who also belonged to M.E. 27., were however retained by Prince Bernhard at the Royal Palace at Het Lo, Apeldoorn, to maintain his wireless link on Northaw with the U.K.

The Missions initial function was the collecting of the agents who had been overrun or liberated, interrogating them and sending them to the U.K., liaising with Prince Bernhard, S.H.A.E.F. Mission to the Netherlands, Netherlands District, B.B.O. and the S.I.S. Mission at the Hague. Redundant wireless material was collected throughout Holland and all Regional Commanders, and their areas visited.

Brigadier Mockler-Ferryman, C.B.E., M.C., accompanied by Mr Millar and Major Willard of O.S.S. visited the Mission on 6th June and remained until the 9th June. On the morning of the 7th June the visitors inspected the local Resistance sights of interest in Utrecht, including the famous underground telephone exchange used during the German occupation. They returned to the Mission for a luncheon party which was attended by:

Lieut. General H.R.H. Prince Bernhard of the Netherlands.
Major-General Koot. C.B.S.
Brigadier Mockler-Ferryman. S.F. H.Q.
Mr Millar. O.S.S.
Lieutenant Col. de Rome. O.C. 2 S.F. Det.
Lieutenant Col. R.I. Dobson. O.C. M.E.27.
Lieutenant Col. Van Houten. Prince Bernhard's Staff.
Lieutenant Col. Six. N.B.S., H.Q. A'dam.
Lieutenant Col. Klijzing. B.B.O.
Major P. Borghout. Agent *Swish*. Dep. C.B.S.
Major de Boei. Delta Centrum.
Captain Tivey. Adjutant M.E. 27.

This was followed by a small ceremony during which the agent Lieutenant De Goede (*Rummy*) was invested with the Order of the M.B.E. (Military) by Brigadier Mockler-Ferryman.

In the afternoon a reception was held at the Mission H.Q. which was attended by all the principal Resistance personalities throughout Holland and also the following:

Lieut. General H.R.H. Prince Bernhard.
Lieut. General Ch. Foulkes, G.O.C. 1st Canadian Corps.
The Regional Commanders and one saboteur leader of each of the
13 N.B.S. Regions.
Staff Officers of Prince Bernhard.
Staff Officers of the B.B.O.
Staff Officers of M.E. 27., and 2 S.F. Det.

On Friday June 8, Brigadier Mockler Ferryman and party accompanied
by Lieut. Col. R.I. Dobson made an all-day tour comprising visits to the
Resistance H.Q.s' at Rotterdam and Amsterdam.

The Mission completed its work of collecting surplus explosives,
Regional Commanders' reports and disbanded on the 7th July, 1945
and returned to the U.K. on 10th July.

List of Casualties January 1944 to May 1945

Year and date.	Killed or died.	Arrested, escaped or liberated.	Remarks.
1944			
May 19	Faro	*Cricket, Ping Pong*	Swale (Missing)
May 31	*Poker*		Aircraft shot down and occupants killed.
	Football		Aircraft shot down and occupants killed.
July 5	*Fives*		Aircraft shot down and occupants killed over Ijsselmeer.
	Racquets		Aircraft shot down and occupants killed over Ijsselmeer.
	Bowls		Aircraft shot down and occupants killed over Ijsselmeer.
	Halma		Aircraft shot down and occupants killed over Ijsselmeer.
Aug 28	*Skating*		Captured after aircraft shot down.

Sept 20	Captain Greenwood		Killed whilst on Arnhem Operation.
Nov.		*Podex*	During Razzia.
Dec 20		*Cribbage*	
Dec	Sergeant Austin		Executed with political P.O.W.s.
Dec 27	*Turniquoits*		Missing.
1945.			
Feb.	*Trapping*		Caught and shot.
	Coursing		Caught and shot.
Feb 10	*Draughts I*		Died of wounds after arrest.
Feb.		*Bezique*	
March 5	*Dudley*		Shot whilst escaping.
April 11	*Scrape*		Killed whilst attacking S.D. HQ.
April 11	*Jingle*		Drowned after dropping in lake.

Sabotage Summary

Zone 1   *Region 1*
Railway lines cut at Buitenpost, Dronrijp, Heerenveen, Oudega-Nijhuizum and St. Nicolaasga.

Two telecommunication cables cut between Leeuwarden and Kroningen.

Local P.T.T. establishments saved by tampering with demolition charges.

Explosive charges removed from several bridges in the Friesland area.

Attacks on German lines of communication, small patrols and straggling enemy elements – the Germans suffering a considerable number of casualties.

Region 2
Attack on the prison at Leeuwarden on 8 Dec 44 and effecting the release of 50 members of the local Resistance movements.

Region 3
Railway lines sabotaged at: Junction South of Meppel on lines running in direction of Friesland, Drenthe and Groningen; Between Hoogeveen and Assen; South of Coevorden, at the junction Zwolle-Coevorden and Coevorden-Almelo; Coevorden-Germany.

Sabotage of Water Communications:
Lock at Stieltjescanal rendered useless, also the lock in the Zwindersche Canal, causing an interruption in the traffic to and from Coevorden for three months.

Sabotage of Telecommunications:
Telephone lines cut in several places along the railway lines.

Zone 2   *Region 4*
Some 150-ton barges sunk in the Twentsche-Rhein Canal.

Draining of the Almelo-Hengelo Canal by opening the locks
at Wiener, near Delden and destroying the electrical machinery
controlling them. A delay 4/5 weeks was caused.

Successful attack on the lock gates at Klooster, near Almelo.

A number of successful attacks on railroads in the area.

Transport on roads crippled by tyrebursters, blowing down
trees and using bent nails.

In March 45 the whole Railway system in Overijssel was put
out of action and cuts effected at Borne and on the line Almelo-
Zwolle at Nijverdal.

German efforts to divert rail traffic via Deventer-Zutphen
to Hengelo was frustrated by a derailment carried out between
Delden and Goor.

Removal of signposts on crossroads and minefields.

Sabotage of telecommunications.

Successful attacks on German demolition squads at bridges
and a number of bridges held including two over the canal from
Almelo to Coevorden.

Region 5
Three derailments after September 1944 on the line Ruurlo-
Winterswijk and one derailment on the line Aalten-Winterswijk.

Delays caused on the railways by removal of signal and Block
system apparatus.

Fuses removed from a charge on the bridge at s'Heerenberg.

Bridges at Aalten occupied to prevent destruction.

Zone 3   *Region 6*
Derailment of a troop train on the line Apeldoorn-Zwolle.

Enemy communications disrupted in the suburbs of Apeldoorn.

Region 8
Having tapped the German telecommunications, the N.B.S. learned
that an ammunition train was leaving Rotterdam for the Arnhem
area. They decided that it had to be stopped before it reached the
Ede De Klomp area. They blew the line up near Driebergen, near
Zeist, and as a precaution, also nearer Arnhem. The attack was
successful, and the train had to return to Rotterdam.

Railway office at Utrecht raided to supply Resistance Forces
with money. The sum of 1½ million Guilders was seized.

Complete dislocation of all railway traffic to and from Utrecht by the cutting of lines at some 200 places in the area.

Destruction of a large number of Wehrmacht cars in the area.

Region 9

Three cuts on the line Amersfoort-Amsterdam.

One cut on the line Hilversum-Utrecht.

Three derailments on the line Bussum-Weesp.

Two cuts on the line Hilversum-Bussum.

Small railway bridge over the canal at Baarn destroyed twice, each time resulting in a derailment.

Small railway bridges at Pruimgracht, Karnemelksloot and Keverdijk destroyed resulting in the escape of some 600 political prisoners.

Bridge over the Vecht on Merwedecanal destroyed.

60 German cars and lorries damaged by tyrebursters and bent nails.

40 cuts in German field telephone lines.

Two kilometres removed from the Hilversum-Berlin telephone cable.

Two munition barges sunk by limpets.

Zone 4   *Region 7*

Nothing to report. No material was ever sent there, and as no specific information trickled through, the area was not built up. In addition, owing to the defences, the Air Ministry would not entertain air operations in the area.

Zone 5   *Region 10*

Attack on a battery charging installation. Two chargers were blown up and the factory set on fire.

Attack on the Pander factory for glider bodies at Rijswijk and by using bottles of phosphorous and benzol the factory was completely burned out.

Continual attacks on the Amsterdam-Haarlem railway line delays caused, varied from one day to some weeks.

Destruction of the railway bridge at Diemen, near Amsterdam.

Hundreds of German cars destroyed by sabotage. In April and May the number varied from 10 to 12 per day.

Destruction of a school building containing labour conscription registers. The records were completely destroyed.

Sinking of a barge loaded with 200 tons of Gun Cotton in the River Amstel.

Region 12

D/Fing station at Ardenhout attacked and burned out.

Five derailments on the lines Leyden/Haarlem-Haarlem/Amsterdam-Haarlem/Ymuiden.

In March 45, forty Wehrmacht cars destroyed in garages in and around Haarlem.

Telephone lines were sabotaged.

Region 13

Railway sabotage. Points cut were: Railway bridges at Zevenhuizen, between Hekendorp and Gouda, Het Haantje near Delft.

These lines were destroyed by means of explosives during the months of March/April 45 when a great deal of transport of V.2. material was taking place. Lines were blocked for periods varying from 1 to 8 days.

Derailment of train loaded with A.A. material and troops, blocked the Utrecht/Rotterdam and Utrecht/Hague for 24 hours. Four derailed trucks loaded with A.A. material lay on the rails for some time.

A number of German cars destroyed by tyrebursters and nails.

German telephone lines cut at several places.

Region 14

In November 1944, the Resistance, supplied with limpets from the U.K., sank the blockade ships *Schonfeld* and *Hansa* in the port of Rotterdam, vessels of 11,000 and 9,000 tons respectively. As they were only able to place one limpet on the *Hansa*, the Germans were able to refloat her fairly quickly. Three limpets were used on the *Schonfeld* and it took the German engineers ten weeks to refloat her.

In January 1945, the *Westerdam* fully laden with gravel and cement and destined for the final blocking of the River Maas, was sunk by means of limpets on the 18th at her mooring berth in Rotterdam. She is still in the same position, upright but sitting on the bottom of the dock.

Resistance men sank the 180-ton floating crane Titan in order to prevent its removal to Germany. She has since been refloated.

A small railway bridge over the canal between Schiedam and Vlaardingen, 3 kms from Schiedam, was blown up and prevented the further use of this line for onward traffic to the Hoek of Holland up to the time of the German capitulation.

Raids on ration book depots producing the following:

Kloosterzande – 48,00 books and 150,000 coupons.

Maassluis – 10,000 books and 200,000 coupons.

Doorn – 12,000 books and 200,000 coupons.

The destruction of 300 bags of cement used for road blocks.

Preservation of an electric pumping station at Maassluis by cutting the underground detonating fuse.

Destruction of 80 H.E. containers intended to blow the dykes surrounding the land below sea level near the Hoek of Holland.

Removal of fuses leading to explosive charges under a railway bridge across the harbour at Maassluis.

Removal of H.E. charges from lock gates just outside the Hoek of Holland.

Rails cut at Achterdijk.

Rails cut at Gorkum and Arkel.

Barge, containing 300 Dutch political prisoners, sunk near Dordrecht enabling them to escape.

Bridges at Slikkerveer and Alblasserdam saved from demolition by cutting of fuses leading to the charges.

About 200 Wehrmacht cars destroyed or damaged by abrasives, tyrebursters and bent nails.

In April 45 all railway lines around Rotterdam were cut simultaneously. A 1000 ton lighter loaded with iron was sunk at the Boompjes near the Leuvehaven, Rotterdam.

Two lighters loaded with engine parts, iron and copper, moored opposite the Posthoornsteeg, R'dam, were sunk.

A lighter loaded with engines (believed to be for U. Boats) was sunk in the Katendrechtsche Harbour at Rotterdam.

With the co-operation of a German, quay mines in the Schiehaven, Merwedehaven and Waalhaven, were rendered useless.

Zone 6   *Region 11*

Railway tracks were cut at several places and, during the two months preceding the German capitulation, railway traffic was practically paralyzed.

Attack on a railway bridge resulting in its complete destruction and also the derailment of the engine.

Changing of signposts, placing of road blocks and sniping.

Landmines placed on main roads.

Large lorry carrying Diesel Oil completely burned out.

All enemy cables destroyed North of the Schagen-Medenblik.

A lighter loaded with machinery sunk and recuperated after liberation.

Dropping Grounds Used in Holland 1 January 1944 to 24 April 1945

Name of Ground.	Location	Number of successful		
	Map ref 1:50,000.	Sorties.	Containers.	Pkgs.
Bertus	Sh.32.-526:028	2	30	5
Fencing	Sh.50-852:273	1	2	
Faro	Sh.14-191:745	1	2	
Podex	Sh.27-755:170	1	2	
Rowing	Sh.19-235:550	1	2	
Yew (Rolls Royce)	Sh.32-528:039	4	75	3
Sculling	Sh.14-180:765	1	1	
Shooting	Sh.32-522:013	1	1	
Acacia	Sh.29-470:255	1	12	1
Kees	Sh.48-733:628	1	6	2
Evert 2	Sh.28-185:235	2	33	2
Mandrill	Sh.19-137:579	12	258	34
Pear/Rummy 3	Sh.27-709:135	4	81	10
Rhododendron/ Rummy 4	Sh.12-098:909	2	33	3
Apple/Rummy 5	Sh.17-243:664	3	66	8
Plum/Rummy 6	Sh.17-295:679	4	60	8
Xantippe/Rummy 8	Sh.11-043:000	1	15	1
Pluto/Rummy 10	Sh.17-302:773	3	54	2
Sunbeam/Rummy 12	Sh.31-914:903	5	102	11
Evert 3	Sh.22-179:379	9	155	44
Robin/Rummy 13	Sh.31-936:954	3	63	6
Whiskey/Rummy 11	Sh.37-774:853	5	74	4
Currant/Rummy 14	Sh.29-469:210	3	63	4
Marmosette	Sh.31-105:025	2	39	6
Koos	Sh.28-145:091	2	39	5
Nico (Jura)	Sh.38-910:738	6	150	23
Arie	Sh.34-102:050	1	24	2
Paamdens Lengte	Sh.28-416:278	2	39	4
Leede (Sculling)	Sh.31-066:865	2	48	7
Gerard (Dudley 3)	Sh.20-626:588	3	74	9
Cadillac (Rummy 16)	Sh.19-093:488	4	77	9
Magpie, Sculling 1	Sh.27-773:144	1	24	3
Oliver, Draughts 5	Sh.19-214:577	8	174	24
Alfred, Gobbo I	Sh.10-499:016	2	48	6
Ingram, Gobbo 2	Sh.11-709:843	5	105	15
Timothy, Gobbo 3	Sh.6-841:287	3	54	7
Bluebottle	Sh.41-166:745	3	72	7
Vesuvius, Rummy 18	Sh.33-024:004	4	78	8
Chevrolet, Rummy 19	Sh.43-674:606	3	69	9
Madeline, Draughts 6	Sh.31-034:023	4	82	7
Lafayette, Rummy 20	Sh.37-810:843	3	72	9
Maxwell, Rummy 21	Sh.30-804:902	4	77	12
Paris, Sculling 3	Sh.31-081:002	5	111	11

Laloe 2, Draughts 7	Sh.19-264:532	3	76	11
Lammert 2, Draughts 8	Sh.34-062:942	1	15	2
Albertecin, Rummy 22	Sh.19-130:361	1	24	2
Medan, Sculling 4	Sh.19-101:537	1	24	3
Poodle, Podex 5	Sh.38-901:767	1	24	3
Kaas, Sculling 5	Sh.19-127:367	3	63	4
Mercedes/Snowdon	Sh.31-917:968	4	108	17
Gin, Sculling 6	Sh.31-077:989	2	46	6
Spa, Sculling 7	Sh.31-047:880	1	24	3
Sideboard, Necking 1	Sh.11-857:834	3	71	6
Washstand, Necking 2	Sh.10-485:963	3	72	13
Martini, Draughts 9	Sh.19-078:543	1	15	7
Sally, Draughts 10	Sh.19-246:524	6	115	22
Wardrobe, Necking	Sh.11-795:975	1	14	3
Curtain, Necking 4	Sh.6-845:295	1	24	3
Buick/Taurus	Sh.31-989:969	3	60	9
Trojan, Rummy 29	Sh.31-924:918	1	15	5
Ryn, Cubbing 1	Sh.31-003:969	6	189	33
Waal, Cubbing 2	Sh.31-067:942	1	24	-
Maas, Cubbing 3	Sh.31-050:020	11	174	27
Austin/Eiger	Sh.31-951:958	1	24	4
Lek, Cubbing 4	Sh.31-072:023	3	66	11
Chevrolet/Everest	Sh.30-787:888	1	24	4
Willow/Dudley	Sh.28-281:294	1	24	7
Hudson/Draughts 12	Sh.25-167:343	2	48	8
Lancaster/2 13	Sh.19-137:374	1	24	5
Winton/Matterhorn	Sh.31-959:022	5	106	18
Winnipeg	Sh.19-103:532	1	13	3
Cod/Checkers 1	Sh.31-986:007	4	87	18
Rolls Royce 2	Sh.32-516:017	1	17	3
Flint (Scrape)	Sh.37-780:860	1	-	-
Popeye, Rowing 3	Sh.31-148:025	3	66	14
George, Gueuze i	Sh.32-590:910	2	37	9
Karel, Eduard I	Sh.34-277:917	1	24	6
Otto, Eduard 2	Sh.21-013:487	2	48	3
Frying Pan, Neck 6	Sh.16-772:823	1	24	4
Primus, Neck 7	Sh.10-582:867	1	24	3
William, Medico 1	Sh.31-986:052	2	42	7
Monty, Medico 3	Sh.31-992:057	1	13	3
Ike, Medico 4	Sh.31-928:025	2	42	7
Elgar, Whimper 1	Sh.21-768:349	1	15	6
Haydn, Whimper 2	Sh.32-443:932	1	24	4
Stork, Medico 7	Sh.32-302:084	1	15	4
Klaas, Medico 8	Sh.25-198:178	1	18	3
Foxtrot I	Sh.38-964:692	1	15	4
Ararat, Scrape 1	Sh.38-890:775	1	13	3
Dustbin, Neck 9	Sh.11-904:950	1	24	4
Joyce, Dicing 1	Sh.12-216:837	1	22	1
Trout, Checkers 2	Sh.31-036:987	1	22	6

Lonecastle, Med 10	Sh.25-137:314	1	13	3
Dolomites, Hoot 2	Sh.30-835:897	1	22	3
Rockies, Hoot 1	Sh.37-759:833	1	24	3
	Totals	239	4793	701

Summary of Dutch Section Personnel

January 1944 – end August 1945.

On the 1st January 1944, the Dutch Section consisted of the following personnel:

Major S. Bingham.	Section Head.
Jnr. Cmd. S.I. Bond. A.T.S.	Training Officer.
Captain A.G. Knight.	Operations' Officer.
2/Lieutenant D.G. Mortlock. U.S.	Asst. Operations' Officer.
Mr. B.H. Olink.	Communications.
Sergeant W.A. Thomas. F.A.N.Y.	Asst. Communications.
Captain W.E. Mills.	Admin. and Finance Officer.
Captain J.W.C. Kay.	Conducting Officer.
Lieut. A. Snewing.	Conducting Officer.
Lieut. A.C. Parr.	Conducting Officer.

On the 26th February 1944, Major S. Bingham relinquished his command of the Dutch Section and Major R.I. Dobson, who transferred from the Belgian Section, took charge.

The section underwent the following changes in additions, departures and promotions:

1944

January	Departures	Captain J.W.C. Kay.	
February	Departures	Major S. Bingham.	
	Arrivals	Major R.I. Dobson.	
April	Arrivals	Captain C.F. Dadley.	Assist. to S.H.
May	Arrivals	2/Lieutenant H. Hooper.	Conduct. Officer.
	Promotions	Lieut. A. Snewing.	To Captain.
July	Promotions	Mr. B.H. Olink.	To Captain.
September	Promotions	Lieut. H. Hooper.	To Captain.
	Promotions	Lieut. A.C. Parr.	To Captain.
Oct.	Arrivals	F/Lieutenant E. O'C. Tandy.	Assist. Ops.
Nov.	Arrivals	Lieutenant H.S. Gardiner.	Wireless Off.
1945			
January	Arrivals	Major W.A. Murphy.	Assist. to S.H.
	Arrivals	Captain C. Tivey.	Assist. Ops. Off.

	Arrivals	F/Lieutenant R.H. Flower.	Assist. Training Off.
	Arrivals	Captain A.P. Irby	. Assist. W/T. Off.
	Promotions	Major R.I. Dobson.	To Lieut. Colonel.
Feb.	Nil.		
March	Arrivals	Ensign J. Dane F.A.N.Y.	Training Assist.
	Arrivals	Captain G.C. Bowden.	Assist W/T Off.
	Departures	Captain A.C. Parr.	
	Departures	Captain A. Snewing.	
	Promotions	Captain C.F. Dadley.	To Major.
April	Departures	Captain G.C. Bowden.	
	Departures	Captain A.P. Irby.	
May	Departures	Ensign J. Dane F.A.N.Y.	
June	Departures	F/Lieutenant E. O'C. Tandy.	
July	Departures	Captain D.G. Mortlock. U.S.	
	Departures	Captain B.H. Olink.	
	Departures	Jnr/Cmd. S.I. Bond.	
	Departures	Captain A.G. Knight.	
	Departures	Lieutenant H.S. Gardiner.	
	Departures	Captain C. Tivey.	
	Departures	F/Lieutenant R.H. Flower.	
Aug.	Departures	Major C.F. Dadley.	
	Departures	Lieut. W.A. Thomas F.A.N.Y.	

Nucleus of Dutch Section as at 1 September 1945 – engaged on liquidation matters:

Lieutenant Colonel R.I. Dobson.
Major W.A. Murphy.
Captain W.E. Mills.

Attached to H.R.H. Prince Bernhard's staff as Wireless Communications' Officer:

Captain H. Hooper.

Chapter 6

DUTCH SOE GENERAL EVALUATION

Morale

The attitude of the Dutch population under the German occupation in 1941 and 1942 was, in the main, apathetic and the people were not resistance-minded. To those few clandestine agents who were functioning at the time, the population was neither dangerous nor helpful. The people were not sure of their attitude towards the Germans who were trying to be as friendly and as correct as possible and to interfere as little as possible with internal conditions in the country. Thousands of Dutch civil servants and businessmen were confirmed in their appointments by the Germans. Whilst disliking the sight of German troops and tanks in their cities, the Dutch had no great incentive to resist, and it was difficult to obtain assistance for resistance movements.

After the big strike in Amsterdam in 1942, which called forth very severe repressive measures, and the anti-Jewish drive which began in 1942, and grew in intensity throughout 1943, the people began to realise that the same repressive measures would ultimately be applied to everybody and, guided by the B.B.C. and Radio Oranje, they began to seek the means of actively resisting the Germans.

Two groups of people were affected in particular by the German decrees. Firstly, the young men who were liable for conscription to work in Germany, secondly, ex-officers who, in early 1943, were ordered to register at Amersfoort to be subsequently shipped off to Germany under arrest. These two affected groups provided most of the malcontents who went underground in 1943 and who began to organise methodically against the Germans.

Prior to 1943 there was no effective underground movement functioning against the German occupation. Generally speaking, the population was extremely patriotic and throughout 1943 their pro-resistance sympathies grew to such an extent that by April 1944 50% of the people were working clandestinely in some way or other against the Germans. A large Catholic population was responsible for much of the propaganda in favour of resistance. Up to the middle of 1944 the population was united in its desire to rid Holland of the enemy and morale was high, but later, when it became clear that Holland would have to wait for its liberation, morale sagged badly. In early 1945 the population became less willing to assist resistance groups as they were beginning to fear reprisals which were becoming more and more brutal. Also, there was a tendency in some areas to regard the N.B.S. as a terrorist organisation in view of the ruthless methods sometimes adopted by N.B.S. members. Other factors which weakened the will to resist were the under-nourishment, fear of street fighting in the towns the Allies were approaching and a reported conflict between the R.V.V., K.P. and O.D. leaders who were said to be working for their own ends and their own prestige.

Resistance activity varied according to areas. In the country, where food was relatively plentiful, morale was much higher than in the towns. Activity in Rotterdam, where there was a large working-class population, was more intense than in the Hague where resistance was confined to less active measures such as propaganda and similar forms of passive resistance.

Operations before September 1944 were not carried out to any great extent but grew in number and importance in December 1944 and early 1945. Targets were attacked by groups of determined full-time resistance members, while the bulk of the people were suffering at the time from lowered morale due to disappointment at the failure of the Allies to eject the Germans earlier.

Some sections of the population were by January 1945 adopting a critical attitude towards the Allies. It should not be overlooked that food was the main pre-occupation at the time and how to get more food was the question paramount in everybody's mind.

In April 1945, thousands of recruits came into Resistance believing that once they were accepted by the N.B.S. they would stand a better chance of being fed.

Propaganda

Throughout the occupation the B.B.C. was widely listened to on illegal sets and, in the latter phases, when electricity was cut off, batteries were used to supply the necessary current. Listening parties were organised and an illegal news distribution centre existed for the dissemination of Allied propaganda.

Most of this propagation of news was done by intellectuals who listened to the B.B.C. English service, but rumour-spreading was indulged in by the working-class population, who listened to Radio Oranje in Dutch. Criticisms of these Dutch broadcasts from Radio Oranje were, however, widespread and the Station was accused of being completely out of touch with the real situation and viewing things through rose-coloured glasses. Radio Oranje had, apparently, overlooked the fact that resistance movements in Holland were illegal and that the penalty for participation was death. Frequently it gave away clandestine projects by premature announcements and was guilty of certain inaccuracies in the statements which were broadcast. On one occasion, after intensive German C.E. activity had resulted in the arrest of hundreds of people in a certain area, Radio Oranje broadcast the boast that resistance was still functioning and that the Germans had by no means caught everybody. This naturally resulted in a renewed burst of C.E. activity on the part of the Gestapo. On another occasion the Station broadcast the news of the arrival in Rotterdam of certain agents two days before they were to be dropped in the area.

From 1942 onwards Radio Oranje terminated all broadcasts with the words "Keep Courage, we are coming" and this phrase became a standing joke among the resistance workers. The belief is widespread in Holland that the heavy casualties sustained in September 1944 were due to over-optimistic announcements by both the B.B.C. and Radio Oranje to the effect that Holland would be free by October. These announcements led to open revolt in some areas and careless, indiscriminate recruiting in others with disastrous results.

Pamphlets dropped by the R.A.F. were widely read by the Dutch and passed round but there were many casualties to people picking up these leaflets. The penalty for retaining R.A.F. tracts, or passing them on, was death and the unfortunate Dutchmen caught perusing one of these leaflets was usually shot at once. These tracts were unequally distributed, and the view was taken by the underground movement that if they had been dropped to Reception Committees the Dutch themselves would have known how and where to distribute them. Many were lost as they were collected immediately they were dropped by special squads detailed for the purpose by the authorities.

A very active and efficient underground press existed in Holland throughout the occupation and the organisation controlling the underground press remained in touch with London for all matters of policy. The Dutch clandestine papers had a wide circulation, and the underground press was responsible for two things – i) to raise funds for the underground movement and ii) to boost the morale of the population.

German morale was affected adversely by slogans in use by the general population and tracts were issued deliberately by the Dutch in order to mislead the Germans as to the real number of Dutchmen working in the underground movement. The numbers of people in active resistance were given as being much greater than they really were. In the latter days of the occupation no propaganda was needed to demoralise the Germans as their demoralisation had become complete through lack of food and transport.

Growth of Indigenous Clandestine Movements
Many spontaneous resistance groups came to light in the early days of the occupation, the principal ones being the ex-officers' organisation which existed to aid officers who had been forced to live underground in order to avoid deportation to Germany and the student aid groups which were formed to assist young Dutchmen who were refractaires from the German labour laws.

Due to the needs of these groups other organisations grew up which were concerned with acquiring false papers, accommodation and supplies for those living illegally. The clergy were active in this respect and later did splendid work in aiding Allied airmen in the same way. Later organisations like the Doctors' Illegal Committee came into existence. This was a committee formed to assist doctors in trouble and also to provide clandestine medical facilities for wounded patriots.

Many people in the liberal professions formed similar groups. A nation-wide clandestine movement grew up with branches in every town to protect members of technical trades, telephone engineers, mechanics, toolmakers, etc.

Up to 1943 none of these groups were in any way organised and most of their activities were concerned with defensive rather than offensive resistance. In 1943, however, most active resisters began to cast about for offensive methods of resisting the German repression and while the ex-officers busied themselves with attempts to acquire military information, the students began to commit small acts of sabotage, such as misplacing signposts and puncturing the tyres of German transport.

The underground press organisation had meanwhile grown to be a powerful weapon. Security at the time was negligible. One man might be a member of several different groups and there was much overlapping. People were often indiscreet and most people in resistance knew far too much about other people's business than was good for security. One incentive to better security was the presence of large numbers of N.S.B. informers. These Dutch Quislings were hated by the Dutch far more than the Germans and the first attempts to form really secret and secure clandestine groups were made as a result of penetration and betrayals effected by the N.S.B. spies.

All these early scattered groups which grew quite spontaneously served their apprenticeship in underground work quite independently but later the members were absorbed by larger groups organised on a national basis for active offensive resistance. These organised groups will be discussed later.

Enemy Forces

Forces employed by the enemy to control underground activity were as follows:

The Grüne Polizei,
The G.F.P.,
The S.D. and Gestapo,
N.S.B. – civilian agents,
Dutch and Fleming S.S.,
Feldgendarmerie,
Landwacht and Wehrmacht.

The list indicates the degree of importance attaching to each particular force. The Grüne Polizei were most feared by the Dutch underground movement, and the Wehrmacht, last on the list, was considered by the underground movement to be relatively unimportant. The Grüne Polizei were apparently a branch of the S.D. and the letter directed their activities. They were very active and conducted most of the razzias which were made for obtaining forced labour. The G.F.P. were controlled by the Abwehr and operated sometimes as civilians and sometimes in uniform. They were far more active than the Gestapo and were used for house arrests, searches and interrogations. The S.D. in uniform, comprising many former members of the Kriminal Polizei and the Grenz Polizei were in evidence all over Holland. Many of them were Gestapo men using S.D. uniform as cover. Those members of the S.D. who wore civilian clothes became known fairly quickly to the general public. Civilian members of the N.S.B. were used extensively by the S.D. to act as informers and street watchers and were extremely dangerous, although most of them were known to the underground movement.

The Dutch and Fleming S.S. was not particularly astute but had the advantage of knowing local customs and the language and were feared because of their great brutality. The Feldgendarmerie were used in the towns for street patrols as was the Wehrmacht but neither of these forces constituted any real danger. The Landwacht was composed of Dutch Nazis either very young or middle aged and was a nuisance but not greatly feared. They always preferred to avoid conflict with resistance unless in great strength. In general controls were relatively few until the middle of 1943 when restrictions began to be tightened up but, even then, the country districts were fairly safe and remained so throughout the occupation.

In 1943 the S.D. and the Gestapo became particularly active and after D-day in France thousands of C.E. personnel were imported into Holland. Conditions became very difficult, especially in the towns. The control of identity papers, however, became, if anything, easier after September '44 as, in view of the increase in arms receptions the Germans were searching diligently for arms and restricted the body search to weapons which might provide clues as to the whereabouts of arms dumps. There was some rivalry between the various enemy forces and just prior to the liberation fighting broke out in the Hague between the S.S. and the Wehrmacht.

The Native Police

In general, it can be said that the Dutch police were not an obstacle to resistance. 20% had Fascist tendencies and were dangerous, 50% were afraid of German reprisals if they assisted the underground movement and were neither helpful nor dangerous. 30% helped actively and provided valuable assistance. Those policemen who were members of resistance groups acted as guides, transported stores, W/T sets, clandestine documents and newspapers and also frequently instructed the underground movement in the use of weapons and explosives. Their uniform was a valuable screen for their clandestine activities. Rank and file were usually reliable, but the heads of departments were pro-Nazi and had been placed in office by the Germans. A high percentage of policemen were willing to render occasional services but withdrew their support when the Germans began to place informers in all the police offices.

In 1944 and 1945 new police battalions were raised by the Germans from predominantly N.S.B. sources. The new police force was known as the P.O.B. and wore slightly different uniforms. They were very dangerous and much feared by the Dutch underground movement.

Collaborators

There were in Holland at the time of the occupation approximately 600,000 members of the N.S.B. Most of them were young hotheads and there was a high proportion of criminal types. There was also a large number of middle-class people who believed sincerely that the

New Order would benefit their country. It was from this hard core of National Socialism that the Germans recruited the new police battalions, the Landwacht and the thousands of informers and street watchers used by the S.D. and the Gestapo. One report states that every Gestapo or S.D. agent employed 15 civilian Dutchmen who acted as his informant service. Most of these informers were, however, known to the underground movement and in September '44 nearly all ceased their activity and searched for a means of changing over to resistance.

Their activities in 1943 and 1944 were, however, very successful in penetrating underground movements. Although many farmers and peasants were of great assistance to resistance movements there were quite a number with Fascist tendencies who lost no time in denouncing people who took in refractaires or escaping Allied airmen, or who picked up and circulated R.A.F. tracts in the country districts. Many people recovered parachutes and hid them, using the silk for their own purposes. Quite a number of people were denounced for this alone by N.S.B. farmers and peasants. Many farmers were dealing in the Black Market and supplied the underground or the Germans quite indiscriminately and for their own ends.

After the liberation there were thousands of borderline cases, and it is extremely difficult to decide whether these people collaborated willingly with the Germans or not. Thousands of people in the underground movement worked legally for the German administration and used their employment as cover for their clandestine activities. Equally thousands of people worked willingly for the Germans and now say that they did it in order to assist the resistance movement.

Organised Clandestine Groups

From the many scattered and unorganised clandestine groups which sprang up in the early days of the occupation grew large nationwide movements, well co-ordinated and fairly well disciplined, each movement confining its activity to a type of resistance activity in which it specialised.

From the needs of refractaires in search of false papers, funds and accommodation grew first the L.O. which catered especially for 'under-divers'. This organisation needed small coup-de-main parties for raiding food offices and arbeits bureaux and the K.P. organisation came to life to supply this need. The L.O. and K.P. organisations subsequently merged to all intents and purposes, K.P. being the shock troops of L.O.

A movement which absorbed most of the amateur saboteurs was the R.V.V. which worked in Maquis style in the country districts.

Many ex-army officers, businessmen and politicians joined the O.D., a movement which planned to take over the administration of the country when Holland had been liberated.

These four groups were subsequently merged to form the N.B.S. who directed all resistance activity on instructions from Prince Bernhard in London.

Other national movements which grew up during the occupation were N.C. which was concerned with welfare and social problems; N.S.F., which was the resistance movement's treasury; A.C., the Action Committee of the Dutch underground press and C.I.D. which was the organisation controlling the black telephone system.

All these movements were represented during the latter stages of the occupation by P.A.R.I., an Advisory Committee to the Dutch underground movement consisting of 12 members representing all types of resistance activity, as shown below:

L.O. and K.P., false papers etc., aid to refractaires.
R.V.V., Receptions and sabotage.
O.D., Post-war planning, these in Autumn 1944 became:

N.B.S., Netherlands Forces of Interior.
N.C., Welfare and Social Aid.
N.S.F., Finance Organisation.
A.C., Action Committee Underground Press.
C.I.D., Black Telephone System:

Advisory Committee Dutch Underground Movements – P.A.R.I. (Now working for A.M.G. and Civil Affairs).

L.O. – Landelijke Organisatie
This was a particularly active organisation and supplied approximately 200,000 false papers of all types monthly, besides finding accommodation and clothing for refractaires and escapees. Their methods are described at length later but one method of obtaining documents was to raid Government offices, steal supplies of permits, ration cards etc., and either use the originals or copy them. Raids were carried out by the K.P. groups.

K.P. – Knok Ploeg (later it was called Koniglijke Patrouille).

K.P. groups of 7 or 8 men were the shock troops of L.O. and indulged in minor sabotage and small-scale raids, in fact in any minor activities calculated to harass the Germans. They frequently engineered prison breaks and rescued comrades who had fallen foul of the Gestapo.

R.V.V. – Raad Van Verzet.

This movement consisted of cells of 20-25 men, mainly working in country districts on major sabotage and receptions. They worked in some districts on Maquis lines and carried out attacks on military objectives as laid down in directives received from London. They also acquired military intelligence.

O.D. – Ordre Dienst.

The O.D. was not concerned with actively resisting the Germans. It had created a clandestine organisation which was piling up economic and political intelligence with a view to administering the country after the war.

General

Inevitably, since all these organisations had grown in a slapdash fashion, they were by no means watertight and most of the leaders and organisers of different movements knew each other personally. Equally members had at sometime or other worked for some or all of the four organisations and security was, therefore, not all that could be desired. There were also many personal and political feuds and much rivalry existed between the chiefs of the various movements.

O.D. came in for much criticism as active resisters liked neither their programme, which was negative, nor their principles. They were accused of being reactionary and, in some cases, of working for the Germans. Most of the other groups had left-wing tendencies. There was also a certain amount of overlapping, some movements taking part in activity which was nominally the responsibility of others and in some areas where one organisation was stronger numerically than the others, it would engage in a multiplicity of resistance activities and cope with anything from false papers to major sabotage. In the latter stages L.O. had not so much work to do and its members joined the K.P. groups. Similarly, O.D. members, tired of inaction, deserted O.D. for R.V.V. and K.P.

In the Autumn of 1944 liaison officers were sent to Holland with orders from Prince Bernhard to amalgamate all groups in the N.B.S. and not without trouble this was ultimately achieved and the N.B.S., Dutch Forces of the Interior, was created to cover all underground activity in the country.

The N.B.S. was formed on military lines in zones, regions and districts, and Commanders, taken from the K.P., R.V.V., and O.D., were appointed by the Prince. Political rivalry and personal feuds almost succeeded in making the project impossible but the N.B.S. finally came into existence and is now providing the material for the new Dutch Army.

Introduction of London-trained Agents to Existing Groups

Most London trained agents were sent either to one or the other of the existing groups which ultimately became amalgamated into the N.B.S. or to the underground press organisation. Early contacts with indigenous groups were made by agents from England returning to Holland and renewing relations with friends who belonged to one or the other of the underground movements. Later, Dutchmen were exfiltrated to England and brought with them valuable information in the way of known sympathisers and up-to-date information on the resistance movements. A chain of contacts was thus built up and agents were sent out from England with a contact's address and usually a mission which necessitated their placing themselves at the disposal of local underground leaders.

The London trained agents, whilst rendering valuable service as liaison officers, W/T Operators and weapon training instructors, rarely took over complete control of independent groups or areas, as was the case in France but, in the main, were subordinated to regional Commanders of already established indigenous groups. Once regular W/T communication was established with home base by London trained agents, the departure of an agent from this country could be advised to those in the field and his reception arranged.

The Arrival of Individual Agents

Agents were normally dropped by parachute into Holland, although some were dropped in France and Belgium and made their way into Holland from there. Before leaving this country, the agent had many things to consider and was aware of the risks he ran in making the journey and returning clandestinely to his country. An unforeseen difficulty which occurred occasionally was when, due to the nervous tension of the agent on departure, he got into the wrong aeroplane and, consequently, was dropped to the wrong place and Reception Committee. His arrangements were further complicated if his baggage had been put into the correct aeroplane and consequently dropped to another point.

Once in the 'plane there was the danger of A.A. fire, which was intense over Holland and many agents lost their lives as the result of crash landings. There was also the danger of German fighters attacking the 'plane and, on some occasions, fighters followed the 'planes in and signalled news of the dropping operation to ground forces. In some cases, the despatchers were at fault, dropping the stores too late or dropping the agents at too great a distance one from the other. Over the dropping point, if the lighting system was bad the 'plane had to circle once or twice, thus attracting attention and making things difficult for the agent on landing. Agents usually dropped to a Reception Committee, but many were dropped 'blind' and left to their own devices.

Agents dropping to a Reception Committee were given a password for the Reception Committee leader and told to place themselves under his orders until the necessary arrangements had been made to pass them on to the persons with whom they were expected to work. These arrangements did not always function smoothly. Reception Committees in Holland were usually para-military operations, those participating relying more on Sten guns for protection than security measures. Consequently, passwords, if they were remembered, were often ignored or overlooked in the general enthusiasm. There was frequently no security check, the B.B.C. message announcing the dropping being the only guarantee that the new arrival was genuine. Often, however, an agent was received by a friend or a fellow trainee from England and the password was unnecessary. On some occasions agents were dropped in error to a Reception Committee other than the one awaiting them, but usually they managed without difficulty to persuade the Committee that they were genuine agents from London. A complaint received from many agents was that frequently Reception Committees were expecting stores only and the arrival of an agent was quite a surprise to them. This resulted in the new arrival waiting about for instructions until the Reception Committee got in touch with his contact. It is also true to say that it has frequently occurred, even when the agent's arrival had been pre-advised, that local Commanders sometimes made no advance arrangements for the disposal of newly arrived agents. One report received states that agents had been shot by the underground movement, who suspected them of being spies because their arrival had not been announced.

In general, the Reception Committee personnel lacked discipline. The guards would leave their posts to greet the new arrivals and there was much talking and smoking, especially when the 'plane was late arriving. If this happened security precautions were forgotten, and people became impatient. Two other criticisms of Reception Committees are that far too many people attended the Reception. (Often up to 50 people would arrive to collect four or five containers and one agent). Also, far too many people knew the location of the dropping point.

Normally a newly arrived agent would be guided from the dropping point to a safe house by members of the Reception Committee. Subsequently he would be accompanied to a contact address where he would meet his chief to be, or the latter would visit him at the safe house.

Transport to and from the safe house was often available in the form of bicycles, ambulances, P.T.T. vans or milk lorries. Sometimes even police cars. One method which was adopted to transport two agents from a safe house to a contact address in Rotterdam, was to stage an 'arrest' of the two agents at the safe house and transport them in a police van to their destination. The 'safe' houses used were not always particularly secure. Security was often negligible, and people used them as rendezvous points where many people would meet and discuss their clandestine work. The arrival of an agent from England would often start a pilgrimage to a place, curious well-wishers desiring to meet an agent from London.

The Reception Committee, often assisted by the local Police Force, would dispose of the stores dropped with the agent and collect his equipment. The agent dropped 'blind' was free from the anxieties experienced in passing through a Reception Committee, but, on the other hand, he was handicapped in that he had to make his way alone to his contact address. If he were unfamiliar with the country or had been away from Holland any length of time, he needed especially careful briefing about local conditions in his dropping area, which would facilitate his movements during the 48 hours after his arrival. If he were badly, or insufficiently, briefed, he could easily make some error which would attract the attention of the population in country districts for whom the arrival of a stranger was in itself an event and among whom there were many collaborators eager to inform against anybody acting suspiciously. Another worry of an agent dropping 'blind' was the disposal or concealment of his equipment. Cases have occurred where agents being anxious to leave the scene of their dropping as quickly as possible had not concealed their equipment carefully enough and have returned later to the spot to find their kit had been removed. In some cases, due to faulty despatching, equipment had been scattered far and wide and the lone agent has been unable to retrieve it. Equally some equipment, especially W/T sets, was found to be damaged on landing and unusable. This delayed the commencement of the work in some cases for months. Some agents dropping 'blind' discovered that their contact addresses were useless, as the contact had either left or been arrested and many were forced to find accommodation with friends with whom, for security reasons, they would rather not have renewed acquaintance. Finally, one big risk that was taken by the agent dropping 'blind' was the possibility of injury on landing and the necessity of getting medical attention at a hospital or doctor's surgery without betraying himself to the Authorities. One report quotes the case of two agents who dropped together – one sustaining a bad fracture of the leg in dropping. The uninjured agent spent days trying to find a doctor who would cope with the situation clandestinely and also experienced great trouble in acquiring the necessary transport to take the injured agent away from the scene of the accident, where he had been lying for some days.

Relations with local leaders

Having overcome the initial difficulties connected with his arrival, and having made contact with the underground movement, the agent was faced with other difficulties. In some cases, instructions given him in London were ignored by the man on the spot and he was put to work on missions for which he had not been prepared. In other cases, the local leaders were not interested in the agents from London or, lacking pre-advice, did not know how to use the new arrivals. Much time was therefore lost before they started work. One danger was that agents sometimes only had a very vague idea as to what their mission really was and lacked information about the underground movement and its organisation. They were not always sure of their status and not knowing whether they were to advise or take command, felt that they lacked authority and prestige with the groups to which they were attached. Some London trained agents, however, went with too big a sense of their own importance, which did not improve relations with the men on the spot.

The following is an extract from a report on London trained agents, made by a Regional Commander:

"Their training in the use of sabotage material and their knowledge of London's facilities and limitations, helped to give the local men a better idea of possibilities. Their knowledge of specialised weapons etc., was very useful. In the beginning it was not difficult to find them accommodation, but later on this became more and more difficuLieutenant The identity cards they brought with them were very bad. The photographs, fingerprints and other technical details were incorrect, but the worst mistakes were in the professions chosen and in the use of the age 19 which was a most dangerous age to choose. They only carried identity cards and no other papers. It was not understood why London could not provide better cards as grave risks were taken by having to procure new ones for the men as soon as they arrived. Clothing supplied to London trained agents was fairly good imitation, but shoes were obviously made in England and the fact could be noticed 100 yards away. These agents had no idea of conditions in the field. They thought it was all shooting and that there was an S.D. man behind every tree. When they were on bicycles, they expected to be controlled at two-minute intervals. At first, they were very jittery but recovered their nerve very quickly once they saw what true conditions in Holland were like."

Achievements

In spite of handicaps, the agents from this country achieved very good results in liaison work between the different groups and between London and Regional Commanders in Holland. They were of great assistance in the early stages of the formation of the N.B.S. W/T communications with this country, an essential part of co-ordinated underground effort, were also maintained almost exclusively by London trained operators. Agents from this country also did valuable work as weapon training instructors and demolition experts. They also helped to co-ordinate the propaganda disseminated by the Dutch underground press.

Cover and Papers

Indigenous agents

A high proportion of clandestine work was done, not by the 100 per cent clandestine agent but by men still working legally in responsible administrative positions under their own names and whose only precaution was to adopt an assumed name when working subversively and to conceal their address from all intimate associates. Most of these men were of an age which exempted them from the German labour laws.

Indigenous clandestine agents working completely underground adopted a variety of covers which were changed or modified as and when it became necessary through new laws and decrees issued by the occupying authorities. The main consideration was avoidance of conscription for work in Germany, and consequently semi-official jobs were chosen for cover – such as food controller, inspector of transport and communications or policeman. Other professions chosen were teacher, nurse, doctor, engineer or clergyman. Many agents adopted O.T. cover. In general, papers supporting the cover story were duplicates of those issued to legal holders who knew that a double was using their identity. Agents usually had some person to vouch for them in the bureau or administration which nominally controlled their activities, and, by connivance with State servants working legally in responsible positions, obtained the necessary information about their adopted profession which would enable them to talk convincingly if questioned. Thus, they were able to produce day-to-day or hour-to-hour alibis to cover their movements. False papers were acquired through L.O. sources or from one or the other of the groups engaged in producing all types of papers en masse.

London-trained agents

In general, cover stories prepared in London were not retained for any length of time in the Field. Some were rejected on arrival because of flaws pointed out by men on the spot, and many were rejected by individual agents who realised that the story would not have stood up to a serious investigation but could have been cracked wide open inside two minutes. Many agents, therefore, preferred to make up their own cover stories on arrival, with the help of the local men. London was at a disadvantage in the preparation of cover stories as it was apparently impossible to keep up with events in Holland and faulty or incomplete sets of papers were issued to the agents to support their cover stories. Cover stories were often based on papers available, and consequently an agent was frequently committed to a completely false story. A big handicap was the youth of most London-trained agents, as the Arbeitsdienst claimed all men from 18 to 25, and subsequently from 18 to 40. Professions had to be chosen with this in mind. Another consideration was the problem of explaining away a period of absence from Holland while the agent was training in this country. Both of these difficulties were overcome in many cases by adopting the cover of a seaman or ship's carpenter waiting in Dutch ports for a ship, or of a Dutch Merchant Navy Officer on leave from Germany. Some agents were given O.T. cover, according to which they had left other occupied countries to avoid capture by the Allies, and in some cases, they posed as store-masters working for the Wehrmacht. Some explained their absence by claiming to have arrived from the Netherlands East Indies. Others posed as repatriated prisoners of war or clerks employed in foreign firms and visiting Holland to see relatives. Many agents obtained exemption from the labour laws by posing as Category C men.

Although a few agents were ordered to prepare their cover story on arrival, most were given a cover story to learn before they left, and some did not see eye to eye with their Section Officers in the matter. One agent, for instance, was sent out with papers showing him to be a baker, whereas he, knowing the area to which he was being sent, maintained that a better cover story would have been that of a farmer or agricultural worker.

Many agents who, with London's approval, prepared their own cover story, retained their own identity and papers and consequently only had to explain away the period of their absence from Holland. This they did by claiming to have been in Government service in some other part of the country, or persuading friends to vouch that they had been living with them for their period of absence.

Papers given to agents in London were almost invariably considered by local resistance leaders as worthless and immediately exchanged for local products. Sets of papers supplied by London were usually incomplete and, even if retained, had to be augmented by documents obtained on the spot. The faulty watermark of the London identity card came in for much criticism. Some agents never used their London papers at all but kept them as souvenirs. There were cases of agents returning to Holland with papers previously acquired when in resistance before being brought to England for training. Two criticisms made by agents about London papers were the following.

In one case a man's profession on his identity card was indicated as a private secretary without stating by whom he was employed, thus leaving the agent to find his own employer. In another case an agent's address was given as a certain hotel which had in the meantime been requisitioned by the Wehrmacht. The main objection to London papers was the fact that they were entirely false, unregistered, and with no possibility whatsoever of their being vouched for or authenticated.

Fortunately, there was no very thorough check on papers unless by the Gestapo of S.D., and these strict controls were far from numerous. A plausible story was more important than papers, and bluff worked wonders.

EXAMPLE 1

Real name	R. Matthysen.
Code number	D.22
Interrogated by	Captain Mathe and Major Hirsch
Interrogated on	17th June 1945.
Area	Holland

Interrogator's impression of informant
Informant is a keen young Dutchman, highly patriotic, who seems to have done an excellent job of work for his country during the occupation. He gives the impression of complete reliability and good security mind.

Background

Between 1940 and 1942 informant was a chemical student, but when the German control became more severe in 1942, he began to help people to escape. It then became necessary to supply them with forged papers, and it was in this way that he began his work.

A visit was made on June 12th, 1945, to a small printing factory in 27 Oude Gracht, Utrecht. The firm was engaged in dye-setting, photogravure and engraving. Total personnel employed, 5 people, whose functions were, Manager, Photographer and 3 labourers. Prior to September 1944 the firm was working quite legally and openly for industrial concerns in Utrecht and the region of Utrecht, and also producing letterheads and various types of permit for the Wehrmacht. At first, there were many firms in Holland engaged in the production of false papers, but when conditions became difficult owing to the arrest of many people and the cut in electricity, informant's firm carried on with only one other organisation.

The clandestine work was carried out after the ordinary day's work had finished. Some or all of the staff worked every evening to supply the Resistance with all types of identity cards, permits, ration documents, etc., and the finished products were immediately removed by R in order that as little compromising material as possible might be left on the premises. After September 1944 the plant was closed down by the Germans, and all work was then done illegally.

History of organisation

At first only identity cards were forged, but in 1944 when the Germans discovered this forgery, they began to demand more papers, and informant's organisation began to forge ration books as well.

The first forgery of papers was begun when the elimination of the Jews in Holland was attempted. The "J" on the identity cards was obliterated by informant's organisation.

The next forgery was to change the number of the identity cards, as the organisation often used cards which had been lost, and the Germans had a list of the numbers of such cards.

Finally, whole new identity cards were forged, but the Germans discovered this when some of the people implicated were arrested. There were various means of proving that an identity card was forged, and the most effective way of doing this was to use an ultra-violet light.

Ordinary inks were used for writing on these forged documents, but care had to be taken to make the ink as near as possible to the official ink, which was very dark, due to the top being invariably left off the bottle, which tends to darken the ink. To obtain the correct colour, blue and black inks were mixed.

Grafting

Another method of removing entries, especially in the case of the "J" sign indicating that the holder was a Jew, was to peel off the top layer of the card and graft on the top surface taken from another card. This obviously was a very complicated and difficult process, but with practice people became expert in this method.

Watermarks

In the complete reproduction of watermarked identity cards, the real watermark was drawn by the designer, and from this an engraving was made. The identity card was split into two layers, front and back, and the watermark was stamped on the inside of one of the layers. The two layers were then glued together. By this method, an almost perfect copy of the true watermark was produced, but when the Germans became aware of this forgery, they found it easy to detect such cards, as the glue was poor, and the edges were liable to come apart. However, when a rubber solution was used for sticking the two layers together, the forgery was not so easy to detect.

Ancillary documents

Bicycle Permits, Certificates for Exemption from Work in Germany, Certificates issued by employers, etc.

These were obtained easily from legal holders and were copied without difficulty. The German Authorities were in the habit of issuing provisional certificates or permits pending the issue of a final document. This was because of the mass of papers required and the consequent pressure of work. The provisional documents were usually just typewritten sheets of which hundreds of roneo'd copies were taken. The organisation in Utrecht copied this method and produced hundreds of certificates which were entirely false, and which were found to be of great utility in passing through snap controls in the area.

The manager of the firm stressed the fact that the documents had to be stamped, and that the more stamps which appeared on a document the better it was for the holder. Working on this principle, he arranged for all current German official stamps to be reproduced by the organisation, with the result that every stamp in the office of the Gestapo or Wehrmacht had its counterpart in the office of the paper factory in Utrecht.

Ration cards

During the occupation, a master ration card was issued to all Dutch subjects. With the master ration card was issued a sheet of coupons entitling the holder to exchange one coupon for a sheet of tickets covering food issued for certain periods and for certain products. The organisation reproduced hundreds of thousands of coupons entitling the holder to draw ration tickets. No attempt was made by them to reproduce the master ration card as, when presenting coupons, holders were not obliged to show their ration cards, and therefore no difficulty was experienced in this respect.

One drawback in connection with the reproduction of ration tickets was that the paper used contained silk thread and was in very short supply. It was, indeed, almost unobtainable. The organisation, therefore, obtained old, expired coupon sheets or sheets which had been stolen en bloc but declared non-valid by the authorities, and for their illegal purposes, cut from these coupon sheets the blank portion which ran down the middle of the sheet as a dividing line. The width of this strip was just sufficient for the reproduction of the ration cards.

Railway tickets

Railway tickets were forged by the organisation, as they had not sufficient money to buy tickets in the normal way for the people whom they helped to escape.

Production

When the Germans stated that all people born in 1922, 1923 and 1924 were to be taken to Germany to work, there was an influx of work for informant's organisation, and they issued about 40 false identity cards a week. In this instance, they changed the date of birth of all those people.

In Amsterdam in August 1944, 3,000 false identity cards were made.

Finance

Informant was not directly in touch with any organisation from England but, through his friends in Amsterdam, who was in contact with a financial organisation from England, the N.S.F., he received financial assistance for his work. The organisation in Amsterdam received 25,000 guilders a month, and informant asked for and received 1,500 guilders a month for his organisation.

Security

Informant maintained communication with his associates himself. He always ran the risk of being caught with compromising documents on his person, and he might also have found the Gestapo in any of the places which he had to visit, but he judged it safer to run this risk than to have many couriers visiting his house, which would certainly have caused suspicion amongst his neighbours, who might easily have betrayed him. When in contact with political organisations, informant's organisation was careful to remain as anonymous as possible, and provided them with only one address, which automatically became obsolete if any arrest were made. In this way, informant's organisation suffered hardly any casualties, unless a member himself were indiscreet.

EXAMPLE 2

Real Name	Dr. Erne.
Field Name	Van De Weerd.
Area	Apeldoorn (2 i/c to Piet Van Arnhem).
Interrogated by	Major Burnes.
Date	27.6.45.
Code No	HD.15.
	D.42.

Introduction
Informant was a Captain in the Dutch Army reserve on the outbreak of war. When Holland capitulated, he was imprisoned by the Germans in Zeeland and later with many other officers despatched under guard to Germany. After completing part of the journey, the party was ordered to return and individual officers received orders to report back to their garrisons for demobilisation. Many officers who had already reached Germany were afterwards sent back to Holland because of this change of policy. Those officers who had civilian clothes were demobilised and liberated, and later all officers were returned to their homes. Informant, after at first refusing to go home in civilian clothes, was threatened with deportation to Germany and later went home to Utrecht and resumed his profession, which was teacher of languages at a college in Utrecht, where his home was.

Informant reverted to his normal way of life and took no part in active resistance until 1942, when rumours began to circulate about the possibility of ex-officers being rounded up again and deported to Germany. From then on informant decided he would have to do something to assist resistance and cast about for useful contacts.

Resistance at this time was taking shape, but informant had no faith in the rather amateurish efforts of those people he knew to be working in resistance and knew nobody in whom he could have complete confidence.

He had been approached once in 1940 soon after his demobilisation by a stranger who knew of informant through a mutual acquaintance and who asked him to take a command in the resistance movement. Informant was not enthusiastic as the stranger was not an ex-officer and informant rather expected the initiative in this respect to come from a brother officer. In this he was disappointed and preferred not to treat with a civilian he did not know. The latter promised to send someone from the Hague to Utrecht to explain in detail what was required of informant, but nobody from the Hague ever came and having no reliable contacts informant decided to work on his own, and to confine his activities to his own profession, i.e. helping students who had disobeyed the German labour conscription laws. This work he continued to do, among other activities, right up to September 1944, when he became a prominent member of the N.B.S. working with Piet Van Arnhem.

In 1943 the Germans began to put into effect the various threats previously issued with regard to ex-officers of the Dutch Army, and all officers were ordered to proceed to a report centre at Amersfoort for registration. Many of the officers were doing important administrative work for the Government and for this reason were exempted. Thousands of these exemptions were issued, the majority of them completely bogus, and it was even possible, by making the right approach to the Germans, to get an exemption without difficulty. Informant, however, refused in principle to apply for an exemption as the Queen had issued definite orders that officers were not to register, and in any case, he did not wish to ask favours from the Germans. Informant pointed out with regret that thousands of officers were weak enough to ignore the Queen's order and went off to register. They bought return tickets for the journey, but the return half was not used. They finished up in Germany. Those officers who did not register were not in any immediate danger as the Germans did not have complete lists of all Army officers, and in this respect the Dutch Record Offices were obstructive and unhelpful to the Germans. Many important archives had been destroyed deliberately to this end.

Informant, however, like many other officers who had failed to register, thought his arrest was imminent and, as he was well known in Utrecht, he decided to leave his wife and family and go underground in another part of the country. What decided his departure more than anything was the fact that among the students at the college were many sons of prominent N.S.B. officials and he feared that his activities concerned with helping refractaires might be known. In the event of arrest for non-registration, enquiries might result in all his underground activities being revealed.

Most of his friends and acquaintances were under the impression that he had registered but those who knew him well and guessed he had not, tried to persuade him to comply with the law and remain safely in Utrecht with his wife and family. He finally gave out that he was going to Amersfoort to register and one of his friends undertook to look after his wife and family in his absence. The college, after some time, assumed that he had been deported to Germany and struck him off their books.

He left Utrecht in the beginning of 1943 and went to stay at Beekbergen, a small village 6 miles from Apeldoorn, where he stayed with a friend who was already in underground work, also assisting refractaires by obtaining for them papers and accommodation.

Informant's activities prior to working with N.B.S.

On arriving in Beekbergen, informant joined his friend and they, with two other local men, formed a small group to whom parents came for assistance when their sons had fallen foul of the labour laws. Most of the boys were of the student type and informant's main concern was for them to arrange the continuation of their studies or, alternatively, to get them apprenticed to the professions they would normally have taken up. Once the parents had handed the boys over to informant's group, the parents had no further contact with him, and the boys were under strict orders not to attempt to see their parents again.

In and around Beekbergen are a number of small summer houses which informant's group took over and there the boys were billeted under close supervision till other accommodation could be found or situations obtained for them.

Whilst waiting, papers were obtained for them, and in the interim period they continued their studies, some of them even taking correspondence courses. Ultimately, they were placed on farms, in industry, or apprenticed to doctors or chemists, always with the connivance of employers as informant travelled the country seeking out friends and contacts who were willing to accept the boys and give them work. His contacts were usually on a high level, and he had friends in the Arbeits bureau at Apeldoorn, who procured for him stacks of movement orders already signed in advance by the German supervisors, which allowed the boys to travel. These movement orders were issued to boys who had registered to work in Germany and indicated the date on which the bearer was to report for work. Naturally these dates had been arranged by informant to give a handsome margin of time and a boy carrying a movement order of this sort was immune from any sort of enquiry. These papers were issued to refractaires when they were actually traveling and on arrival at their destination informant arranged with friends in the different Arbeits bureau to register them on the books as working for the particular employer chosen by informant from among his circle of acquaintances. In many cases the boys did not change their identity cards as their only crime was in failing to register and this was covered by the bogus movement order they carried. In most of the administrations who employed boys sponsored by informant, only two people knew the boys' real status, the manager and the staff manager, who, in collusion with an Arbeits bureau representative, arranged the records.

The L.O. organisation had by then been functioning on a big scale all over Holland doing more or less the same work as informant but helping not only students but anybody who was leading an illegal life. They did not take the same fatherly interest in their proteges as did informant and once they had dealt with a case, had nothing more to do with the individual.

The Apeldoorn area was not covered by L.O. as they had few contacts there, but they heard of informant's work through a friend of his who was in touch with the L.O. and sent a representative to ask him to work for them. By this time informant had contacts all over Holland and was a very useful recruit for L.O. He agreed to work for them and from then on extended his activities to cover the different types of needy people catered for by L.O. This meant he could no longer devote his time and labours exclusively to students, and this part of his work he delegated to the other members of his small original group of 4. He could no longer give the same attention to his proteges in view of the increase in his work, but one advantage in his link with the L.O. was that he could obtain papers much more easily as L.O. had a very efficient machinery for this particular need. Informant obtained from them over 600 sets of papers for students, and they were his first source of supply on a big scale.

To show the way in which his work increased, informant mentioned that in January 1944 he supplied approximately 600 sets of documents, but in February 1945 2,700 sets which he had at his disposal were insufficient for the needs of his organisation. In the early days informant had acquired false papers from a friend in Amsterdam, who was a chemical student and was doing rather well in an amateurish way. Informant himself took a short course in Amsterdam in the falsification of documents. The methods employed did not differ from those already explained in previous reports forwarded in connection with the Utrecht false paper establishment. Informant's methods are explained below.

Cover

As already stated, informant left Utrecht for Beekbergen early in 1943 and from then on discontinued his teaching and devoted all his energies to clandestine work. He first lived with his friend in Beekbergen but afterwards moved into his own cottage there and subsequently his wife and family came there to live also. He was living on his means as the college in Utrecht no longer paid him. Right up to June 1944 he used his own papers, accepting the risk of enquiries being made. He never altered the name on his papers, but in 1945 when everybody was conscripted for O.T. work and trench-digging, he changed his profession and became a Protestant pastor. He knew something of clerical matters having friends in the clergy who would have spoken for him, and in Christmas 1944 a rest home for Protestant clergymen advertised for a bursar, which post informant obtained and lived at the home for some months with his wife and family also on the premises. He was thus able to acquire enough knowledge to enable him to pass a normal interrogation on the street.

For his clandestine work, although carrying papers in his real name, he assumed various false names for different regions and types of work. He realised the danger here and quoted the case of a friend, Stoffel, who used his own name and papers, being known to friends in resistance by a false name. This man was once interrogated in the presence of a contact to whom he was talking and when the contact was asked Stoffel's name answered promptly that the name was Jansen. Stoffel/Jansen was thereupon arrested as was the contact.

Informant was never seriously disturbed by controls as he is over 44 years old and the Germans were concentrating on young men. The German controls were not particularly clever, the Dutch S.D. man examined his identity card and although informant said his profession was that of a teacher, the S.D. man insisted he must be a butcher as he saw on the card the maiden name of informant's wife, Fleischer. The S.D. and Grüne Polizei seemed to concentrate on young men between 20 and 30 and two of informant's proteges were arrested because they were unwise enough to go to Amsterdam without papers to see their parents.

Organisation and Communications (Internal)

Informant had very few full-time workers. He employed a secretary who was a young refractaire and was living completely underground, 2 or 3 girl couriers and a policeman suffering from a "political" illness, who was on prolonged sick leave. All other contacts or helpers were living quite legally, most of them working in some official capacity.

Although informant himself maintained communication by personal visits to sympathisers, those persons who received assistance never met him but applied through contact addresses, leaving messages which were collected by courier. Material was distributed in the same way.

In order to obtain full information with regard to services required, informant had printed a number of questionnaires in code, asking age, religion, profession, details of papers already in possession etc. In this way he maintained records of what assistance had been rendered and to whom.

The three contact addresses were known to about 20 people in all, but informant's address and name were in general not know to the mass of people being helped. The contact addresses were changed frequently and were usually shops. Messages for informant were placed in an envelope bearing a sign of some sort but no name and left with the shopkeeper for collection later by courier.

Informant had some trouble with people applying for more than their quota of papers and these cases he passed to his Investigation Section, i.e. the policeman, who, with the assistance of the records kept, checked up on applicants.

Informant had a small finance section, which obtained funds from wealthy sympathisers and from sales of illegal newspapers. Later there was a central organisation in Amsterdam with unlimited funds and a representative in Apeldoorn to whom informant applied when he needed cash.

Security Precautions

Apart from an understanding among the members of informant's group and among all contacts that warning of enemy action was to be circulated immediately, no security rules existed in the organisation. Informant's own personal courier knew all addresses and could warn everybody in a very short time.

Methods of obtaining False Papers.
There were three methods of obtaining false papers:
(a) With the connivance of officials, who supplied them in bulk.
(b) By raiding offices and stealing supplies. This was done by K.P. members at the request of L.O.
(c) By reproducing false papers or altering papers to meet particular needs.

In most cases informant resorted to method (a) but L.O. usually supplied him with papers acquired by method (b). Informant had contacts everywhere who could supply him with genuine documents, and by using the same methods as the Utrecht group, which methods were more or less generally resorted to, he was able to alter cards to suit his purpose. Ration cards were in great demand amongst resistance members for when men reported for work in Germany, they were given a movement order, the date of departure being altered illegally by the holder to delay the move to Germany. However, when this was done, the Arbeits bureau took the man's ration card as officially he no longer needed it. The stemcard or ration book was issued before identity cards became compulsory, but the first stemcard was later cancelled and a new one issued. A corner of the old card was clipped off and in exchange for this coupon a new card was issued and at the same time the holder was asked to produce an identity card which was stamped at the same time. L.O. printed thousands of clippings, entitling the holder to draw a new stemcard. Another method adopted by informant was to draw up lists of hundreds of people who had never existed, with full particulars of date and place of birth. These lists he handed to friends in the Town Hall, who created dossiers which were included in the official records and papers were then issued in their names. These false dossiers were removed from the Town Hall if there was any serious inspection of the records and replaced afterwards. Through his contacts in the Town Hall, Food Office and Labour Office informant was more or less in control of the entire administration.

Informant's introduction to N.B.S.

Early in 1944, informant being an ex-Army officer, he decided he would transfer his activities from the civil to the military sphere and passing control of this group to friends, he began to collect information of military value for a small group of friends who were in touch with England by W/T and later in touch with the Albrecht group. These people numbered among them R.V.V. as well as K.P. members and he knew them all as they had previously worked with him.

Informant had previously, in the early days in Utrecht, been an O.D. officer, but he did not like their programme or their principles. He therefore worked with this small group until September 1944 when a series of arrests began in the region.

The O.D. chief had sent a boy messenger to a prominent woman member of the R.V.V., the boy was arrested, searched and the message he was carrying was found. The R.V.V. woman was arrested as was the O.D. chief and anybody visiting either house was also arrested. The result was confusion in resistance circles in Apeldoorn and many casualties. The O.D. chief was shot and many leading R.V.V. members and K.P. men were arrested. From that moment O.D. in the region was blacked out and other groups were quiescent. Some O.D. members, however, said to informant "wait and see the marvellous organisation we shall have after the war". He, however, was still seeking military contacts and some of his friends were helping in the search. Finally, one of his friends introduced him to Piet Van Arnhem, who stated there was no organised resistance at all on the Veluwe and enlisted informant's help in reorganising resistance in the area. This was very difficult as each group which still existed strongly suspected the others of being penetrated and feared also that indiscretions or imprudence committed by the other groups might incriminate them. Piet Van Arnhem, with informants help, finally succeeded in uniting the different groups in the area and his organisation ultimately became the N.B.S.

Informant's work with Piet Van Arnhem

The organisation built up by informant and Piet Van Arnhem was very elastic and there were no watertight compartments. Small groups of men would form themselves into cells and the cell leader would report to informant or Piet Van Arnhem. In the main, they were men who had previously worked for informant for L.O. or other resistance movements and they more or less continued to do under Piet Van Arnhem what they had done before in their own groups. Thus, they would be engaged in all sorts of resistance activities, false papers, sabotage and providing accommodation for escaped pilots and refractaires. Informant himself had little to do with the organisation of the movement after the initial contacts had been made between Piet Van Arnhem and the local leaders. He became the officer responsible for collecting information of military value which he passed to his chief. He used many of the men who had worked with him in the past, but recruited others for this particular work, who had been recommended to him. He trained them in military matters himself and explained what type of information he required. In this he was helped by being introduced to a member of the Albrecht Group, who gave him much assistance and advice on how to collect information and what sort was wanted. If a potential recruit was introduced to him and he was not impressed by the man's manner or qualifications, he did not refuse to use the man but omitted to find him work and did not see him again.

Informant obtained information by having a group in every village responsible to a chief who would collate the intelligence acquired by his group, place it in an envelope marked with a blue cross, but with no mane, and send a courier to Beekbergen, where the courier would leave the envelope in the official letter box at the post office. Envelopes were always deposited before 9.30 a.m. Between 9.30 and 10 the official responsible for the post office extracted the letters, put them aside and a courier called at 10 o'clock at the post office and carried the messages away to informant's cottage. By this manner, by 11 o'clock every day informant had in his possession up-to-date military information for the whole region. The couriers who went with the information only knew they were to put the envelopes in the letter box at Beekbergen. The official at the post office only knew the courier who called to collect the envelopes and asked no questions. He had a perfect alibi as he could always say he did not know who left the letters or for whom they were destined. Informant submitted his reports to Piet Van Arnhem, who sent the information on to Ede, where it was sent to Nijmegen by courier or by black telephone or transmitted direct to London by an operator who was working near Ede, called King and later by another operator – Frans Beckers. Informant was not clear about the methods of onwards transmission of his intelligence as after handing it to Piet Van Arnhem he was no longer responsible.

In the matter of communications, the post office official was very helpful, and informant could use the official telephone at the post office in case of emergency. If informant were needed urgently, a contact could call the post office and the official would send a messenger to informant's home. Another service the official rendered was the handling of correspondence addressed to a Mr. Verstraten at a boarding house in Beekbergen, which correspondence was really destined for informant. These letters were set aside for informant and collected by his courier. This man at the post office had never met informant and only received his instructions from the courier, but he was very discreet and never wanted to know what was going on.

Enemy C.E.

In October 1944 there were 60,000 evacuees in Apeldoorn area with consequent difficulties for the Germans in respect of controlling papers of all kinds, especially temporary passes etc. The job was too much for the Germans and although the Grüne Polizei and especially the Fleming and Dutch S.D. were very dangerous still, control of individuals ceased and mass raids and razzias commenced early in 1945. No warning was possible about these raids, the city would be surrounded, and all young men driven to the market place. Papers and explanations were disregarded and only men working for the Germans were released. The employers of these men had to come themselves to the spot and vouch for their men. The men arrested were deported to Germany but many afterwards returned, having escaped. Foreign workers were apparently not too rigidly supervised. House to house searches were frequent but although informant's own house was searched, nothing was found as all incriminating material was always buried in a tin box in the garden, and a small fire was always burning in the cottage for the destruction of any papers in the event of a surprise visit.

Escapee Pilots

Although much good work was done by informant's organisation in assisting allied pilots to return to allied lines, informant did not himself take part in these operations. There was no organised escape line, but pilots were instructed to try to contact a priest who would pass them on. What usually happened was a pilot took refuge in a cottage or farmhouse, and rumours about his arrival quickly spread. All informant's men were acquainted with the procedure laid down by Piet Van Arnhem and when any men in the organisation heard of a pilot being harboured somewhere, he would go to the house, take particulars and report to informant, who issued the necessary papers and clothing and informed Piet Van Arnhem. The latter arranged for the pilots to be transported on P.T.T. vans or bicycles to other safe houses on a line running from East to West, terminating at a concentration point where batches of refugees were gathered and taken by guides across the Rhine at night to the allied lines. These guides knew the country to be traversed like the back of their hands, but all the people concerned in these escapes were unanimous in their condemnation of the pilots' indiscretion and lack of prudence. They frequently endangered the lives of their helpers. Two things which made escapes difficult were the lack of clothing and the lack of medical necessities needed to help wounded pilots. Informant said all the dungarees in the Veluwe must now be in England.

Recruiting

Prior to September 1944 most recruits were obtained by personal recommendation, and recruiting was on a friendly basis, a member vouching for the integrity of a potential recruit. In some groups the recommendation itself was considered insufficient and a careful investigation followed, information being obtained from the recruit's circle of friends and acquaintances. This investigation was carried out by the group's Intelligence or Security Section. There was never any serious attempt at creating any particular machinery for recruiting, as in 1943 and 1944 the supply of potential recruits was much greater than the demand.

When recruits were required, some organisers could have recourse to youth movements, students' organisations etc., with whom they had been in touch before the war. Others, who occupied prominent positions in administrations or in the liberal professions, had a wide field for recruiting new members. Dr "X" is a typical example. He was a prominent member of the Doctors' Underground Committee, formed to resist German repressive measures, and knowing all the doctors in Amsterdam and the region, he was in possession of a very long list of useful contacts well-placed to assist him in his work. He never approached any of these contacts himself on business connected with the Resistance but instructed one or the other of his assistants to visit a contact and recruit him without mentioning Dr. "X"s name. The person sent to recruit a new member did not even know Dr. "X" himself, and the potential recruit had no idea that his colleague, Dr. "X" had sent someone to recruit him. In this way Dr. "X" succeeded in keeping in the background and becoming known to very few people as an agent working for London, although a number of people knew him as a member of the Doctors' Committee.

Quite a different technique was used by the editor and General Manager of Het Parool in the Hague. His method of selecting recruits was intuitive rather than anything else. After talking to a person for ten minutes he would make up his mind whether or not the person was likely to be suitable. Most of the people he recruited had been recommended in the first place by some friend of his, but sometimes he simply spotted someone and decided that he might be a useful man. Informant did not even bother to check the antecedents or background of new recruits. He worked on feeling and found this very successful. He personally tested all new recruits to the staff and said that they were never penetrated because he could 'smell' a German agent without difficulty.

The N.B.S., after the amalgamation in the Autumn of 1944, recruited on a descending scale, that is, the District Commanders recruited the Company Commanders, who in turn recruited Group Leaders and so on. It was usual to check potential recruits' suitability by making a study of their activities throughout the Occupation, but a thorough check was not always possible. Refractaires moving from one area to another invariably knew somebody in the local group and were often accepted without question.

Some organisations did more recruiting than others. K.P. did not recruit much until August 1944, and at this time they only had about 500 members in the whole of the Netherlands. On the other hand, O.D. in the Hague alone had several thousand members. In September 1944 the need to swell the ranks of the N.B.S. for forthcoming operations led to a period of hasty and insecure recruiting. Previously great care was taken in recruiting, and full information was obtained of potential recruits, but in September 1944 a flood of people came in to be enrolled, and no check was possible. The possibility of penetration during this period is definitely a thing to be considered. In October security with regard to recruiting was tightened up.

Training

Operational Training

Resistance groups received instruction in the use of Sten, U.S. carbine, rifle, grenade, Bren, Bazooka, German weapons and explosives. Training varied from district to district according to the reception of arms and explosives from England. In some areas, where there were few receptions, agents concentrated on stolen German weapons and home-made explosives. In some areas no English weapons and explosives were ever received, and in general, training was hampered by the lack of material. In the whole of the Utrecht region, for instance, there were only 100 Allied weapons.

Weapon training was not entirely necessary as many Resistance members were ex-soldiers or policemen and were familiar with most weapons, but after September 1944, when supplies and instructors were arriving in quantity from England, clandestine classes were organised in most groups.

Some instructors gave their students elementary courses in fieldcraft and tactics. Instruction was given by agents sent expressly for the purpose from England and by ex-officers and NCOs from the Dutch Army, or by policemen. Many agents had already a good knowledge of explosives, and chemists recruited by the Underground Movement worked clandestinely, making up home-made explosives and instructing the Underground Movement in their use. The English-trained instructors were usually attached to Regional Headquarters, where they trained selected men from the districts, and these men in turn would return to their districts and pass on their knowledge to the various groups under their command. Many instructors, however, went round visiting the districts and trained small groups whenever training was required. Much of this training was purely revision.

In 1944 and 1945 larger classes were arranged in towns, and agents were trained in groups of 20 to 30 at a time in swimming baths, gymnasia, dance halls etc. Small classes were held in shops, private houses, stables or garages. In the country men gathered in farmhouses to receive their training, or alternatively in fields well off the beaten track and with guards posted.

London-trained instructors were in great demand in view of their specialised knowledge, but they run a certain risk, especially when instructing large groups of men, as they became too well-known. One instructor in Rotterdam is said to have personally trained 12,000 men, and when he went out he met people he had instructed every few yards.

Arrangements for training were usually made by a liaison officer who would fix the time and place and bring the students and instructors together. Trainees would be brought to a pre-arranged contact address by girl couriers, and from there conducted by another courier to the place where training was to take place. These places would be used three or four times in succession and then abandoned. Lookouts and guards were usually posted when training was proceeding, and in places like swimming-baths the staff provided special facilities and kept watch.

Material for the training would be taken to the spot every night by selected couriers and sometimes, suitably camouflaged, by trainees themselves in broad daylight. In the country, stores and arms would be left at farmhouses for training purposes.

Most instructors provided themselves with some sort of alibi to cover their activities, but trainees rarely took the trouble.

The following extracts from reports on operational training are of interest:

1) "The numbers attending informant's classes varied from 10 to 40. He thought the numbers were often too large. Three armed sentries would patrol the district during the actual training. Hours of training would vary from 2 to 10 hours a day for one or two days. Informant first visited Zone 3 where he stayed for two days in a safe house. These safe houses were nearly always isolated farms, and informant used his same cover story of helping the local farmer as his own farm was flooded. Here he met and trained the local commanders of the region."

2) "Eventually instruction was proceeding at the rate of about 20 to 30 a day under much better conditions. It was arranged that this should take place in a room opening off a large gymnasium hall. About 100 to 150 men would go to the hall for gymnasium, and from these people every half hour they would take 10 or so to a separate room to instruct them in arms. There was a fixed code word for entry. The doors were covered by guards, but gymnastics went on all the time, and the instruction went on in a separate room, which could not be seen from the street."

3) "Training was carried out by informant to groups of about 30 at a time. Different places were used for this instruction. On several

occasions a room at a swimming-bath was used. Students would go singly to the swimming-bath early in the morning, carrying bathing-suits, and the instruction would go on all day, food being brought in. No lookouts were placed, but the attendant was in their confidence and would have given the alarm had it been necessary. They relied more on their weapons than on security measures for protection. The weapons for training were taken to the swimming-pool by members of the organisation in sacks, with an innocent article such as a broomstick protruding from the top."

Security Training
In general, no special security training was given to recruits, who were deemed to be reliable and intelligent people who could be trusted to behave sensibly and who should be, in any case, fully alive to the dangers of the work as a result of their having lived under occupation conditions for some time. Indeed, some members laughed at the idea of security training, and most were more interested in para-military operations than in security. This attitude was largely overcome by instructors combining weapon training with security and giving talks on commonsense security principles. Most organisers gave detailed security briefing to their second-in-command, with instructions to pass on the principles of security in informal talks with their group leaders.

Pay
It was a generally accepted principle in the Underground Movement that only those who were working full-time in Resistance, and therefore had no other means of livelihood, should be paid. Occasional workers would be paid expenses and any members who were out-of-pocket through taking part in active resistance work could count on reimbursement. A courier, for instance, who incurred traveling expenses, would be paid about 200 guilders a month.

The Underground Movement was never short of funds, and had several sources of supply, namely the NSF (Dutch Welfare Organisation), the Underground Press, taxes levied on known Black Marketeers and bank robberies. Payment was more often than not made in kind, for it was impossible to buy food, cigarettes, bicycle tyres, shoes, clothing, fuel or tea, and gifts of one or the other of these commodities would be made in lieu of cash. The NSF, with Headquarters in Amsterdam, controlled all the underground finances and made a monthly allotment to each of the 14 regions. The Utrecht region, for instance, received approximately 30,000 guilders a month. The commanders of each of the three component groups of the NBS, that is KP, RVV and OD, stated each month what money they would require, and lists were sent to the district commander of the NBS, who received the money for distribution from NSF, whose contact with NBS was usually the local LO agent. The money was handed in cash to the group leaders, who passed it down through their cells by personal contact.

In KP an unmarried man would receive 125-150 guilders a month, and this amount might go up to 250 or 300 guilders according to the man's dependants. Payment was never organised in a methodical way but was done according to the merits of the individual case, those receiving payment for their regular jobs not needing to be paid by the Underground organisation. Financial difficulties were very rarely experienced in any of the groups.

Care of dependants was done by NSF in close co-operation with LO agents in the district, and local groups looked after the families of married men who had been arrested or killed until such time as NSF or LO could cope with the matter.

NSF funds were derived from voluntary contributions. Many members of NSF were bankers, big businessmen, accountants etc. The Underground Press was able to contribute considerable funds to Resistance coffers. In the case of Het Parool, for instance, finances were provided by the sale of the paper. Each person who took the paper paid a subscription of 2½ guilders a month. This was not really enough to pay all the necessary salaries and other expenses of the movement, but there were also some wealthy supporters of the paper who would be able to pay special subscriptions of as much as 2,000 guilders a month. Another source of income was the large-scale Black Marketeer making huge profits, who was blackmailed and offered protection in true gangster style in return for his cash contribution to Resistance funds. Finally, when cash was required urgently, KP could usually provide a small-scale raiding party who would raid a bank or a post-office and make off with useful sums of money. In September 1944 one KP group raided a post-office in the Rotterdam area and obtained 1½ million guilders.

As commodities were as important as money for Resistance purposes, the Underground had a special section to deal with the Black Market. This section sent out patrols during the night to farms which dealt with the Black Market, and they once obtained 23 tons of sugar and 16 tons of potatoes. Resistance members obtained their own bicycles, either by buying them on the Black Market, stealing them from the Germans, or borrowing them from friends. Everybody could get food through the organisation. Food was obtained from Black Market sources. Many farmers, however, contributed willingly, and many of them were members of reception committee groups. In each town there was a special food section known as CVD, which stored and distributed clandestine stocks of food. Wehrmacht stores were also frequently raided by KP groups.

Premises
Safe Houses
These were necessary to accommodate agents arriving from England and refractaires forced to live illegally. They were rarely used for any length of time and the proprietor or tenant was usually a member of a group or on the list of sympathisers rendering occasional services.

A newly arrived agent from England was normally housed in a farm or farm labourer's cottage near the dropping point or in a house in or close by the nearest village. The local schoolmaster or priest would usually be of assistance in this respect. Frequently barges or houseboats would be used.

After spending a few days near the dropping point, the agent would journey to the town where he was to make his first contact, and here he would go to a second safe house. This second safe house was often some sort of local headquarters or rendezvous point with much coming and going and too much incriminating material on the premises. In this respect security was bad and often had an adverse effect on the morale of the agent trained in security principles in this country. The curiosity of local men, who visited the safe house merely to see the new arrival, was a constant source of danger.

Refractaires from German labour laws usually stayed in the homes of friends, changing their residence as often as possible, but, when things became too hot for them and their friends and their friends were unwilling to house them, L.O.'s Special Section would find them accommodation.

L.O. had useful contacts with estate agents and billeting authorities and could find billets with legal cover. One organisation in the Apeldoorn area, working independently of L.O., was very active in housing students who were living illegally, having refused to be conscripted. This organisation had a section to whom parents came for assistance when their sons had fallen foul of the labour laws. In and around Apeldoorn there are a number of small summerhouses which the group took over, and there the boys were billeted, under close supervision, until other accommodation could be found or situations obtained for them.

Living Accommodation
Indigenous agents, living quite openly and working legally under their real names, lived with their families in their own homes or with

friends. Some, as in the case of ex-Army officers who had omitted to register their particulars, were, however, obliged to make certain small adjustments on their papers and remove all mention of their Army status. Many of these agents lived quite securely in their own homes throughout the Occupation, their only precaution being to keep all incriminating material elsewhere.

Agents from England and indigenous agents living illegally had the same facilities as the refractaires, and through their group or organisation applied to L.O., who obtained accommodation for them. In many cases this was unnecessary as most agents had friends or contacts who were willing to take the risk of housing them in their own homes.

Headquarters and Office accommodation: In Towns
In towns a variety of premises were used, including private houses, flats, churches, business premises, shops etc. In Utrecht, as in other towns, about 20 addresses were used as headquarters, but not more than three, or at the most four, people lived in the same house at the same time.

Some organisations had a special engineering section which was in charge of securing the houses. They always went to view them first to see what were the prospects of hiding compromising materials etc. They invariably had a cover story for taking over a house – e.g. one was that they had been bombed out of Arnhem – and, armed with false papers to verify their statements, they nearly always succeeded in their object.

Furnished or unfurnished flats or houses were afterwards rented for the organisation by quite innocent people like doctors, dentists or clergymen, and then handed over to the person needing accommodation, a suitable cover story being arranged for the use of both tenant and occupant.

In the Hague, the organisation controlling the issue of *Je Maintiendrai* first duplicated the newspaper in the Peace Palace, where there were the necessary facilities and to which the organisation had access through a woman who held an official position which enabled her to place keys at their disposal. The Peace Palace was looked upon as an international building, and the Germans always respected this. There was never any question of their having access to it. From the Peace Palace copies of the paper were transported to a grocery warehouse from which they were sent out to the distributors.

One organisation in Utrecht had a small office which was one room in a factory making tools and instruments for the Germans. The manager of the factory was the organiser's friend and allotted him this room but accepted no responsibility if the police raided the factory and discovered what was going on. If the police called at the factory the manager would inform them that he had in fact allotted this room to his friend, but he had no idea on what work his friend was engaged.

The group producing false papers in Utrecht used as headquarters a small printing factory. The firm was engaged in dye-setting, photogravure and engraving. The total personnel employed was five people, whose functions were manager, photographer and three labourers. Prior to September 1944 the firm was working quite legally and openly for industrial concerns in Utrecht and in the region of Utrecht and was also producing letter-heads and various type of permit for the Wehrmacht. The clandestine work was carried out after the ordinary day's work had finished. Some or all of the staff worked every evening to supply the resistance with all types of identity cards, permits etc. Finished products were immediately removed in order that as little compromising material as possible might be left on the premises.

One of the principal organisers in Amsterdam used as headquarters an apartment in a boarding-house which was owned by a German lady whom he had known before the War. Up to October 1944 only German officers had lived in the building. When they moved out, no one would take a room there, so the organisers took the whole of the top floor. At first, he used it as his headquarters when he was in charge of transportation of stores and later as the headquarters of the whole of the organisation in Amsterdam. Nobody knew he was there, and the room was rented in somebody else's name. If the house was searched while he was there, he would be a doctor visiting a patient.

Headquarters and Office accommodation: In the Country
In the country districts – notably in the Veluwe and Overijssel – isolated farmhouses were used for all purposes and men lived in fox-holes in Maquis style. Headquarters in these areas were mobile, and groups moved from place to place as and when events made a move necessary. Headquarters in these country districts would usually comprise three farmhouses within 30 minutes' cycling distance one from the other – one farm housing the chief of staff and his assistant, one accommodating the Zone commander, and a third in which the W/T operator functioned. A courier service would ensure communications. Isolated country houses, clergymen's houses, garages or smithies were also used.

Contact Addresses and Rendezvous Points
Most organisations used for internal communications, accommodation addresses which were changed every month, or as and when necessary,

and which were used as courier terminal points. These accommodation addresses were usually banks, large shops, doctor's surgeries or any premisses where a number of people could go in and out without attracting attention. In the main it was thought that the doctor's surgery was the best place to be used as an accommodation address. Private houses were used, however, for this purpose, as were libraries, cafes and churches. The bank's safe deposit system was used by making a safe deposit dox a dead boite-aux-lettres, the necessary keys being given to all users with the connivance of the bank employees.

To maintain communications in country districts, there was always a contact address somewhere near the headquarters of the Zone. Here messages could be deposited without necessitating a visit to headquarters itself. This contact address would often be a shop in a village near to which headquarters was located.

Meetings were held in business premises during working hours, in doctor's surgeries and in private houses. One meeting, for instance, took place in the offices of the Chamber of Commerce in one of the larger towns. The meeting took place in a private room allotted to the organisation and, although work was going on in the offices of the Chamber of Commerce, nobody knew that a meeting was taking place with the exception of the director's secretary, who had been warned about the meeting 30 minutes before it was due to commence.

Training Premises

In 1944 and 1945 larger classes were arranged in towns, and agents were trained in groups of 20 to 30 at a time in swimming baths, gymnasia, dance halls etc. Small classes were held in shops, private houses, stables or garages. In the country men gathered in farmhouses to receive their training, or alternatively in fields well off the beaten track and with guards posted.

W/T Sites

As already stated, most W/T operators were agents newly arrived from England, and in general the group for whom they were working found transmitting sites for them through friends or contacts or again with the assistance of the L.O. Priests and doctors were also of great assistance in finding transmitting sites for operators. In some cases, however, it was left to the agent himself to find places from which to work. Some agents during their mission used as many as 50 different houses, being obliged to move frequently owing to the danger of enemy D/F-ing activity. Consequently, without assistance from the organisation it was very difficult for them to find suitable premises.

Frequently they were forced to transmit from houses in which other forms of clandestine activity were taking place, with obvious danger to their security.

Using a suitable cover story, an operator seeking a transmitting site would visit a home, flat or farm, and, having examined it from a technical viewpoint, would try to rent accommodation without revealing why he needed it. In most cases, however, this was impossible, and the operator was obliged to take the people into his confidence. If they were unwilling to co-operate, he merely asked them to forget the incident and withdrew. Needless to say, the operator would only visit people whose names had been given by friends or acquaintances in resistance.

The following are extracts from reports received from two operators working in Amsterdam:

"A priest, a protestant minister and a doctor did all the searching for addresses. When the two padres and the doctor had found them addresses, the two operators went round inspecting them to see if they were suitable. Some were not high enough, some had too thin walls. It was preferable to have unoccupied flats round the one chosen and operating always had to be done away from an adjoining apartment, especially during the night, so that the neighbours would not hear anything. The occupants of the premises chosen only knew they were being used to operate from but nothing else. The owners of those houses not chosen merely thought that the two operators were young doctors looking for somewhere to live and that the rooms were unsuitable for some reason best known to the operators."

"One agent had a W/T site in a house opposite a school to which he had a key, and there were plenty of facilities in the school for hiding material."

"The other agent's headquarters was situated in the basement of one of the houses of a hospital. Entrance was obtained through the house of the hospital's chief engineer, out into the garden in the centre of the hospital and down some stone stairs leading to an unlit corridor below the nurse's home. At intervals along the passage metal plates, approximately 3 ft. x 3 ft., were riveted to the wall. The first two would not come away when pulled by a hole in the middle but the third let down on chains when a piece of wire was pushed downwards through the hole to release a catch. These metal plates were about waist height. Behind the plate thus removed was a fairly large, low cellar where it was impossible to stand up straight and which was below ground level. No one, not even the director of the hospital, knew what was happening, or that anything was happening, except the chief engineer of the hospital, who helped the agent to set up his C.P. The agent would use various covers to get into his C.P. – either that of a doctor, a nurse or a plumber. He nearly always rang up the chief engineer before coming to see that everything was all right and he enquired again of the chief engineer when he passed through his house before going down to his C.P. if it was still alright. The C.P. was equipped with everything to enable the agent to stay down there, if necessary, for any length of time. He had in it his broadcast receiver and transmitter sets, his T.D. apparatus, inside and outside telephones, spare accumulators and other spares for his W/T sets, food, water, heating, electric light, hand grenades and fire-arms etc. If, for any reason, the warning system failed and the agent could not get out of his C.P. before the police reached the passage, it would be highly probable that they would not find it and if they did, he was prepared to fight it out. All the materials were taken down there at night and special rubber-soled shoes were asked for from England to enable them to walk up and down the passage. It took two months to equip the C.P. fully. The agent had a house telephone in his C.P with a secret number which only the chief engineer knew, so that the latter could ring him up and warn him of any danger. He, though, could ring up anyone from his phone, both inside and outside the hospital, through the secret exchange. The only snag was that certain very high-pitched morse buzzes vibrated on the central heating pipes which run through the cellar and could be heard in the room immediately above, so the occupant of the room above was moved out and a woman put in who knew she must not speak about any peculiar noises she might hear. One of the agent's reasons for choosing this place for his C.P. was that it was safe from bombardment as it had several feet of steel and concrete above. He wanted to be able to go on transmitting even if Amsterdam was being bombarded right until the very end."

Secret Telephone Exchanges

For the manipulation of the black telephone system, which will be discusses later, many secret telephone exchanges existed all over Holland. Old houses and shops were chosen, and for this purpose the solidly built Dutch house, with its thick walls and many steps, stairs and cupboards, was ideal. Houses with suitable facilities were chosen, or, where these facilities did not exist, carpenters and builders were called in to construct hidden rooms and cupboards. The Dutch are very clever at this type of work, and many ingenious hide-outs were thus created. However, in every case two or three men would be required for a number of days to do the work entailed, with obvious security implications. In some cases, an attic or cellar would be sub-divided, and a secret room walled off, entrance being made in the secret room through a cleverly constructed door which could not be found without a long search. In other cases, the rooms would be completely built in, leaving no means of entry other than a secret door constructed in the fireplace of an adjoining room.

The following extracts illustrate security precautions taken by agents in the Field:

"Eduard had his own men in touch with or working in SD offices and was thus fully informed with regard to planned raids or impending SD activity.

HQ and dwelling places were changed as frequently as possible, and the addresses known only to the minimum number of people."

"In the office, informant kept a certain amount of material connected with his Insurance business and had he been questioned would have attempted to explain his presence there by saying that he was continuing to do his work in the office lent him by his friend.

One precaution, however, was taken in that the manager of the factory had a bell push under his desk, by means of which he could warn informant if the Germans were visiting the factory.

In the office itself, informant had, with the connivance of the factory manager's brother, who was an engineer, constructed a cavity in the floor in which a large box containing his weapons, papers and other incriminating material was stored. The cavity was carefully concealed by a concrete slab on which stood a large electric fire. The box itself could be raised to the surface by means of an electrical lift which the engineer had installed in the room. By pressing a switch, the cavity in the floor could be opened or shut at will and the box raised to the surface very quickly and without any trouble at all. In case of alarm, everything would have been put into the box and lowered into the floor."

"Apart from an understanding among the members of informant's group and among all contacts that warning of enemy action was to be circulated immediately, no security rules existed in the organisation. Informant's own personal courier knew all addresses and could warn everybody in a very short time."

"He always had one house, the address of which was known to nobody, where he could go and sleep with no fear of his whereabouts being betrayed. He had a small office consisting of one room which he used as his headquarters and whose whereabouts was never known to more than two or three persons at the most.

He had a chain of rendezvous addresses where he could meet and discuss his work with other resistance leaders. These meeting places were never used more than twice running, and new rendezvous addresses were acquired as often as possible."

"Informant's organisation was careful to remain as anonymous as possible, and provided them with only one address, which automatically became obsolete if any arrest were made."

"With regard to meetings in houses, they had certain safety signals (e.g. ringing of the doorbell) and in addition a girl was posted at a second-floor window, from which she could see who was ringing the bell, and in the case of a stranger, she would immediate sound the alarm before going to open the door thus giving them time to hide all compromising material. When it was impossible to hide everything in time, they went to the door armed with their Sten guns and pistols, etc."

"Source remarked that the most important qualifications for a house were that entrance might be made unobtrusively, that bicycles might be taken inside, and that there should be a means of escape in case of a raid. Source had one safety house which he used only as a refuge, and not for training.

The only safety signal used was the ringing of the doorbell in a special way to obtain admittance. Only certain men were allowed to visit HQ."

"Informant used his own home as his headquarters throughout the occupation and kept all illegal material in a suitcase which never left his side. His plan if the police called was to lower this suitcase from a window into the garden of his next-door neighbour.

As regards the concealment of illegal material at the printing office, informant said that it would have been easy enough to hide anything among the masses of material in the office."

"At first security was exceedingly poor – e.g. as many as 20 or 30 men would attend for arms instruction, each bringing a bicycle and leaving it outside the premises! Agent forbade this and instructed all trainees that they should arrive on foot, in small groups and at different times.

On arrival in Rotterdam, agent found that only one central arms depot, containing the entire supply of arms, existed. Agent at once decentralised, in case of a razzia.

An agent should never know the address of his chief and should know as little of the organisation as is compatible with efficiency. (Agent says that an exception to this rule was to be found in the case of couriers, who, of necessity, knew several addresses.)"

"As far as possible he changed houses from time to time and had his set moved. This was always done by a girl, sometimes by Jos.

When the agent was going to transmit from a house where he was not known a password was used and at certain premises the safety signal was always used. At one time he was using the old Belgian Legation, which was inhabited only by a concierge and where he fitted up the set between the ceiling and the roof, thus working in complete concealment."

"With regard to the first four places mentioned, informant had nothing of interest to say. At the farm where he was living in Vlieden, there were four means of egress, and from his own room he had a very clear view of the surrounding countryside and could see for very long distances. He arranged with the farmer's son that if anything should happen while he was away from the farm, a message would be sent through to headquarters who would contact him by messenger. There were no other safety precautions and informant relied on the service of people in the organisation who quickly circulated news of enemy activities.

He had several hiding places, all well scattered, in outhouses and stables. At the headquarters at Deurne the smith was always working during the day, in the front of the house, and his wife worked at the back. At night the headquarters at Deurne was never used.

There was no material stored at headquarters, in the house, but arms and explosives were hidden in a waterproof box in the garden. Informant knew of no other material which was kept at the house."

"This man took the house over in his own name and allowed informant to live there. Bob and Meta lived in the house as a "jeune menage", informant passing himself off as Meta's brother. The neighbours accepted them without question. Nobody knew of this address except informant's reception committee chief. It was impossible to find hiding places in the house and they were always armed in the house and ready to repel any attack made upon them. The only security precaution taken was a vase of flowers placed in a particular position in the window which would indicate to any of the residents returning home that it was safe to enter."

"When the agent had an appointment at the second flat he would go there before the appointment and await the arrival of the person he was going to see. The safety signal used was that the hall of the flat, a very dark place, was kept in semi-darkness unless there was danger, in which case the electric light was lit, and could be seen from outside. It would have been normal for the light to be lit when someone was admitted to the flat, so that had any unwelcome visitors arrived before the appointment it would have been perfectly possible for the person coming for the appointment to see that there was danger."

"Only five people knew the H.Q. building – the organiser, the liaison officer, a girl courier, a girl secretary and a despatch rider."

"Informant's home after he left the 'safe house' in Rotterdam was a ground floor flat in a block. His friend Van Velzen knew the neighbours, who evinced no curiosity when informant arrived there. To them he was just another refractaire, and they did not talk. This also applied to the middle-aged couple whose flat it was. There were two exits from the apartment. Informant was unable to find a suitable hiding place in his room for incriminating material and hesitated to ask the owners of the flat. He therefore locked his codes in a metal box, which he placed, together with his other belongings, in a locked suitcase. He always locked the door of his room when going out and was always very alert and careful when leaving or returning to his home. He always called first at a neighbour's house before going home to find out if anything interesting had happened in the neighbourhood during his absence."

"Zwarte Wim once slept for three weeks in a different house every night because nobody dared to have him. He got his addresses from L.O. He asked them for 10 or 12 and used some as cover addresses and some to live in. He had no time to find addresses for himself."

"Together with the boy whom he was given as his assistant, he organised a system of guards for the various safe houses. They were four girls who cycled round the house reporting every car which appeared in the immediate neighbourhood. If all were well, they carried a handkerchief in their hand but, the absence of the handkerchief indicated danger. Informant made this arrangement bearing his security training at Group "B" in mind."

"They had to be very careful to keep the group as small as possible; when they made outside contacts, they never allowed outsiders to know where they were living or what their real names were. Appointments were always made away from their own homes.

Informant never made any really serious effort to conceal her materials and papers when she had them in her room, because she knew that there was no way of hiding them from any thorough search. She simply scattered them about the room, hidden under other objects."

"At the beginning private houses were always used for meetings, and when this was the case members always arrived singly and at different specified times, the leader, Erkens, always being the last to arrive. The safe houses were always the property of a personal friend of the organisation whom they knew they could trust. These people did not know exactly what was going on but realised that whatever and whoever they saw or heard, they must be discreet about it, and knew that in some way they were helping the resistance. Informant states that at these meetings cover stories were not arranged beforehand, but as soon as the members were assembled the first thing, they did was to arrange one, such as playing cards, etc. These safe houses were selected by all members, Captain Pieters acting as courier between the other members."

Internal Communications

Couriers

Girl couriers were used extensively by the Underground Movement, and indeed, they maintained 50% of internal communications. In general, couriers and the "black" telephone provided practically all internal communication facilities. The girls would travel about on bicycles, carrying verbal or written messages, and using as cover a pretended visit to relatives, or an expedition in search of food, milk, etc. They were not specially trained but acquitted themselves admirably of their tasks. In their own districts they were well-known, and their excursions aroused no interest or suspicion. Only in the later stages of the occupation did the Germans begin to stop and search women. Many cases were known in the later stages of women being stripped and thoroughly searched. Written messages were usually carried in the frames of bicycles or concealed in handbags or shopping baskets, or frequently in the lining of a costume. The messages were taken to a courier terminal point, where they were collected by another courier or cut-out. Most Regional Commanders maintained a separate courier service consisting of about 20 girls who covered their own particular areas on foot or on bicycles. An agent would thus only need to send his own personal courier with a message to the Headquarters of the Internal Communications Section, and the latter would then take on the responsibility of delivering the message to the addressee. The couriers were trained gradually by experience and worked out their own alibis. In the towns, many posed as housewives doing their daily shopping. Organisers were unanimous in their high praise of the girls' achievements and their courage and devotion. The girls frequently accepted missions which the men refused to undertake. The girls were not trained but relied on their thorough knowledge of local conditions and on their natural resource to get them through.

As a precautionary measure, the couriers were often rested for some considerable time whilst new couriers were used in their place. By this means no courier could learn too much about locations, nor did they become familiar figures in any one place for any length of time. Another precaution taken was that each courier had instructions to say that she did not know where to deliver the message if she were stopped and searched en route. Her story would be that she had been given a message by some unknown person with a request to deliver it to another person in the town or elsewhere at a fixed rendezvous. Each courier normally knew a number of addresses which were unknown to other couriers, and only the Chief of the Internal Communications Section would know all the addresses used. He always knew where each courier should be, and how long the courier's job should take, and if the courier did not return punctually a search was made. Couriers were sometimes arrested with their letters upon them, but the system worked sufficiently well in that no further arrests were made as a resuLieutenant In the case of an arrest, all addresses known by the courier arrested were warned and the people living there immediately moved elsewhere. Couriers frequently changed their clothes to confuse possible followers, and inconspicuous girls were chosen for the work. There was little risk of women being picked up in razzias.

Live letter-boxes were used as contact addresses and collecting points with the necessary security precautions (see Premises). Cut-outs were frequently used for the collection of messages left by couriers at these points. One very ingenious live letter-box was used by an agent at Apeldoorn, who obtained military information by having a group in every village responsible to a chief, who would collate the intelligence acquired by his group, place it in an envelope marked with a blue cross, but with no address, and send the courier to a small village near Apeldoorn where the courier would leave the envelope in the official letter-box at the post office. Envelopes were always deposited before 9.30 a.m. Between 9.30 a.m. and 10 a.m. the official responsible for the Post Office extracted the letters, put them aside, and the courier called at 10 a.m. at the Post Office and carried the messages away to the organiser's address. In this manner by 11 a.m. every day the organiser had in his possession up-to-date military information for the whole region. The courier who went with the information only knew they were to put the envelopes in the letter-box at the Post Office. The official at the Post Office only knew the courier who called to collect the envelopes, and he asked no questions. He had a perfect alibi, as he could always say he did not know who left the letters or for whom they were destined.

Personal Meetings

Much clandestine work was planned at personal meetings between agents who knew each other's addresses and called openly to discuss their work, but always with a suitable alibi, and having previously fixed the time and the reason for the meeting by telephone, employing veiled language. Meetings were very often arranged by telephone, using conventional phrases to indicate the time and place. Most meetings took place indoors, and when more than three or four people were to meet, suitable cover stories were always arranged collectively for all the people concerned. Some organisers, having fixed a meeting, took the precaution of sending a cut-out to transact business for them, providing him with the necessary means of identification. One method of arranging a meeting was to mail a business letter fixing a business appointment, but with the necessary conventions pre-arranged. This was, of course, only possible when the post functioned normally.

Post

Up to 1943, when the official post functioned normally, it was used as a means of intercommunication. After 1943, however, there were to all intents and purposes no facilities for public use except inside towns. In the early days of the occupation letters in connection with clandestine work were sent through the normal Post Office system, but veiled language was always used. Frequently the Post Office officials worked hand-in-glove with the Underground Movement. One service rendered by the Postmaster in a small town was the handling of correspondence addressed to a certain name, the addressee supposedly living at a boarding-house in the town. This correspondence was really destined for the local organiser. These letters were set aside for the organiser and collected by his courier. The Postmaster had never met the organiser, and only received his instructions from the courier. He was, however, very discreet, and never wanted to know what was going on.

A group in Rotterdam had a contact in the Post Office who handed over to them all the letters sent from civilians to SD Headquarters. There were sometimes 10 or 20 a day, usually letters of denunciation, which would be destroyed, the people denounced being warned. Any harmless letters were put into new envelopes and sent on.

If agents had recourse to the post, they usually had letters sent to accommodation addresses, so that their homes could not be traced.

Telephones

Telephones were used extensively prior to September 1944, when all lines were disconnected by the Germans except those in use by the Wehrmacht, the police, administration, hospitals etc. Conversation was in veiled language and most agents had some contact with the P.T.T. officials, who would warn them if their line was being tapped. In the small towns and in the country districts even when normal facilities no longer existed, Post Office officials were very helpful, and agents were allowed to use the official Post Office telephone in cases of emergency. If agents were wanted urgently, a contact called the Post Office, and the man in charge would send a message to the agent's home.

Black Telephone: After September 1944, when the normal telephone service was withdrawn from the general public, a "black" telephone exchange was installed in most of the principal towns and was worked by an NBS operator with the connivance of the telephone manager. There were in some towns up to 30 or 40 illegal extensions. One flaw in the system was that the telephone manager and the operator at the "black" exchange knew all the people who had access to the "black" telephone. The organisation controlling this secret telephone network was known as CID, and only one man in each town knew how to get in touch with its local representative. This telephone system was used freely, and in this way the Commandant of the NBS in Amsterdam received his orders by telephone from Prince Bernhard in clear from Almelo when this town was freed. The system was of great help to intercommunications and was even used in conjunction with W/T sets in the system of radio transmission by remote control which is discussed later. So secure was the "black" telephone that urgent letters could be read over the line from one town to the other

General

Trunk calls on local telephone lines, telegrams and the official postal services were avoided in principle, although most agents are unanimous in declaring that there were no signs of any form of censorship of correspondence. Trunk calls were, however, frequently tapped by the Germans, and this means of communication was therefore not utilised. One reason for not using the post when it did function was the delay involved, and the inefficiency of the postal services, which made receipt of a letter by post very uncertain. Dead letter-boxes were not used as most agents regarded them as unsafe. Codes and ciphers were rarely used for internal communications due to the delay entailed and, in most cases, to the limited staff available for cipher work. Routine messages were sent in veiled language by post, and couriers carried massages in clear or in veiled language. They sometimes carried important messages in code or reports in microphotograph form with all names and addresses in the report reproduced in code. In these cases, they were ignorant of the details of the messages they carried. Combinations were used for time and place conventions used to arrange a meeting. One method employed by a food controller was to send a veiled language letter by post announcing the place of the meeting, and later on send a bill of certain expenses in which certain figures would indicate the time of the meeting.

External Communications

Ninety per cent, if not more, of external communications was maintained by wireless transmission. Other methods were used but were relatively unimportant.

Innocent Letter seems to have been used very infrequently; some agents confessed to having forgotten their conventions, whilst others admitted having overlooked the possibility of using this method of communication. There was also a feeling that the strict censorship of foreign mail made this form of communication impracticable. In any case, postal facilities ceased to exist for the general public a long time before Holland was liberated. One agent, working through Holland into Germany, used Innocent Letters utilising Playfair conventions. Postcards reached London via Switzerland and Sweeden, in which countries he had been given addresses before leaving London, and they took about a month or three weeks to arrive. He never had a reply, but he learned subsequently from his Country Section that they had reached their destination. The messages were about 30 letters in length, and in order to post them in Germany it was necessary to produce all his papers at the Post Office. As his identity in Germany was "legal", the production of a sheaf of documents enabled him to post his mail. Another agent sent Innocent Letters into Sweden but never discovered if they arrived in London.

Pigeons were rarely used owing to the difficulty of housing them, and, although London often promised to despatch consignments of carrier pigeons to the Field, the promised consignments did not arrive. An agent in the Rotterdam area sent some messages by pigeon but he never heard if they reached England. Altogether he sent about 20 pigeons carrying microphotographs. On one occasion he sent 10 pigeons, each carrying the same picture of the defences of the North Sea coast of Holland.

Some information was smuggled in and out of the country by courier lines working through Belgium and France into Switzerland, and after D-Day in France by infiltrating and exfiltrating agents through the battlefronts. Information smuggled through in this way was normally in the form of microphotographs sewn into the lining of the agent's coats. The editor of the underground press in The Hague had a line of communication with Switzerland which ran from Paris. Couriers carrying false German papers would travel by train to Paris and there get in touch with a former K.L.M. colleague of the editor who was able to send them on by train to within 40 km. of the Swiss frontier which they crossed on foot. Some agents with wives and families in Belgium or France had permits to pass backwards and forwards between the two countries and were thus able to pass communications through contacts in France and Belgium to England.

Other means of external communication were never actively sought after, for it was always possible in the underground movement to link up with W/T operators almost anywhere. Even when they had no direct communication with England, the groups knew that constant radio contact was maintained and knew how to get messages passed to a W/T operator if it was required to send a message to England. When a group did want to get in touch with England, they simply wrote out the message en clair and handed it in to a contact who was in touch with the W/T operator. Replies would frequently be passed back to them on the "black" telephone.

Wireless Transmission

Some aspects of the W/T operator's difficulties in the matter of W/T sites have already been dealt with under "Premises". The question of guards and D/F-ing will now be discussed.

In general, the same precautions as in use elsewhere were practised in Holland, namely frequent change of site, duration of sked reduced to a minimum, bodyguard or team of watchers, spare sets installed for use at site, and transport of set and accessories effected when necessary by couriers.

In view of the fact that many operators were nervous of D/F-ing, a guard armed with Sten or pistol would often stay in the room during the sked. There was usually someone on watch outside the house during transmission, generally patrolling on a bicycle and with someone in the house looking out of the window for a signal in case of danger. In spite of these precautions, and in spite of being on the air for only 20 minutes or half an hour for each sked, operators were frequently D/F-ed in a very short time. It was not always possible, however, to obtain a sufficient number of people to form a team, and operators were often obliged to rely on their own personal couriers for protection. In these cases, the couriers would leave the premises and wander about outside. On the arrival of anything suspicious, the courier would re-enter the premises at once with a key and would warn the operator, who usually had a hiding place for his set. In country districts the operator would often be assisted by only one person, and he and his bodyguard would frequently live together in the same house. Sets would always be transported by girl couriers, who were invaluable in this respect.

If caught, they would merely say that they did not know what they were carrying.

It was an accepted principle of underground life that reports should be circulated immediately on any suspicious activity on the part of the Germans, such as a concentration of vehicles or anything which might possibly have some connection with D/F-ing. By means of this intelligence service operators were warned immediately there was any danger.

Enemy D/F-ing activity varied from place to place. In the early days of the occupation, and even up to the end of 1943, it was comparatively rare, but in 1944 it grew in intensity and reached its peak in early 1945. Activity in the Hague and Amsterdam in 1944 and 1945 was intense, whereas in Rotterdam, even in 1945, only six to eight cars were operating. In the country districts, notably in the Overijssel, there was little, if any, activity. In the Autumn of 1944, there were only about 12 D/F cars in North and South Holland and the Utrecht area, but this area was very efficiently covered by them.

The cars were often Wehrmacht cars or civilian armoured vehicles camouflaged as ambulances or laundry-vans. The cars' number plates were changed almost daily. The cars were always petrol-driven and worked in two's and three's, frequently drawing a characteristic trailer behind them. Inevitably, both cars and drivers became known to the underground intelligence service who reported changes in number plates or other details to the appropriate quarter immediately. In this way their presence in any locality was immediately notified, and they were not much feared, provided the operator worked with a bodyguard and had a place where he could quickly hide his set and material.

Another form of D/F activity was the portable apparatus carried about by Luftwaffe personnel, who could be seen wandering in the streets with earphones and suspicious-looking suitcases.

In general, there was no serious D/F-ing before December 1944, but when the Germans first began on a big scale, they caught quite a lot of operators napping.

The following extract on D/F-ing is of interest:

"The agent had considerable difficulty in achieving a state of security from the point of view of safe houses, as these were difficult to obtain. He was transmitting from the same place for days at a time without changing the address and at one time was transmitting for 4 months (September to December 1944) from the Belgian Legation. However, as far as possible he did move about, although this was always very much limited by the lack of accommodation. Partly as a result of this and partly because he found home station tended to prolong the skeds unduly, he was D/F-ed on three occasions that he knows of. The first time (in September 1944) was while he was working in the Belgian Legation and a D/F car was observed in the vicinity by someone looking from the window. He stopped transmitting and that was the end of that. On the second occasion (in December 1944) he was still in the Belgian Legation and a D/F car stopped at the end of the street. A Dutch policeman was going into each house along the street, and he decided that to stop would have betrayed to the listener in the car the fact that the man was entering the house where the set was, so he continued to transmit and as he was in a completely concealed place he was not found. About half an hour later, when he had finished his sked and gone, five Germans in civilian clothes came and searched the house and spent about an hour doing so, including a visit to the roof where they found several pre-war serials, but not the agents own, which was concealed in the same place as the set.

"About a fortnight later, the agent was sending from another house in a street of 5 houses. He had been using the same signal plan for nearly five months, but this was the first time he had used the house. About ten minutes after he come on the air the immediate vicinity was surrounded by 5 D/F cars and 75 Grüne Polizei. They began to search the five houses from the other end of the street, and they went about it very thoroughly indeed, practically pulling the first four houses to pieces. The agent had only time to hide his set under some coal. The search began at about ten past 11 in the morning, and at about 3 o'clock in the afternoon the agent took his hat and coat and went out. One of the policemen asked him where he was going, and he said he was going to work and was allowed to continue. Although they searched the ground floor of the house where the agent was, for some reason they did not go upstairs and so the set was not found and the next day the organisation was able to move it elsewhere. The agent stopped transmitting on the signal plan because he knew that a new one was on the way, and he was able to start the new plan five days later. He was never again D/F-ed as far as he knows.

"At one time the agent tried to use guards outside the house from which he was transmitting, but he found that these people were constantly interrupting his skeds with false alarms about slow-moving cars and so he abandoned this method and merely used a guard in the house, looking out of the window."

Coding

In general, organisers did the coding themselves, using their own conventions, or they entrusted this work to reliable girl couriers. The operator used his conventions only for personal messages. Messages, therefore, arrived and left the W/T operator in cipher and he was thus ignorant of their contents. O.T.P. cipher was used and was quite satisfactory. Some agents burnt all copies of messages immediately after despatch or receipt and had no difficulty in referring back to previous messages as they had memorised the content. Others kept copies long enough for a repetition to be provided if required. Copies were kept for five to fourteen days and then destroyed, but in most cases some precautions were taken against a sudden search, and if possible, a fire would be available to burn both messages and code. One agent always had an incendiary bomb handy when decoding or encoding. In a few cases, where a really secure hiding place could be found, all copies of messages were kept.

Inter-Communication

Organisers kept in touch with their operators by means of a courier service, by legal or illegal telephone, or by each visiting a contact address known to both. A courier would bring the organiser's already enciphered messages to a contact address and the operator's personal courier or bodyguard would collect them and leave at the address any incoming messages, also in cipher. Some organisers lived in the same house or flat as their operators, or, when this was not so, visited their operators quite openly.

General

In most parts of Holland, there was no electricity in flats or private houses after September 1944, and even before that current was not always available. Batteries were, therefore, used and some difficulty was experienced in getting them re-charged. Establishments still using electricity, such as hospitals, breweries, bakeries etc., were contacted, and with their help batteries were re-charged. Girl couriers carried the sets and batteries from place to place – but always suitably camouflaged, as the operational suitcase was well-known to the Germans. Later, pedal generators were dropped, but in many cases, they arrived too late to be of assistance.

The following is an extract from a report received from an organiser in Amsterdam:

"There was no current in Amsterdam after October except in hospitals and certain big buildings. The batteries were charged with steam generators, bicycle generators or from hospitals. It was dangerous, though, to tap electricity mains as this could be detected. However, they had special contacts with the electricity company. They applied for generators from England in October and did not get them until

March. Three generators were sent but they were too heavy and were smashed on landing. The most suitable accumulator sent out was a British accumulator and that had stamped on it "Not to be dropped", and this always arrived in the best condition. They had to buy one-tenth of their accumulators before these began to arrive from England. It was very difficult to buy them on the spot. Some were stolen from the Germans and some from telephone offices. Operators often pointed out that the technical side of their work was far more difficult than the security side. Certain operators stated that skeds fixed for transmission after 5 or 6 o'clock in the evening were inconvenient, especially in winter, owing to the difficult conditions under which they worked. It was suggested that the best time for skeds would have been between 8 a.m. and 4 p.m."

T.D. System

In the Autumn of 1944, when the Germans began to intensify their D/F-ing activity, certain operators asked England for suggestions and were told to go out into the country. This, in the opinion of the operators, was one of the worst things to do, as the D/F-ing car would find the area where they were operating and then the police would throw a cordon round and there would be no chance for the operator as there would be so few houses in the area to be searched. On the other hand, in the town the D/F-ing cars would only track the operator down to a block of flats and it would take the police so long to search everyone that the operator would have plenty of time to conceal his set.

As an answer to D/F-ing, the T.D. system was introduced. They built up their own telephone exchange to which each W/T set was connected. This enabled an operator to sit in a room and tap out a message which would actually go out on a set situated some distance away. The set was tuned by somebody on the spot. These secret lines were connected partly by P.T.T. experts and partly by the electricity company, neither knowing exactly what the other was doing. Where there were existing telephone lines these were used but diverted so as not to go through the central exchange. Sometimes new cables had to be laid and, as most of the lines had been disconnected, some had to be reconnected. This special secret telephone exchange was used in the Amsterdam area instead of the ordinary underground exchange, as they expected the latter might be blown and they did not want to be without communications. With the T.D. system it was possible for each set in a different part of the city to work in rotation for say, five minutes. This completely foxed the German D/F-ing cars.

A full report on the T.D. system is attached.

T.D. in Holland

In Holland it was found that in many cases it was not possible for a W/T operator to work in the country. The country is so densely populated that it is almost impossible for an operator to work or live in the country without getting known. People began to talk – probably with no wrong intention – but in the end it would reach the ears of an informer. Travelling was also very difficult, and couriers making regular journeys to and from the operator and his chief found it harder and harder to find suitable cover for these journeys. For these reasons many operators were forced to work in towns. Here an operator was able to work quite successfully until the end of 1944, when the Germans improved their methods of D/F-ing to such an extent that it was considered unsafe to be on the air for more than 10 minutes. At the same time the traffic increased daily and, although there was a sufficient number of houses from which an operator could transmit, it was found impossible to pass all the traffic during the short time an operator could be on the air, even if he worked two or three times a day. The danger from D/F-ing was overcome by having an efficient protection service which was able to give danger signals to the operator well in time to prevent the risk of arrest, but 10 minutes per sked was too short a time, and the traffic to be sent began piling up more and more.

To meet this difficulty the following system, called the Transmission Dispersal System, was used:

Several transmitters were ready to go on the air at the same time from different places with the keys substituted by relays which were worked from one central point. These transmitters were tuned by people specially trained in this work who were in constant telephonic communication with the W/T operator at the central point during each sked. The T.D. operators would be at their posts an hour before sked time and would then ring up the W/T operator for their instructions. The W/T operator would work out his sked beforehand, deciding on which frequencies, for how long and from which T.D. points he would transmit. Each T.D. operator was supplied with a number of crystals and, according to the instructions he received from the W/T operator, would tune up his set. Five T.D. stations were prepared, and these would be tuned as follows:

Stations A. and B., to Frequency 1.
Stations C. and D., to Frequency 2.
Station E., to Frequency 3.

Station A was as far as possible from Station B. and Station C. was as far as possible from Station D. At sked time the W/T operator from the central point would begin his transmission, using Frequency 1. From Station A. After about 5 minutes he would switch over to Station B., using the same Frequency. A few minutes later he would switch over to Station C., using Frequency 2., followed by Station D., also on Frequency 2. In the meantime, Stations A. and B. would retune their sets to Frequency 4. The W/T operator at the central point, after having worked for 10 to 15 minutes on Frequency 2. – one half of the time from Station C., and the other half from Station D. – would switch back to Station A. and continue transmitting on Frequency 4. Station E., tuned to Frequency 3., would be kept in reserve. In this way the traffic was being sent without interruption but from a different part of the town every five minutes, with a change of frequency every 10 minutes. Thus, a sked of, say, 40 minutes could be worked with very little danger from D/F-ing.

Only one set of wires was laid to the T.D. stations and these had to be used both for telephoning to and from the central point and for taking the relay. For this reason, a private, five-line exchange had to be installed. If the wires had passed through the ordinary exchange, the A.C. current passing through when being used for relay would have caused great interference. Having tuned up their sets, the T.D. operators would listen in on the telephone and, as soon as they heard the loud hum denoting that the relay had been switched on to their particular sets, they immediately switched the connection over to "Send". They would go on listening until they heard the hum cease, when they knew their set was no longer being used. According to arrangements previously made, the T.D. operator would then retune his set to a new frequency and listen once again for the sign that his set was again on the air.

There was a broadcast receiver working at the central point which was tuned in to the frequency on which the W/T operator was sending. Thus, the operator would listen in to his own traffic which was being transmitted from the T.D. station, and in this way, he could be sure, when changing from one station to another, both working on the same frequency, that the T.D. operator had not omitted to switch his set on. He could also check his own keying. The various T.D. addresses were guarded as normal W/T addresses, but, as the time worked from each address was very short, the T.D. operators who had to tune the sets were not exposed to much danger. In order to speed up traffic as much as possible, a second broadcast receiver was also fitted up at the central point and this was tuned up to Home Station, so that the latter could "break-in" at any time during transmissions.

The technical side of T.D. was not very complicated. At the central point a power pack of a 3/II set was used and from it was tapped 90 v. A.C. which was passed over the telephone line to the relay point together with a normal telephone apparatus. At the relay point the inductor coil of the relay was connected parallel to the telephone on the line. This line was, therefore, used for normal telephone conversations as well as for the relay.

Security Precautions, Enemy C.E. and Casualties

Security Precautions

Some idea will already have been gained regarding the various security measures adopted by the Underground Movement and made necessary by German C.E. activities. In the early days of the occupation and during the early struggles of the Resistance Movement, security was almost negligible, and most groups, although taking common-sense precautions, had no knowledge of the most elementary rules of security. Few groups, if any, had at any time during the occupation any definite rules which were observed by all members, but agents gradually became security-minded, the process being assisted and accelerated by the knowledge of casualties sustained in movements where few precautions were taken, and also by personal experience of narrow escapes.

There came into existence, therefore, a list of "do's" and "don'ts" for the underground worker, principles being generally accepted and practised by most agents. Agents would try and be discreet and know as few people as possible, and then only by their field names. Real names were avoided and addresses as far as possible kept secret. Couriers were, of course, always in possession of a number of addresses, but it was forbidden to carry lists of names or addresses or, in fact any incriminating material at all unless absolutely necessary. Agents were not expected to carry arms if this could be avoided. Individual agents were not given information more than was necessary for the efficient handling of their immediate task and were not expected to find things out which did not concern them. The agents became expert in the use of cover stories and alibis. Precautions used in connection with premises have already been discussed, but one rule which was generally followed for meeting was to reduce the number of people convened to a minimum and to take care in arriving and leaving the meeting place on account of possible surveillance. Punctuality was always stressed for personal meetings.

Agents usually had a hideout somewhere where they could retire in comparative safety, and whose whereabouts was known only to a few people. Visits to agents' homes were discouraged, and hiding-places and means of quick get-away in case of trouble were always considered when premises were chosen. An attempt was made to keep the groups as small as possible, and recruits had to be vouched for before being accepted. Some groups had a small security section, numbering about a dozen men, who made it their job to keep watch over enemy activities, and who were responsible for the security of the organisation. These men acquired intelligence which would be useful in the self-preservation of resistance members. For this purpose, a number of them were installed in various police, SD and Gestapo offices, and in this way the Underground was always warned in advance of impending raids, controls, arrests etc. Also, there was a general warning system whereby members passed on any information relating to casualties of any sort which were the result of any form of enemy activity, and because of this grape-vine system the Underground workers usually contrived to be just one jump ahead of the enemy police.

One very definite rule which was observed by everybody was that in case of arrest, the person taken by the police would endeavour to keep silent for at least 48 hours, and thus give his colleagues time to make their own get-away, or if possible, to make arrangements for the release of the arrested person.

Enemy C.E.: Controls

Snap controls carried out by one or the other of the enemy C.E. bodies already mentioned, often assisted by the Dutch Police or Landwacht, were frequently encountered in the cities. If the control was effected by Dutch Police alone, irregularities were often overlooked, but if German or NSB police were present this was not likely. There was no point in trying to avoid the controls as they were to be found everywhere, on bridges, main streets, road crossings, stations and on trains. One had no idea where they were likely to take place. The towns were patrolled by policemen on foot and in cars, but less of them in the centre of the town than in the outskirts. The personnel employed sometimes worked in civilian clothes but usually there would be a uniformed soldier or SD man working with them. The controls operated mainly for obtaining forced labour for Germany. Papers, even if in order, were often disregarded, and people arrested and deported for no reason at all. A lot depended on the individual who effected the control.

Body searches were not thorough, weapons and W/T sets being objects which most interested the Germans. Certain people would be picked out for a thorough search and completely stripped. Anybody carrying arms was likely to be shot immediately.

Controls in the trains were frequent. Sometimes they would pick out one person in each compartment and go over his papers very thoroughly, but sometimes they would just pass along the carriages glancing at the papers of everyone in each compartment and take no further action.

Controls differed widely, some being dangerously efficient, others being merely routine verifications of papers, which were often only subjected to cursory examination. Some agents spent months in the field without ever being controlled at all, and outside the towns few controls were ever encountered except at strategic points on main roads or near Wehrmacht camps or barracks.

The following incidents illustrate different types of controls encountered:

1) Once, when returning from a dropping operation carrying compromising material in the form of a piece of silk and a pistol concealed in a basket of onions, they had to pass through a control. This was about 8 a.m. and when the Germans stopped them and asked them for their papers, they were suspicious, and asked why they were so dirty. They merely replied that they had been collecting onions and were allowed to pass.

2) On another occasion, when travelling by car from the Hague to Rotterdam together with certain high officials in the Underground Movement on their way to see the head of Resistance for All Holland, they were stopped by a control which had happened to include the Chief of the Gestapo in the Hague. They were immediately told to alight from the car and were separated and interrogated in turn for about half-an-hour, being asked who they were, what they were doing and how they all came to be together in a car. They had fortunately prepared a cover story for just such an emergency, and it was that they had all separately asked for a lift. After half-an-hour's questioning they were permitted to pass on, but not before the driver had received a warning about giving strange people lifts, being told that had one of the passengers been revealed as a terrorist, the whole lot of them would have been shot.

3) Informant was several times controlled, sometimes while carrying illegal papers. She always carried such papers round her waist, and since she was never made to strip, these were never discovered. Once or twice controls were very thorough indeed and the police felt all her pockets and examined her papers very carefully, holding them up

to the light and studying the signature and watermark. She always carried a forged identity card for a non-Jewish person. At first, she was nervous that her appearance might betray her Jewish origin, but although during such controls the police were particularly on the look-out for Jews, she was never suspected.

Enemy C.E.: Razzias

In the later stages of the occupation there were thousands of evacuees in the cities, with consequent difficulties for the Germans in respect of controlling papers of all kinds, especially temporary passes. The job was too much for the Germans, and although the Grüne Polizei and especially the Fleming and Dutch SD were still very dangerous, control of individuals ceased and mass raids and razzias commenced in late 1944 and early 1945. No warning with regard to these raids was possible. The city would be surrounded, and all young men driven to the market place. Papers and explanations were disregarded, and only men working for the Germans were released. The employers of these men had to come themselves to the spot and vouch for their employees. The men arrested were deported to Germany, but many afterwards returned, having escaped. Foreign workers were apparently not to rigidly supervised.

If a suspect was taken in a razzia and removed to Police Headquarters he would be stripped, thoroughly searched, and interrogated. The raids were usually made by Dutch Police supervised and controlled by SD and Grüne Polizei.

Enemy C.E.: House searches

House-to-house searches were frequent. Sometimes whole streets of houses were blocked and cordoned off, and frequently the Germans would without warning surround and search a building which they had under supervision. People whose papers were not in order would be sent to Germany. Houses would often be selected at random on the pretext that some proof existed of the occupants' illegal activities, and the house would be subjected to a very thorough search. Most of these house searches were the result of W/T activity in the area.

Enemy C.E.: Informers and Street Watchers

The Germans made use of Dutch informers up to September 1944, but afterwards no Dutchmen would work for them in view of the then certain victory of the Allies. Most informers were NSB members and were known by sight to the Underground workers. They were often employed as street watchers to report anything suspicious that they noticed. They were also used to listen to conversations in trains or trams and in all public places. Many were used to watch certain houses and follow the people who came out. These informers counted among them many women and former Underground workers who had been turned by the Germans. They were used everywhere in official positions, in the Police, and generally in places where their work would permit them to overhear conversations and observe any unusual behaviour.

They were to be found among the peasants and farmers as well as in the towns. Quite a number of policemen were acting as informers because of their NSB tendencies, and members of the Landwacht kept their eyes open and were always ready to denounce people to the Gestapo. One instant of a peasant's activities is the case of a man living near Deurne who was well known by everybody as a man who had denounced to the Germans certain people who had looked after British airmen and removed parachute silk for their own use. He had threatened to denounce others but having mentioned his opinions to an acquaintance who happened to be a member of the organisation, he was subsequently liquidated.

Enemy C.E.: Surveillance

Plain clothes men of the NSB, Landwacht, SD or even Dutch Police were used for this work but were apparently badly trained and not particularly effective. Few agents report cases of being followed, although certain arrests were made as a result of this form of C.E. activity. One agent reports that followers often picked him up outside his house or office, and when he knew that he was followed he would give up any subversive work he had planned for that day. The agent does not think more than two people were ever employed to follow him and he was always able to pick them out, and even came to recognise them when he saw them again. The methods employed by followers rendered them rather conspicuous. For example, one man would stand on a street corner watching a building for a long time, and another man would come up to him and ask him for a light for his cigarette. The first man would then go away, and his place would be taken by the newcomer. It was not difficult to shake them off once having noticed that followers were on the trial.

The hide-out of a Resistance chief in Rotterdam was once discovered through a plain clothes policeman following a girl courier who went to the house with a message straight from the correspondence address, where she has been picked up by watchers.

Enemy C.E.: Agents provocateurs

Agents provocateurs were used extensively. They went round offering people arms and false papers and arrested those who accepted their offer. A favourite trick was to cycle beside girls and engage them in conversation in connection with Underground work. More than one unwary courier has been arrested as a result of indiscreet conversation. The Germans frequently used Dutch Jews for this work, and in Utrecht one young Jew was notorious for his A.P. activities. He had been taken under the protection of the German Commandant who, like many of the SD men, was known to be a homosexual. This young Jew acted as A.P., informer and spy for the Germans.

Enemy C.E.: Impersonation

Very few cases of impersonation were known, but this was a method used by many enemy C.E. personnel to trap the unwary. A German agent closely resembling a prominent Underground worker and on a bogus mission would arrive in a town and try to make contact with the Resistance Movement. The method sometimes succeeded and resulted in a number of arrests. The following case was possibly a German attempt at impersonation: A farmer who was harbouring refractaires received a visit from two men, one of whom stated he was Van Kleffens, Minister of Foreign Affairs. The other man gave only the name Jan. They requested introduction to Resistance leaders, and a woman from Utrecht introduced the two men to a local W/T operator, who is said to have recognised Van Kleffens from a photograph he had previously seen. A local organiser later met Jan, and there was some talk of London methods and personalities, but the organiser was not convinced of Jan's sincerity. The latter stated he was running an escape line. The organiser contacted London and received the news that Van Kleffens was not in Holland. He therefore made arrangements to liquidate both Van Kleffens and Jan at a future rendez-vous, but neither turned up, and were not heard of again.

Enemy C.E.: Penetration

Methods of penetration of Underground organisations were many and varied. Impersonation was one method which has already been discussed. Another way of getting on the inside of a subversive group was to employ Dutchmen who, through bad recruiting on the part of the Underground movement, became members of a group and subsequently betrayed its members to the police. Fortunately, although the lower levels were often penetrated by this method, security was sufficiently good to prevent the penetration going any higher.

There were many cases of Dutchmen having fallen foul of the police for minor offences being blackmailed and forced to act as police spies for penetration activities. The most successful agents used by the Germans for penetration were former Underground workers who had been caught, tortured and forced to rejoin their organisation after having been released from prison. One man caught by the SD and turned, sat in public places and quietly and unobtrusively pointed out former colleagues to the German police. Among the cases of released agents used by the Germans for penetration were those of a girl courier who had been in prison for some weeks and who was "persuaded" by the German prison Commandant to co-operate, and a man who was kept in prison for 18 months and who embarked on subversive work immediately on his release. Both rejoined their groups and were afterwards instrumental in turning over to the Germans many former colleagues.

The practice in the Underground Movement of employing SD contacts to provide them with information on German activity was often dangerous, as these contacts worked in both directions, and there was much leakage of information. Thanks to some of these bad contacts the SD knew more about the organisation than was generally supposed. On one occasion there was a disastrous raid on a Gestapo Headquarters which, incidentally, had for object the theft of the lists of Dutch informers used by the Gestapo. This raid was expected by the Gestapo, the proof being that whereas normally only two or three guards were posted there at night, on the occasion of the raid there was a strong guard, and everything had been done to receive visitors. Members of the group involved in the raid were certain that there was treachery of some kind, and the organiser must also have suspected it, hence the raid to acquire information from Gestapo records.

A full report on the penetration of SOE set-up in Holland from June 1942 to December 1943 is attached and shows how organisers and W/T operators were caught and their sets and radio plans used by the Germans.

Casualties

Before September 1944 most casualties were sustained by results of agents' provocateurs activity, informers gaining information from talkative and indiscreet agents, and by controls falling accidentally upon a resistance member with some tell-tale material on his person. If one man was arrested it usually resulted in a number of other arrests although the Germans were not particularly good at following up clues and facts. They would arrest someone carrying a pistol and question him on that, but never ask him about his papers. On the whole, Resistance members were very imprudent. Strict orders were issued with regard to indiscreet talk, but without avail. Everybody talked far too much, and finally full-time workers were threatened with death for indiscreet disclosures.

One very real danger was that the principle of one man one job was entirely ignored, with the result that in a small village would be found about 4 men engaged on a multiplicity of Resistance activities such as housing escapees, obtaining papers, doing Reception Committee work, sabotage etc. It was unavoidable under the circumstances that the men became well known not only to their neighbours but to police informers.

Before September 1944 more care was taken in recruiting and full information was obtained on potential recruits, but after September a flood of people came in to be enrolled and no check was possible. It was during this period that penetration became a very real danger.

Heavy casualties were suffered in the Autumn of 1944, when there were rumours everywhere that the Allies were 10 kms away from almost every town in Holland. Resistance groups threw caution to the winds and rose in open revoLieutenant Unfortunately, although there was a good stock of explosives, the arms available were insufficient to protect the Resistance groups from German attacks, and the revolt was suppressed with heavy casualties. It was not thought that the Germans had started the rumours of Allied successes, but Underground workers put all the blame on the BBC and Radio Oranje for broadcasting the official view that by October Holland would be free. Most of the subsequent casualties were due to repercussions from the September rising. Many men had been arrested, some had talked, and the unavoidable chain of clues led on to still more arrests.

Many casualties were the direct result of information obtained by the interrogation of arrested agents; the usual methods were employed. Among the various methods already mentioned which were adopted by the enemy, penetration was responsible for a big proportion of casualties, but bad luck played a big part also. There were many cases of police accidentally stumbling on some clue which led to a chain of arrests. For example, an agent taken in a razzia and selected out of hundreds for close search and interrogation; an agent unwittingly living in the same house as a suspect and being found in possession of incriminating material when the house was searched; a farmhouse as H.Q. being visited as the result of an investigation of clandestine slaughter of cattle. One group of agents was arrested as the result of incriminating material being found in the debris of their burned-out premises after an air raid.

Casualties were also sometimes caused through panic. An agent stopped at a control, on being questioned as to his papers would take off at high speed with the police after him, and frequently nervous agents would begin to shoot on the first sign of a house search, though these house searches were often routine measures, and a plausible alibi would have sufficed.

Unfortunately, the Germans were often assisted in their C.E. work by the agent's bad security and, in many cases, sheer bravado. As already stated, a sort of "grapevine" information service existed in the Underground Movement which enabled news of enemy activity to be very rapidly passed round, but many cases were known of people refusing to take evasive action on receipt of a warning, through bravado and with disastrous consequences. The most common security mistakes made were: premises used too often and without proper precautions or safety signals; carrying arms unnecessarily; being in possession of incriminating written material, lists of addresses etc.; and not having carefully concealed incriminating material in houses or flats. Indiscretion in conversation was prevalent and one agent was arrested after a public discussion he had had on the subject of BBC news items. Contact in spite of warning with already suspected persons, assisting Jews and too open complicity in Black Market transactions also had disastrous consequences. One agent was arrested for living too near a prison camp on the grounds that he was smuggling information into the prison and attempting to arrange the escape of certain prisoners.

Bad recruiting was, of course, responsible for many casualties, but the use of untrained couriers also resulted in casualties. One girl sent with a message and without proper means of finding the addressee called at a strange house to make enquiries, and walked straight into a Gestapo Headquarters, where she was interrogated, searched and arrested with the message on her.

Some incredibly foolish things were done. In one case an arms dump was located in a hut on a football ground, and a note pinned on the gate stating where the key could be found for obtaining entrance. This attracted the attention of the police, who gained admittance and discovered the arms dump. In another case the organiser attended a Reception Committee, his presence being entirely unnecessary and extremely dangerous. He was wearing at the time a pair of Canadian parachute boots, and when returning from the reception he, together with 4 other people travelling in the same car were stopped by a routine control who examined their papers. The occupants of the car had no alibi to explain their journey together and all 5 occupants of the car were carrying doctor's papers, which fact was sufficient to arouse the suspicions of the police, and the party was interrogated more fully, with unpleasant results.

The following is an account of the ill-fated meeting in Utrecht in November 1944 when over a dozen prominent Resistance chiefs were arrested:

The Utrecht NBS decided that in view of certain difficulties which existed in the region, especially with regard to friction between OD and KP, the dual command of the area, shared by Destembres and Cor, should be replaced by a sole Commander-in-Chief, in the person of Krikke, who in turn appointed Destembres chief of civil administration and Cor chief of sabotage. Krikke was an ex-regular colonel of the Dutch Colonial Army, and as such was not the ideal person to command a subversive organisation. He was a thoroughly reliable man but had no training or background for this particular type of work. He insisted, immediately he took command, on meeting personally all the district commanders, and ordered a meeting in Utrecht at which all the district commanders were ordered to be present, together with prominent Utrecht staff officers including Cor and Destembres, and at which meeting *Cubbing* was also present.

Informant pointed out to Krikke that the meeting presented very real dangers and that for security reasons he did not wish to attend. In this he was backed up by *Cubbing*. Krikke, however, was adamant, and the meeting was therefore convened. It took place on 22nd November 1944, in a private room allotted to Krikke at the offices of the Chamber of Commerce in Utrecht. Although work was going on in the offices of the Chamber of Commerce, nobody knew that a meeting was taking place with the exception of the director's secretary, who had been warned about the meeting 30 minutes before it was due to commence.

Fortunately for some members of the group, they arrived late and were able to make off without entering the building and being taken by the Germans. Unfortunately for the others, they arrived on time, and five minutes after the meeting had begun, the SD surrounded the premises and arrested all those present. The only people to escape were *Cubbing* and one other person (name unknown), who hid in a cupboard and made their escape at night over the roofs.

According to informant, the district commanders were summoned to the meeting by written messages in clear, carried by couriers who took the messages to the addresses of the district commanders. Informant states that, in his opinion, the SD found out about the meeting because a girl courier carrying one of these messages was sent to Veenendaal to warn one of the district commanders that he was expected to attend. On arrival at Veenendaal, not being certain of the exact address of the district commander, she enquired at the house of a stranger for information as to his whereabouts. The house at the moment was either being searched by the SD or was a house which had been requisitioned by them, because immediately the courier knocked at the door, she was confronted by uniformed SD who arrested her, searched her, found the written message and possibly found on her the address of other members due to attend the meeting. Whatever were the true facts, it appears certain that the meeting place was betrayed to the Germans by an insecure means of internal communication.

Note on the activities of Abwehr IIIF, The Hague, against S.O.E.
This note on the activities of Abteilung IIIF, The Hague, is not intended to constitute a full report, which could only be prepared against all the available S.O.E. records on the activities in Holland, and, more important still, against the whole of W/T traffic which has passed between this country and Holland. The note is slender and gives no more than an indication of the methods employed and the problems with which both sides were faced; it does, however, illustrate certain points which may be useful in conducting other activities from this end and some lessons can be learned from its perusal. During the period under review a battle was being fought between S.O.E., who were engaged in setting up a secret army in Holland, and Abteilung IIIF of The Hague, who were engaged in frustrating that enterprise. The German objective was, not only to defeat the particular enterprise in which the British had embarked but also to penetrate, control and preserve the organisation which was being set up in order to ensure that Allied activities would not be diverted into other less well-known channels; in this endeavour Abteilung IIIF had a very considerable measure of success.

The S.O.E. Project
In June of 1942 a certain Johannes and a W/T operator to whom he was attached arrived in Holland. Johannes had been sent to contact O.D., an indigenous loyalist organisation. He was to tell its leaders that he had come from a joint Dutch/British mission and was to disclose to them the "Plan for Holland" which had been worked out. He was to obtain their comments upon this plan and to emphasise that the Dutch Government in London had approved it in principle and expected it to be accepted in substance. After introducing himself to the leaders

of the O.D., Johannes was to make contact with its various sub-groups operating throughout the country. Johannes was to report to London and London was to send out trained organiser instructors to the groups as and when Johannes reported they were ready to receive them. The members of the secret army were thus to be recruited from the O.D., but once so recruited they were to be debarred from their previous activities and were thereafter to regard themselves as part of a separate organisation controlled from London. For the purpose of carrying out this mission Johannes had to organise reception committees for the weapons and supplies and additional personnel which were to be sent. Such was the ambitious plan and during the next 18 months the whole of S.O.E. activities in Holland were directed towards making it a success. Its failure at the end of that period would mean the failure of by far the greater proportion of Allied activities against Holland directed from London.

As events have shown the plan had in it a flaw which proved fatal. If Johannes or the man sent to relieve him were to be captured and turned round the plan would not merely be defeated but might be successfully used by the Germans for the penetration of the O.D. itself. The way was opened for a German agent of Abteilung IIIF, not merely to pose as an Allied agent, but to do so with all the authority and character of an S.O.E. agent in direct touch with, and under orders from, London.

The Organisation of Abwehr IIIF
Abwehr IIIF was the organisation whose business it was to counter such Allied activities in Holland. Two of the principal officers responsible for penetration work were Hauptmann Ernst Keisewetter, aka Baden, and Oberstleutenant Giskes, aka Gerhard. Keisewetter had been in the Balkans and joined the Abwehr in Holland in about April 1942.

He was a German and in peacetime was owner of a glove factory in Erfurt. Oberstleutnant Giskes, on the other hand, was a German professional soldier. Prominent also was Huntermann, aka Huetner, known in the office as "the Englishman". This man, who was a shipping agent on the West Coast of Africa before the war, appears to have directed the activities of a certain Kupp and Van Vliet and to have controlled the working of the transmitters dropped in Holland which came under Abwehr control, of which wireless links there were a number; in all ten different lines were maintained on this traffic and were kept up for approximately eighteen months, being finally closed down in February 1944. Under Huntermann were a number of characters who worked outside the office and performed the actual task of making contact with members of resistance with a view to penetrating the organisations for which they were working. The principal among these were Van Vliet, a Dutchman, and Arnaud, a German who appears to masquerade as a Dane and who had worked for the Abwehr since 1939. Posing as a member of the Underground Movement, Van Vliet, who appears to be the principal penetration agent, managed to trace a number of W/T agents and the Germans were always very quick to turn them round. Abteilung IIIF could count on a substantial number of other individuals who were prepared to perform similar functions.

Evidence that S.O.E. Organisation was under control at an early date
The history of the agents who were sent to the field from England to establish the secret army illustrates the methods adopted by Abteilung IIIF and shows that the enemy were not merely successful in frustrating the enterprise but in disguising their successes and turning it to their advantage. Johannes arrived in Holland in June 1942 and there are indications that he never operated except under the control of the Germans. Whether this is correct or not, the organisation was under control by the beginning of November of the same year. Although suspicion was aroused in London that all was not well in July 1943 when, after consideration the conclusion was reached that Johannes's successor *Kale*, was in danger, it was not until later that S.O.E. had any serious doubts regarding the organisation as a whole. In fact, the organisation was certainly under German control from the end of 1942; was most probably under control from the summer of that year (possibly August 1942) and it is very likely that it never operated at all except under control and that the Germans captured Johannes on or shortly after his arrival.

Johannes was dropped in June 1942 when the "Plan for Holland" was set in motion. He was followed by another S.O.E. agent, a certain *Broadbean*, who arrived in the field in February 1943, being dropped to a reception committee arranged by the agent *Parsnip*. *Broadbean*, who was identical with a man called Frans, and two other agents, one of whom was recruited locally in the field, were arrested and worked for the Germans as double agents. After they had worked in this way for a few months a message was received from England congratulating them on the good work they had done and instructing them to return, and the steps taken by the Germans to deal with this situation are interesting. It is certain that at some date *Broadbean* did come under control, and if he came under control on arrival in the field, as appears probable or at least possible, the task of the Germans must have been fairly simple.

An examination of the facts which are set out hereafter supports the view that IIIF were in control at a very early date and that the month of August 1942 would not be very wide of the mark. We also have the evidence of the agent *Chive*, who was arrested by the Germans on making his descent in Holland at the end of November 1942 and who was then sent to a concentration camp.

The interrogation of *Chive* when he ultimately escaped and returned to this country made it abundantly clear that at least by the end of 1942 the whole organisation was hopelessly penetrated.

History of S.O.E. Activities and Abwehr Counter Activities
From the outset it had been intended that Johannes should return to the U.K. and report after a few months in the field and on the 24th September 1942, *Kale* was sent to relieve him together with a W/T operator named *Cucumber*. During the next few months some ten organiser instructors or W/T operators arrived in Holland. The control by the Germans of the organiser Johannes or of his substitute *Kale*, whose mission was similar to that of Johannes and comprised the organisation of the secret army, involved the control or potential control of the whole of that secret army; and it appears that these men must all have fallen into enemy hands. The recall of Johannes did, however, inevitably present a problem which was repeated on more than one occasion and to which on separate occasions Abteilung IIIF found different answers: Johannes was notionally shot while resisting arrest on 8th November 1942 and his death was reported to S.O.E. on the *Cucumber* W/T set. This date has hitherto been accepted in London as being the actual date of *Cucumber's* arrest. There is, however, no reason at all to think that this view is correct. What is probable is that if Johannes was arrested at this date, and his arrest cannot have been much later than that, Johannes gave away everything he knew, which must have been everything about the secret army including the identity of *Kale*. It is hard to understand how the presumed death of Johannes could have been accepted in London without question, had he been arrested instead of being killed it must have been obvious that it was quite hopeless to endeavour to continue the undertaking which he had launched and of which he was the chief organiser, since to act upon the footing that a captured agent has not been broken is to court, not merely peril to all concerned, but disaster to the whole enterprise.

Thereafter the duties conferred upon Johannes by S.O.E. and the part assigned to him by the Abwehr were carried out in the name of *Kale*. Upwards of twenty-five receptions were arranged over *Kale's*

W / T set and contact was maintained with London through *Cucumber's* set, down to the middle of July 1943.

In the meantime, however, the Abwehr had been presented with a further problem of a similar kind to that which had been dealt with on the recall of Johannes. In consequence of Johannes' disappearance *Kale* was asked by S.O.E. to send to England some other person thoroughly well informed about the progress of the secret organisation. In the face of this requirement the Abwehr decided to go through all the motions of supplying such a person. On the one hand this would serve the purpose of allaying any suspicion which might be felt in London regarding the security of the S.O.E. organisation and on the other hand S.O.E. could be made to disclose to the Germans, through *Cucumber*, the methods by which agents could be evacuated from Europe.

On 14.3.42., S.O.E. were informed that *Kale* would send his chief assistant, who was called *Anton*. When asked for full particulars of *Anton* the reply was that *Anton* was Nicolaas de Wilde, Charlotte de Bourbonstrasse 228, The Hague, born 5.10.03. The Germans perhaps made an error and took a risk in giving these particulars regarding *Anton*. In fact, no such person as Nicolaas de Wilde lived at 228 Charlotte de Bourbonstrasse and steps had been taken to guard against the risk of anyone being sent to contact him at that address. Arrangements had been made by Keisewetter and Kupp whereby if anyone should call at that address, he should be told that de Wilde was away but would return in a few days. There is, in fact, a man called de Wilde working for Abteilung III who was born about 1903, and when the necessity arose, he could, and perhaps did, play the part of *Anton*. And when S.O.E decided to arrange for *Anton's* evacuation through Belgium and Holland someone was found by the Germans to fill the part, and he left Holland about 12.5.43. and travelled to Paris. We do not know the details of the arrangements nor the route he took except that *Broadbean* was told to carry out the evacuation and it is apparent that that route and those who operated it became known to the Germans. We know that the spurious *Anton* was accompanied by a certain *Arnaud* who has been an Abteilung IIIF agent since 1940 and who we also know was regarded by S.O.E. as a passeur of theirs having been notified to them by *Broadbean's* W / T operator (the German controlled set *Golf*) as *Broadbean's* best helper.

On arrival in Paris *Arnaud* and *Anton* made contact, in accordance with directions given by S.O.E. to *Broadbean*, with another agent, Marcel by name. It was impossible to evacuate the party that moon, and they had to wait a month. *Arnaud* and *Anton* returned to Brussels for that purpose – a step which to the uninitiated appears unusual – and on return to Paris they met the S.O.E. agent, Marcel, by appointment in a café. We know from Marcel who subsequently arrived in this country that so soon as he had sat down in the café with the others, three German soldiers came in and started to examine the cards of those at the back of the café. *Anton* got up and walked out. *Arnaud* said "They have arrested *Anton*". Marcel looked out and saw *Anton* crossing the road in company with a man in civilian clothes. Such was the account, given by Marcel when he arrived in this country, of *Anton's* disappearance. A great deal of trouble was taken to decide whether *Anton* had been arrested because he had been followed or whether it was sheer bad luck as a result of a snap check of identity cards. A great deal of trouble was taken to assess the dangers which would fall upon the organisation as a result of this arrest, regard being made to the fact that *Anton*, according to Marcel, had been carrying compromising papers. It never occurred to anyone that *Anton* was nothing but a German agent, and that *Arnaud* was lying when he said that *Anton* had been arrested. *Arnaud's* stock inevitably rose in the eyes of London and Marcel was sent back to the continent to fall into enemy hands. The problem raised by S.O.E.'s request for the sending to England of a man who was well acquainted with the secret army had been answered by the Abwehr with conspicuous success. So far were we baffled by this German trick and so far were we from understanding the nature of the game that was being played and the high stakes involved, that in commenting on the arrest an investigator remarked "If the Germans had known beforehand of this rendezvous it is hard to believe that they would not have arrested Marcel and *Arnaud*."

Indeed, so great had been the success of the Germans in carrying out this ruse that it may well have encouraged them to carry out an even more impertinent and daring transaction. On this occasion the request of S.O.E. for sending to this country of another man who had full knowledge of the secret army was anticipated by the Germans themselves who offered to send a man in close touch with the O.D. Furthermore, on occasion instead of choosing a fictitious individual or an individual who on arrival here might be shown up as a German agent, there was chosen for the part a man against whom nothing adverse could be known in London and who believed himself to be, and was in fact, a bona fide patriot: a man, Knoppers by name, whose case when he arrived in England aroused a great deal of interest and no little perturbation in our minds. Knoppers had been approached at the end of 1942 or the beginning of 1943 by the Abteilung IIIF agent, Van Vliet, who is referred to in the early part of this note. Knoppers had been doing some resistance work and had been in contact with a certain Colonel Koppert, when Van Vliet, representing himself as a member of the resistance, asked him if he might use Knoppers' address as a boite-aux-lettres. Thereafter Knoppers continued to see Van Vliet regularly about once a week until he finally left Holland. Van Vliet, on his first approach, claimed to be working for a General Mahieu and stated that he had been commissioned by the General to find out all he could about the requirements of secret organisations in Holland. He was in possession of what he alleged were forged documents purporting to have been issued by the Gestapo on production of which he obtained frontier passes enabling him to travel between Holland and Belgium on behalf of the General. He asked Knoppers to assist him in this work and to obtain as much information as he could regarding secret organisations to hand over to the General. This Knoppers agreed to do and got in touch with several organisations for this purpose. On 20th July 1943 Van Vliet asked Knoppers, who had by then collected quite a volume of information and passed it to Van Vliet, if he would travel to England and would return with instructions for these resistance organisations. As Knoppers understood it, the idea was that several resistance movements needed co-ordination and central direction and official recognition and support from London. This could be best obtained by sending an emissary from Holland and securing his return as a liaison officer with London credentials. The merit of such a journey from the point of view of the Germans do not need stressing. In order to facilitate Knoppers' journey Abteilung IIIF had already, through the instrumentality of *Broadbean's* W/T set, made contact with London on the subject; and on 5.6.43., a message had been sent to London purporting to come from the agent *Broadbean* via another agent, *Golf*, stating that the sender had come into contact with Colonel Koppert, a leading man of the O.D. He wished urgently to send over his best man for a few weeks. It was suggested further that he should be sent over with the spurious *Anton* De Wilde. S.O.E. immediately gave their approval, ordered *Broadbean* to make the arrangements for the journey and advise him that the new man (Knoppers) should not come with *Anton* de Wilde but should be ready to leave alone in about 4 weeks. S.O.E. would give further instructions. The Germans allowed him almost one month to pass before sending a message ostensibly from *Golf* giving Knoppers' cover name and stating he urgently required to leave as soon as possible. In reply *Broadbean* was given a password and an address to which Knoppers was to call. A week later on 13th July Knoppers had a meeting with Van Vliet at Breda, there he was handed over to a so-called police inspector who took him to Turnhout where they again met Van Vliet who in turn took Knoppers to a flat in Brussels. Two days later a new passeur turned up in the person of Hollevoet (who is possibly identical with a character of that name known to have been working on behalf of Abteilung II of Brussels in passing German agents to Paris en route for this country). Hollevoet took Van Vliet and Knoppers to Jeumont where Knoppers was handed over to *Arnaud* while Van Vliet and Hollevoet returned to Brussels. Knoppers was held up in Paris for some weeks and was then brought by S.O.E. channels over the Pyrenees to Spain. For the purpose of facilitating Knoppers' mission, and also no doubt in order to build up *Arnaud*, Knoppers was provided with documents purporting to come from resistance circles. These comprised of a note to the Dutch or English authorities concerned, suggesting the desirability of establishing an escape route over which important Dutch intellectuals, industrialists and officials in Holland who, without themselves acting in a rash manner, had assisted in the sabotage of the German war effort, might be got out of Holland, not necessary to England but to some neutral country. For this purpose, it was suggested information should be obtained from *Arnaud* "who you know as the chief passeur for Belgium". There was also included a memorandum regarding resistance in Holland which made general statements about loyalist activities in Holland but no specific information of any kind.

The German object in sending Knoppers to this country was defeated, not because of any inherent defect, but because of what, from their point of view, was an unfortunate accident. Unfavourable, and possibly incorrect, reports had been received by the Dutch in London regarding Colonel Koppert. Knoppers' contact with Colonel Koppert accordingly made by him, to a limited extent, suspect. The fact that the message from *Broadbean* stated that Knoppers was Koppert's right hand man, though incorrect in fact, further prejudiced Knoppers in the eyes of those who had to interrogate him. Koppers being suspect was not allowed to return to Holland; and then when investigation was still proceeding, information, which had been in possession of S.I.S. for many months but which had not been distributed by them and which showed Van Vliet to be, if not a German agent, at least highly suspect was brought to our notice. We came to the conclusion that Knoppers had been planted on S.O.E. by Van Vliet and that *Broadbean* was working under German control. *Arnaud*, however, escaped suspicion and the suggestion that the S.O.E. escape route from Paris onwards might have been blown was not accepted.

There are two points in connection with this enterprise to which it may be worth calling attention as indicating the fallibility of Abteilung IIIF. In the first place, when Knoppers came to be interrogated, there was an inconsistency between his story of the origin of his mission and the account which *Broadbean* had given of him as right-hand man of Colonel Koppert. In the second place the timing was bad. The proposition put forward by *Broadbean* for the sending of Knoppers to this country was first put forward on 5.6.43., whereas Knoppers stated that it came not until the 20th of that month that he had been asked to come to England; and then of course not by Colonel Koppert but by Van Vliet. It is curious to find these two mistakes being made, but the fact that they were made, may have prevented us from spotting the fact earlier and the whole arrangement had been made by the Germans. It could hardly be supposed, if the venture was being controlled by the Germans from above, that such clumsy mistakes could have been made.

Knoppers' visit was a rebuff for the Germans. Further difficulties followed. *Anton* had been intended to come here to report on the progress of the secret army. *Anton* had been "arrested" and S.O.E. never accepted Knoppers, who knew nothing of the secret army, as a substitute. According to *Kale*, who was supposed to be in charge, one Steak recruited in the field, had taken *Anton's* place as second-in-command. S.O.E. determined to get Steak over here and on 31.7.43 *Broadbean*, who was supposed to be in charge of evacuation, was told to bring out Steak together with the agent *Pumpkin*. He himself was to come with *Pumpkin*. Before any further steps had been taken *Broadbean* was also instructed by London to send *Tennis* out with Steak. *Broadbean*, *Pumpkin* and *Tennis* were at this time either interned or under control and we have only the word of the Germans that there was ever such a person as Steak. The Germans were therefore placed in the position of having either to make excuses for the failure of *Broadbean* to obey these instructions, an almost impossible task; to arrange the "arrest" of the four men concerned in circumstances which would inevitably suggest that the S.O.E. organisation had been blown; or to adopt some other and more suitable course. In fact, they adopted a technique similar to that adopted when *Anton* was called to London but carried it to a further extreme. Four substitutes, agents of Abteilung IIIF, were provided for the four S.O.E. agents. They were Damen, Harger, an unknown Frenchman, and one De Wilde, who was probably the man who had played a similar role when a substitute had to be found for *Anton*. Three of the four men were taken by Keisewetter by train to Paris where they met the fourth man. There they were handed over to *Arnaud* with instructions to find out by what route they would be evacuated from France. *Arnaud* handed them over to a member of the VIC escape organisation and the four men, after being handled by a number of members of this organisation, were taken to Perpignan staying at VIC safe houses en route. The last stage of the journey was in a lorry across the frontier. Before they reached the frontier Harger and Damen jumped off. A little later the Frenchman jumped off and hailed a car belonging to the Feldgendarmerie showing his papers. He made this car follow the lorry and in due course the driver was arrested. The four German agents returned to Paris and made their reports to *Arnaud*. Subsequently S.O.E. were informed by a member of the VIC organisation that the four agents had been arrested in the Pyrenees while attempting to escape. This was accepted as a sufficient explanation of the failure of this, the third attempt, to bring to England someone who was fully informed regarding the organisation of the secret army.

The suspicion engendered by Knoppers' connection with Colonel Koppert prompted S.O.E. to enquire of *Broadbean* whether he knew Kloppert or Van Vliet. The Germans gave a reassuring reply stating that Van Vliet was only known to Kloppert from conversations regarding Knoppers' journey, but that Van Vliet was a collaborator of *Arnaud*. On November 7th, 1943, following information which had been received from S.I.S. to the effect, *Golf* was informed that Van Vliet was an enemy agent; a statement which *Golf* roundly repudiated stating that these suspicions were unintelligible, that Van Vliet was a great patriot etc.

Van Vliet had indeed, with the knowledge of S.O.E., became so well informed regarding the S.O.E. organisation that it would have been, from the German point of view, fatal if he became known to us as a German agent; and it must be assumed that it was in face of the suspicions that had been aroused in London that the Germans determined to take steps to rehabilitate Van Vliet. It so happened that the S.O.E. agent *Apollo* landed by mistake in Belgium on 18.10.43., when the aircraft that should have dropped him, together with *Brutus*, in Holland was shot down. *Apollo* reached the contact address which had been given to him in Brussels, which was none other than the address of a safe house of Van Vliet, Mme Mertens; he was there duly visited by Van Vliet. Van Vliet successfully played the part of a patriot and one can only suppose that *Apollo* knew nothing of the business of Knoppers before he left for the field. *Apollo* was fortunate in the part which the Germans designed for him in that his arrival offered them the opportunity of building up Van Vliet by assisting his return to this country. On 6.11.43., *Apollo* was taken to Paris by *Arnaud*. The two men stayed in VIC safe houses and were both taken to Lyons by the VIC courier Jeanne. There they met VIC's second in command and *Arnaud* returned to Paris, *Apollo* traveling to Spain. *Apollo* brought a tolerably good account of Van Vliet and recounted it on his arrival here. At almost the same moment a further opportunity arose to carry out a similar trick. The night after *Apollo* came down, Lieutenant John Kennard Hurst, a U.S.A. airman, made a forced landing in Holland. A boy took him to a house and he was passed on by unknown individuals and eventually taken to a bookshop in Doorn where he met one Dodo who claimed to be a Dutch officer. Dodo told Hurst that he had been in the U.K. for three years and had recently returned by parachute. He had gone to an address in Brussels, where he had been contacted by Van Vliet. Dodo introduced Hurst in Doorn to a man who sent him to Tilburg. At Tilburg a uniformed policeman took him to the frontier on a motor bicycle and then, after changing into civilian clothes in a wood, the man took him, travelling on bicycles which had been hidden for them in the wood, across the frontier to Turnhout. There Hurst was met by Van Vliet who motored him to Brussels and established him at the safe house of Mme Mertens. On 25.11.43., Hurst was picked up by Louis Debray and taken to Charleroi. Debray bribed the guards on the Belgian frontier and the two men crossed on foot near Jeumont. There Hurst was given a false identity card by a woman and then, still with Debray, taken to a railway junction (Aulnoye?) where they were met by *Arnaud* who took Hurst to Paris. In Paris Hurst was put up and then taken by the VIC passeuse, Jeanne, to Lyons.

The escape from the German concentration camp in which the S.O.E. agents captured in Holland were interned of the agents *Chive* and *Sprout* in August 1943 made it impossible for the Germans to continue with their deception unless these men could be re-captured. Both men were fully aware of the true facts, both from the terms of their interrogation by the Germans and from their conversations with other captured agents. Furthermore, *Chive* had a transmitter which the Germans had been playing back. No doubt in the hope that *Chive* and *Sprout* would not succeed in leaving occupied territory, the Germans proceeded upon that footing and in fact continued to transmit on the *Chive* transmitter down to February 1944. *Chive* and *Sprout* did, however, actually reach this country in February 1944 and at some stage the Germans became aware of this.

Huntermann who was in charge of all the German-controlled S.O.E. W/T sets, continued to play them all back until February 1944 and then closed the traffic by a message on all lines addressed to two S.O.E. officers by what in fact was their correct names, thanking them for their long mutual co-operation and promising them that if they came to the continent they would be received with the same care as their agents; this course was adopted because Hunterman thought that his false play must have been known to England since November 1943 because of the two agents who had escaped then.

Comment

In putting the above story together some consideration has inevitably been given to the question how far, what appears to have been a series of disasters, could have been avoided from the London end. Their story is a fair illustration of the fact, which is sometimes forgotten, that counter-espionage is very much easier than espionage, and that an espionage organisation in enemy occupied territory is extremely vulnerable to penetration. If that penetration is skilfully done it can remain undiscovered for a long period. These are inevitable risks. Moreover, espionage and sabotage no doubt require a habit of mind in those who direct them which must disregard the individual and, if the target is sufficiently important, must count casualties as a matter of insignificance. Risks must be run. The suggestions put forward are not designed, so to speak, to strike a balance between ruthless action on the one hand and faltering timidity and indecision on the other; but to ensure as far as possible that enterprises, such as that which was set afoot in Holland are not defeated by lack of reasonable precautions.

What strikes one first is that the vulnerability of the organisation in Holland was apparently not appreciated; secondly that the probable and possible implications of minor mishaps upon the security of the organisation as a whole, were not considered and thirdly that no steps were ever taken by means of trap questions or otherwise to find out whether the operators were or were not under control. With the exception of very few messages containing both true and bluff checks the traffic from the field relating to the evacuation of Knoppers (*Golf* and *Broadbean*) only contain bluff checks. Now, although, the use of a true check ought not to be taken as evidence that an agent is operating freely, persistent absence of the true check, ought, at least, to raise the presumption that the agent is under control. This inference was never drawn. Incidentally it says much for the quality of the agents sent to the field that they did not apparently divulge their true checks to the Germans. Experience of combatting the German espionage activities in this country has taught us that an agent's controller is always most unwilling to believe that his agent has been blown or has betrayed him and this may lie at the route of the failure to appreciate the true significance of the absence of signals showing the agents were operating freely. Consideration should also have been given to the possibility of Johannes not having been killed at once or to his having given something away to the Germans, this if only because any information which the Germans might have gained from him might easily have necessitated the abandoning of the whole enterprise, not because it was dangerous and involved risks but simply because it was foredoomed to failure.

Not only, however, does there appear to have been a failure to look the facts squarely in the face but also a failure when suspicion had once been aroused to test those suspicions. It would not have been difficult to have put a few trick questions on the traffic with a view to seeing whether the reaction was that which would be expected if the agent was not under control. In this connection it is worthy of notice that we know that some of the W/T operators who had been captured did not themselves operate on behalf of the Germans, their sets being taken over by the Germans for that purpose. No trick questions, however, seem ever to have been put even to the agents who were under suspicion.

Had the whole of the W/T traffic been under constant review in the light of all the known facts; had trick questions been put to the agents; had each mishap been examined with a view to appreciating its possible implications on the position of the others and the organisation as a whole; above all had a record been kept which set out in chronological order all the known facts regarding the enterprise and the sources from which such facts were known; a record which would have been readily available for consultation in considering all the above matters; had all this been done then there is little doubt that the S.O.E. organisation in Holland would not have met the fate which overcame it.

If it were possible there would be much to be said for an officer familiar with the difficulties of running a controlled transmitter to be sitting alongside those who were in contact with a W/T operator in the field. Short of that it is suggested that the traffic could be examined by such an officer from time to time. In any event it is submitted that it should be the primary duty of some officer to examine and keep under constant observation all the happenings in the field, as well as the mishaps, with a view to satisfying himself as to the true security position and advising those responsible for the offensive accordingly. These precautions would, however, be of little avail in the absence of a record or records in the form of a journal setting out all the known facts regarding the organisation in the field as a whole and the characters taking part in the activities. The need for this is clearly illustrated by the case of *Arnaud* who was accepted as an S.O.E. passeur in the absence of any record which set out all that was known of *Arnaud* and the circumstances of his recruitment; the fact that *Arnaud* was one of the lynchpins of the Abteilung IIIF penetration sufficiently illustrates the point.

Chapter 7

EVALUATION OF S.O.E.
OPERATIONS IN HOLLAND

S.O.E. operations in Holland were subject to the following important factors:

i) Lack of co-operation from the Dutch authorities, especially during 1941-1943, which had a very adverse effect on operations and above all on recruiting.

ii) The small size and dense population of Holland, which makes the selection of dropping grounds very difficult and pick-up operations virtually impossible.

iii) The geographical situation of Holland rendered it a difficult and dangerous area from the operational point of view.

iv) Lack of co-ordination between S.O.E. and S.I.S. during 1941-1943, which had an adverse effect on S.O.E. activities.

As a result of these factors S.O.E. operations in Holland were very difficult. These difficulties were unfortunately aggravated by the fact that the first W/T operator despatched to the field was arrested by the enemy and played back. In spite of this agent's efforts to warn the Home Station, the Country Section continued to have confidence in him and as a result dropped about 48 agents and some stores to enemy controlled reception committees during the period 1941-1943. As a result, there was in 1943, no British contact with Dutch resistance and from the beginning of 1944 to the end of the war a new organisation had to be built up and operated with great haste and under difficult conditions.

In spite of these handicaps an efficient organisation was built up and carried out successful attacks against road, rail and water communications, as well as industrial installations. In addition, the

220

organisation was responsible for useful counter-scorching activities, particularly in port areas.

Although the results obtained were not as great nor as widespread as those in some other countries, they were nevertheless significant and, considering the circumstances under which they were achieved, the Dutch Section who were working from 1944 onwards should receive full credit for them.

Container Operations

Period	Containers	Packages
1941	-	3
1942	282	21
1943	262	50
1944	2,759	336
1945	2,034	365
Total	5,337	775

Note: almost all 1941-43 deliveries were dopped to enemy controlled reception committees.

Agents and Casualties

Period	Agents sent to field	Killed	Missing	Survived	Note
1941-43	55	34	13	8	
1944-45	86	15	4	67	Excluding Jedburghs
Total	141	49	17	75	

Note: Nearly all agents dropped in the period 1941-43 were dropped to controlled reception.

Planning

During the period 1942-1943 all plans were directed to establishing contact and building up an organisation. Unfortunately, the plans adopted depended on too great a centralisation in the field and early penetration by the enemy resulted in the destruction of the whole organisation.

From 1944 to the end of the war, the planning of the Dutch Section appears to have been sound and methodical. This is confirmed by the results obtained in a short time and working with haste under difficult circumstances.

Briefing
S.O.E. briefed agents on their missions and the Dutch authorities briefed them on general conditions.

Seven agents stated that they were satisfied with their briefing and seven were dissatisfied, but of these seven two were handled by Airborne Forces.

The Country Section comments that up to early 1944 very little detailed information was available on conditions of work in Holland and that for that reason briefing was not as good as it became later. This is true, and it was one of the prices paid for the early disasters in this country.

False Papers
The Country Section provided false papers which were to serve until new papers could be secured in Holland. Agents were informed that the papers issued were not perfect and should be changed as soon as possible. Most agents understood the necessity for this system and there were no major complaints about papers.

D-Day Plans
a) Agents were almost unanimous in saying that the D-day plans issued were clear and satisfactory. The only complaints came from two regions which were not in direct touch with London.

b) It would seem certain that it would be disastrous to call out resistance under the circumstances which existed more than 48 hours before the arrival of Allied troops.

Training
1. W/T.
Agents generally considered the W/T training which they received to be satisfactory. Several of them felt that more time could have been spent on learning maintenance.

2. General.
Most agents stated that they were very satisfied with the training which they received. Group 'B' training was felt to be most useful.

The only adverse comments received were:

a) Several men reported that the Group 'B' course overstressed the need for security measures. (The history of the Section scarcely supports this contention).

b) Several wished they could have had training in driving motor cars and motor cycles.

c) A number felt that training in S-phone and Eureka was a waste of time as these devices were seldom used in Holland.

d) One or two expressed the need for further military training if they were to engage in guerilla warfare.

Despatch
Agents were satisfied with the arrangements for despatch as a whole.

The arrangements for searching seem to have been unsatisfactory. A number of agents report that they were not searched before departure. It may be that this was in part due to the fact that they were despatched from various aerodromes and that the system was not always the same. Nevertheless, some system should be devised by which searching is never omitted. This is essential, not only for the security of the agent, but also for national security.

A number of complaints were made that leg bags gave trouble. This was partly due to inexperience on the part of despatchers in affixing leg bags and adjusting them, but there is no doubt that the leg bag needs improvement.

Arrival
There are many complaints of bad despatch from aircraft. Despatchers were reported to be inefficient and sometimes indifferent. There were also many complaints of drops being either too high or too low.

The Country Section state that this was because Dutch operations were done by 38 Group who did not have the technique used by Tempsford. Nevertheless, this failure on the part of 38 Group to despatch efficiently was a serious one and in future every effort must be made to prevent such incidents which are bound to affect the agents' morale.

In two instances agents were dropped to the wrong committee. It seems that some system should be instituted by which such an accident cannot take place.

Amphibious Operations
Although two agents escaped by sea and various small boat operations were mounted across rivers there are no points of general interest to record under this head.

Signal Communications

a) From the technical point of view W/T communication with Holland proved reliable and no special difficulties were experienced.

b) One W/T operator used a remote-control system by which he could operate any one of five stations from a central control. He used assistants to tune the individual stations and could switch from one to another if enemy D/F activity made it desirable.

c) In the early stages of S.O.E. work in Holland one W/T operator was arrested by the enemy and played back successfully for a long time. Other operators, who were arrested as a result of this original capture, were also played back. This serious sequence of events shows how necessary it is to produce a good system of safe checks and also how important it is for any suspicious messages received to be subjected to critical scrutiny by high authority.

d) One report emphasises the importance of broadcasts being issued before curfew to facilitate the work of couriers and messengers.

Codes and Cyphers

All operators agreed that the O.T.P. was completely satisfactory.

Internal Communications.

The two main systems used were couriers and telephone.

a) The courier system was quite satisfactory. Girls on bicycles proved the most useful messengers.

b) The use of the telephone on a wide scale for clandestine communications was peculiar to Holland. It was made possible by the fact that responsible officials of the telephone service were members of the Resistance and were able to arrange for lines to be connected to secret switchboards worked by Resistance operators. The extensive Dutch telephone system, with a great number of underground cables, facilitated this system. In addition to its use for communication, this use of the telephone system proved very valuable in obtaining information on enemy intentions.

Secret Inks

There is no report of the use of secret inks in Holland. Probably the system of telephone communication referred to above rendered such methods unnecessary.

Pigeons

S.O.E. did not use pigeons in Holland.

S-phone

A number of instruments were despatched to the field, but results were disappointing. Later on, S-phones were used most successfully for communications between the enemy-occupied area of Holland and the advancing B.E.F. This was really an S.I.S. operation, although the personnel were from S.O.E.

The reasons for failure in S.O.E. operations appear to have been:

a) A reluctance on the part of the R.A.F. to employ the S-Phone. This was aggravated by the use of 38 Group, which seldom had S-Phones fitted.
b) The fact that the S-phone is not so simple to operate as it appears, and that S-phone training was not sufficiently thorough.

Eureka

Several successful operations using Eureka were reported, but it was not widely used. This seems to have been due to two causes. One was the fact that Dutch operations were carried out by 38 Group, who do not seem to have been very keen on the use of Eureka. The second was that not many S.O.E. agents were in direct contact with reception committees and that the Country Section did not therefore send many Eurekas to the field. Some agents reported having asked for Eurekas but not receiving them.

Stores Reception

a) There are a number of complaints of loads being dropped to the wrong reception committee.
b) One agent complains that one delivery was laid on at short notice without an opportunity for him to confirm that he could accept. This led to a number of arrests.
c) There are an unusually large number of reports of parachutes failing and containers breaking up in the air. This may be due to the fact that the Group carrying out the operations were not accustomed to the work.
d) Although many successful deliveries are reported there are a large number of reports of very bad deliveries, some loads being dropped into the sea or up to 20 miles away. Scatter was often excessive and seems to have been due to high drops and inaccurate running up onto the lights.
e) There are several reports that containers and packages were not correctly numbered.

f)   A few containers exploded or caught fire on landing. One package of hand grenades exploded in the air and betrayed the committee to the enemy.

g)   Packages were frequently difficult to find, owing to scatter.

h)   Several agents complained that the aircraft circled for too long, thus prejudicing security.

i)   There are a few complaints that stores specially requested were never received. This was probably due to the need for standardising container contents.

j)   Packing was on the whole satisfactory but there are a few complaints that Stens were rusty and that medical kits and MCRs were not well packed. Fog signals were sometimes found to have deteriorated while packed.

k)   Reception committee torches proved reliable.

l)   A waterproof container would have been valuable for work in Holland.

Stores.

General.

All agents expressed their satisfaction with the quality of the stores received. No failures were reported, and the only complaints were that the proportions received were not always suitable and that greater quantities were required. The first complaint is inevitable when standard cell contents are employed. The second was caused by the higher priorities allotted to other areas and to the difficulties of store deliveries in Holland.

a)   Many agents expressed the view that the most useful time pencils were the 10 minute and 30 minutes.

b)   Tyre-bursters were found very useful by several operators.

c)   Incendiaries were praised by two operators.

d)   Rail charges were found efficient and easy to handle.

e)   White cordtex was considered too noticeable.

Arms

a)   For clandestine work the ·32 Colt was preferred, but one or two men liked the Luger on account of its accuracy.

b)   The Welrod was used successfully for liquidation.

c)   The Silent Sten was also used successfully for liquidation.

d)   Several agents expressed preference for Brens and Rifles over Stens but complained that Brens were often damaged on landing.

e)   Bazookas were often received with flat batteries and do not seem to have been very popular in Holland.

Camouflage

a) Several agents complained that the clothes with which they were supplied were too new.
b) Camouflage of tyre-bursters was praised by one man.
c) Several operators used disguise with success. This usually consisted of wearing spectacles, changing hair style, growing or cutting moustaches and other simple changes.

Cameras

35mm. cameras were used for intelligence work but require skilled operation.

Medical Stores.

These were found very useful.

Dogs

One agent reports being searched for by Germans using dogs. He attributed his safety to a friendly gamekeeper who hid him and then took a bitch in heat over his trail.

Sabotage

Sabotage in Holland was not as widespread as that in other countries. This was in large part due to the late start of an effective S.O.E. organisation in the country. Nevertheless, many useful operations were successfully carried out.

A study of the methods used in operations shows that there must have been a shortage of fully trained sabotage instructors. No doubt additional training in this subject would have produced enhanced results.

Counter-Scorching

Reports show a number of successful counter-scorching operations, of which the most important were the sinking of blockships at Rotterdam and the immobilisation of a very large floating crane in the same port.

Propaganda

Few agents had anything to say about propaganda. Two mentioned seeing German notices and signs mutilated.

One man pointed out that dropping propaganda leaflets endangered the population, who might be shot if found with a leaflet or seen picking one up. He considered it would have been better to distribute leaflets through the underground movements.

Bribery and Blackmail

The most effective form of bribery, both with Germans and collaborators, was the promise of a favourable report on them when the Allies arrived.

This promise was used on several occasions – to obtain the release of arrested resisters, to prevent enemy demolitions, to adulterate enemy petrol and to obtain stores and materials.

Financial Operations

One operator stole a large sum of money which was to be used by the Germans for paying railway employees.

The same man stole the title deeds of a large sum of Dutch money which was available for German use in Spain for the purchase of wolfram. The documents were stolen in the train from the man who was about to take them to Spain.

Personal Attacks

No special reports were received on this subject other than statements that Welrods and Silent Stens were successfully used for liquidation.

Appendix 'A'

SUMMARY OF OPERATION IN THE NETHERLANDS

ZONE 1

Region 1
- Railway lines cut at Buitenpost, Dronrijp, Heerenveen, Oudega-Nijhuizum and St. Nicolaasga.
- Two telecommunication cables cut between Leeuwarden and Groningen.
- Local P.T.T. establishments saved by tampering with demolition charges.
- Explosive charges removed from several bridges in the Friesland area.
- Attacks on German lines of communication, small patrols and straggling enemy elements – the Germans suffering a considerable number of casualties.

Region 2
Attack on the prison at Leeuwarden on 8 Dec 44 and effecting the release of 50 members of the local Resistance movements.

Region 3
- Railway lines sabotaged at, a) Junction south of Meppel on lines running in direction of Friesland, Drenthe and Groningen; b) Between Hoogeveen and Assen; c) South of Coevorden, at the junction Zwolle-Coevorden and Coevorden-Almelo; d) Coevorden-Germany.
- Sabotage of Water Communications, namely a lock at Stieltjeskanaal rendered useless, also the lock in the Zwindersche canal, causing an interruption in the traffic to and from Corvorden for three months.

- Sabotage of Telecommunications in that telephone lines cut in several places along the railway lines.

ZONE 2

Region 4

- Some 150-ton barges sunk in the Twentsche-Rhein canal.
- Draining of the Almelo-Hengelo canal by opening the locks at Wiener, near Delden and destroying the electrical machinery controlling them. A delay 4/5 weeks was caused.
- Successful attack on the lock gates at Klooster, near Almelo.
- A number of successful attacks on railroads in the area.
- Transport on roads crippled by tyre-bursters, blowing down trees and using bent nails.
- In March 45 the whole railway system in Overijssel was put out of action and cuts effected at Borne and on the line Almelo-Zwolle at Nijverdal.
- German effort to divert rail traffic via Deventer-Zutphen to Hengelo was frustrated by a derailment carried out between Delden and Goor.
- Removal of signposts on crossroads and minefields.
- Sabotage of telecommunications.
- Successful attacks of German demolition squads at bridges and a number of bridges held including two over the Canal from Almelo to Corvorden.

Region 5

- Three derailments after Sep 44 on the line Ruurlo-Winterswijk and one derailment on the line Aalten-Winterswijk.
- Delays caused on the railways by the removal of signal and Block system apparatus.
- Fuses removed from a charge on the bridge at s'Heerenberg.
- Bridges at Aalten occupied to prevent destruction.

ZONE 3

Region 6

- Derailment of a troop train on the line Apeldoorn-Zwolle.
- Enemy telecommunications disrupted in the suburbs of Apeldoorn.

Region 8

- Having tapped the German telecommunications, the N.B.S. learned that an ammunition train was leaving Rotterdam for the Arnhem area. They decided it had to be stopped before it reached the Ede de

Klomp area. They blew the line up near Driebergen, near Zeist, and as a precaution, also nearer Arnhem. The attack was successful, and the train had to return to Rotterdam.

- Railway office at Utrecht raided to supply Resistance Forces with money. The sum of 1½ million Guilders was seized.
- Complete dislocation of all railway traffic to and from Utrecht by the cutting of lines at some 200 places in the area.
- Destruction of a large number of Wehrmacht cars in the area.

Region 9

- Three cuts in the line Amersfoort-Amsterdam.
- One cut on the line Hilversum-Utrecht.
- Three derailments on the line Bussum-Weesp.
- Two cuts on the line Hilversum-Bussum.
- Small railway bridge over the canal at Baarn destroyed twice, each time resulting in a derailment.
- Small railway bridges at Pruimgracht, Karnemelksloot and Keverdijk destroyed resulting in the escape of some 600 political prisoners.
- Bridge over the Vecht on Merwedekanaal destroyed.
- 60 German cars and lorries damaged by tyre-bursters and bent nails.
- 40 cuts in German field telephone lines.
- Two kilometres removed from the Hilversum-Berlin telephone cable.
- Two munition barges sunk by limpets.

ZONE 4

Region 7

Nothing to report. No material was ever sent there and as no specific information trickled through, the area was not built up. In addition, owing to defences, the Air Ministry would not entertain air operations in the area.

ZONE 5

Region 10

- Attack on a battery charging installation. Two chargers were blown up and the factory set on fire.
- Attack on the Pander factory for glider bodies at Rijswijk and by using bottles of phosphorus and benzol the factory was completely burned out.
- Continual attacks on the Amsterdam-Haarlem railway line, delays caused varied from one day to some weeks.

- Destruction of the railway bridge at Diemen, near Amsterdam.
- Hundreds of German cars destroyed by sabotage. In April and May the number varied from 10 to 12 per day.
- Destruction of a school building containing labour conscription registers. The records were completely destroyed.
- Sinking of a barge loaded with 200 tons of Gun Cotton in the River Amstel.

Region 12
- D/Fing Station at Ardenhout attacked and burned out.
- Five derailments on the lines Leyden/Haarlem-Harlem/ Amsterdam-Haarlem/Ymuiden.
- In March 45, forty Wehrmacht cars destroyed in garages in and around Haarlem.
- Telephone lines were sabotaged.

Region 13
- Railway sabotage. Points cut were: Railway bridges at Zevenhuizen, between Hekendorp and Gouda, Het Haantje near Delft. These lines were destroyed by means of explosives during the months of March/ April 45 when a great deal of transport of V.2 material was taking place. Lines were blocked for periods varying from 1 to 8 days.
- Derailment of train loaded with A.A. material and troops, blocked the Utrecht/Rotterdam and Utrecht/Hague lines for 24 hours. Four derailed trucks loaded with A.A. material lay on the rails for some time.
- A number of German cars destroyed by tyre-bursters and nails.
- German telephone lines cut at several places.

Region 14
- In Nov 44, the Resistance supplied with limpets from the U.K., sank the blockade ships *Schonfeld* and *Hansa* in the port of Rotterdam, vessels of 11,000 and 9,000 tons respectively. As they were only able to place one limpet on the *Hansa* the Germans were able to refloat her fairly quickly. Three limpets were used on the *Schonfeld* and it took the German engineers ten weeks to refloat her.
- In Jan 45, the *Westerdam* fully laden with gravel and cement and destined for the final blocking of the River Maas, was sunk by means of limpets on the 18th at her mooring berth in Rotterdam. She is still in the same position, upright, but sitting on the bottom of the dock.
- Resistance men sank the 180-ton floating crane Titan in order to prevent its removal to Germany. She has since been refloated.

- A small railway bridge over a canal between Schiedam and Vlaardingen, 3 kms. from Schiedam, was blown up and prevented the further use of this line for onward traffic to the Hoek of Holland up to the time of the German capitulation.
- Raids on ration book depots produced the following: Kloosterzande – 48,000 books and 150,000 coupons; Maassluis – 10,000 books and 200,000 coupons; Doorn – 12,000 books and 200,000 coupons.
- The destruction of 300 bags of cement used for road blocks.
- Preservation of an electric pumping station at Maassluis by cutting the underground detonating fuse.
- Destruction of 80 H.E. containers intended to blow the dykes surrounding the land below sea level near the Hoek of Holland.
- Removal of fuses leading to explosive charges under a railway bridge across the harbour at Maassluis.
- Removal of H.E. charges from lock gates just outside the Hoek of Holland.
- Rails cut at Achterdijk.
- Rail cuts at Gorkum and Arkel.
- Barge, containing 300 Dutch political prisoners, sunk near Dordrecht enabling them to escape.
- Bridges at Slikkerveer and Alblasserdam saved from demolition by cutting of fuses leading to the charges.
- About 200 Wehrmacht cars destroyed or damaged by abrasives, tyre-bursters and bent nails.
- In Apr 45 all railway lines around Rotterdam were cut simultaneously.
- A 1000 ton lighter loaded with iron was sunk at the Boompjes near the Leuvehaven, Rotterdam.
- Two lighters loaded with engine parts, iron and copper, moored opposite the Posthoornsteeg, Rotterdam, were sunk.
- A lighter loaded with engines (believed to be for U-boats) was sunk in the Katendrechtsche Harbour at Rotterdam.
- With the co-operation of a German, quay mines in the Schiehaven, Merwedehaven and Waalhaven, were rendered useless.

Region 11

- Railway tracks were cut at several places and, during the two months preceding the German capitulation, railway traffic was practically paralysed.
- Attack on a railway bridge resulting in its complete destruction and also the derailment of the engine.
- Changing of signposts, placing of roadblocks and sniping.
- Landmines placed on main roads.

- Large lorry carrying diesel oil completely burned out.
- All enemy cables destroyed North of a line Schagen-Medenblik.
- A lighter loaded with machinery sunk and recuperated after liberation.

The following additional acts of sabotage have been reported:

- In Mar 44 as a result of a sabotage attack on the factory at Hoek Pierson, the consumption of oxygen was cut by half.
- In Sep 44 the line Roosendaal/Breda/Tilburg/s'Hertogenbosch was seriously affected – railway traffic in South and South-Eastern Holland was at a standstill and lines in Eastern Holland were cut nightly.
- Lines cut between Veenendaal and Rhenen, Amersfoort and Apeldoorn, Amersfoort to the South. Sabotage carried out on the railway bridges over the Dedemsvaart and Zwolle-Meppel.
- The three blockade ships the *Borneo*, *Westerdyk* and *Axenfels* were sunk at Rotterdam.
- On 4 Oct it was reported that since 10 Sep thirty rail tracks had been cut and five major canals put out of action.
- The railway between Amersfoort and Apeldoorn was cut, derailing a train and causing two days' delay on the line. A railway bridge two miles south of Amersfoort was blown up by the Resistance on 13/14 Oct. The line between Amersfoort and Zwolle was cut in four places on the night 20/21 Oct 44.
- The railway bridge between Rijswijk and Delft was sabotaged.
- The lift bridge at Wijk bij Duurstede was attacked, damage being caused to the lifting machinery.

The following was reported for November 1944:

- ix) Train derailed at Heerde-Eppe.
- x) German troop train derailed at Budel and Weert – several Germans killed and wounded.
- xi) Both tracks on the Grosbeek-Nijmegen line blown up.
- xii) Several waggons on the Maarsssen-Breukelen line derailed.
- xiii) Railway line Meppel-Zwolle sabotaged.
- xiv) Railway line Zwolle-Marienberg sabotaged.
- xv) Derailment of one locomotive and 20 waggons at Ede de Klomp.
- xvi) Raid on the Wehrmacht bank at Almelo – 46,000,000 guilders seized.

The following was reported for January 1945:

- In Jan 45 a successful attack was reported on the Atlanta building, Amsterdam, which contained registers of personnel due for labour service in Germany. Similar attacks were carried out on another building on 5 Jan. Another registration building in the Paseerdergracht,

Amsterdam, was also destroyed on 7 Jan and various registers of the population brought to a place of safety.

The following was reported for February 1945:

- Transformers supplying current to German Naval Establishments and important factories working for the German War Industry had been sabotaged.
- Rotterdam reported the sinking of newly launched 3,000-ton vessel.
- Utrecht reported the sinking of four barges loaded with 180,000 litres of oil.
- 5 H.E. charges were placed in the S.D. office at the Singel, Dordrecht – 16 S.D. personnel being killed.

The following was reported for March 1945:

- Utrecht reported the cutting of all railways from Amersfoort to the East to impede the transport of political prisoners to Germany.